The Collector's Voice:
Critical Readings in the Practice of Collecting

Perspectives on Collecting
Edited by Susan Pearce
University of Leicester, UK

The Collector's Voice:
Critical Readings in the Practice of Collecting

Volume 1
Ancient Voices

Edited by
SUSAN PEARCE AND ALEXANDRA BOUNIA

Ashgate

Aldershot • Burlington USA • Singapore • Sydney

Published by

Ashgate Publishing Ltd
Gower House, Croft Road,
Aldershot, Hampshire GU11 3HR
England

Ashgate Publishing Company
131 Main Street
Burlington, Vermont 05401
USA

Ashgate website: http://www.ashgate.com

ISBN 1 85928 417 5

069.4
PEA   0239 13 3

British Library Cataloguing-in-Publication Data
The collector's voice: critical readings in the practice
   of collecting
   Vol. 1: Ancient voices
   1. Antiquities – Collection and preservation – History
   2. Collectibles – History   3. Collectors and collecting in
   literature   4. Europe – Antiquities
   I. Pearce, Susan M. (Susan Mary), 1942–   II. Bounia, Alexandra
   069.4'0936

US Library of Congress Cataloging-in-Publication Data
The collector's voice : critical readings in the practice of collecting / edited by Susan Pearce and Alexandra Bounia and Ken Arnold.
      p.   cm. Contents: v. 1. Ancient voices — v. 2. Early voices.
   Includes bibliographical references and index.
      1. Collectors and collecting—History.   2. Collectors and collecting—Europe—History.   3. Collectors and collecting—Philosophy.   4. Collectors and collecting—Social aspects.   I. Pearce, Susan M.   II. Bounia, Alexandra.   III. Arnold, Ken.
   AM221.C65 2000
   790.1'32—dc21   00–0044169

This volume is printed on acid-free paper.

Typeset by Manton Typesetters, Louth, Lincolnshire, UK.
Printed in Great Britain by MPG Books Ltd, Bodmin, Cornwall.

Perspectives on Collecting

Contents

III   Roman voices

IV   Early medieval voices

V Voices from the twelfth to the fifteenth centuries

General Preface to Series

The study of collecting is a growth point in cultural studies. Like most exciting developments, it is on the cusp where older studies meet and stimulate each other; but it is also conceived as a study of practice, of the ways in which people make sense of the world by bringing elements together. Because we and our world are material, and our ways of understanding are tied to the physical reality of material, one of the prime ways in which this sense is created is through the accumulation and juxtaposition of material things. Following the seminal publication of Benjamin's essays and Arendt's Introduction to them (1970), a range of studies have been important in the development of our understanding in this field. Some have been in the broader field of material culture (for example Appadurai, 1986; Miller, 1985; Hodder, 1986). Others have contributed to our understanding of museums, as the institution *par excellence* which sustains and is sustained by the practice of collecting (for example Hooper-Greenhill, 1992; Bennett, 1995; Pearce, 1992). Closely related to this has been the whole People's Show Project which brought contemporary collectors into museum galleries and opened up an important range of popular collecting issues (for example Lovatt, 1997). This climate of interest, linked with important studies by Baudrillard (1984), Pomian (1990) and Stewart (1984) have stimulated a number of specialised studies in the collecting field. Elsner and Cardinal have published an important collection of essays on individual collecting topics (1994) and Pearce has produced a broad analysis of collecting practice (1995) and a study of contemporary popular collecting practice (1998), while Martin has published an analysis of the relationship between collecting and social institutions at the end of the twentieth century (1999). Arnold has produced a study of the 'cabinets of curiosity' phenomenon, and Bounia and Thomason have turned their attention to ancient collecting, Bounia of the classical world (1998) and Thomason of the ancient Middle East. Flanders is working on the collecting processes associated with nineteenth-century museums, and a number of similar pieces of work are in progress.

This intellectual realisation has been matched by a flood of popular interest in collectors and collecting. The *Independent, The Times* and the *Guardian* now run regular collecting columns. The BBC sees ever-increasing spin-offs from the *Antiques Roadshow* programme, and the other channels, television and radio, have their own series. A parallel reverberation of the same phenomenon is seen in the extent to which collecting, used in a variety of ways, appears as a recurrent theme in contemporary fiction.

The four volumes of *The Collector's Voice: Critical Readings in the Practice of Collecting* series take the perspective of the long term. The first, *Ancient Voices*, addresses collecting practice in ancient northern Europe, ancient and classical Greece and imperial Rome, and the post-Roman period through the early and high Middle Ages to the beginnings of European early modernism in the fifteenth century. The second, *Early Voices*, covers collecting during the sixteenth and seventeenth centuries, and into the early eighteenth century. The third, *Imperial Voices*, concentrates upon nineteenth- and earlier twentieth-century collectors up to about 1960. The final volume, *Contemporary Voices*, focuses attention upon the nature of collecting in the closing decades of the twentieth century. In all four volumes the written, or sometimes recorded, voices of the collectors themselves are paramount, but it is hoped that the editorial content which surrounds each text will place the quoted material in its appropriate context.

Two issues emerge clearly from what has been said: the definition of 'collecting'; and the idea of a 'European tradition' of collecting, which presupposes that the notion of a continuity of ideas and practices from one generation to another over a period of several millennia within a particular, and relatively limited, geographical area is a valid premise on which to mount investigation. Benjamin in his essay on his library (1970), and Arendt in her Introduction to his essays, both of which stand at the head of the contemporary critique of collecting practice, make the point that 'insofar as the past has been transmitted as tradition, it possesses authority; insofar as authority presents itself historically, it becomes tradition' (Arendt, 1970: 38). But this line of thought undermines the notion of tradition as an essentially valid element in the historical process; it does not break out of the human predicament which means that the only way in which to behave newly or differently is to do so in relation to a past, which is inevitably perceived as a powerful influence upon the present. And, of course, through most generations, people have not particularly wished to break dramatically with the past, but rather to improve upon it.

The generational link is essentially one of perception: individuals in each generation have an idea, by word of mouth or by reading, of what their predecessors did, and make their own use of what comes to them as the traditions of the past; and it should be recognised that the capacity to accumulate goods, and to access the traditions of the past, tend to rest with the same restricted class of people, for whom the past as they perceive it is of importance because it provides the legitimisation for their present position. To put the point slightly differently, the fostering of the notion of a broad European tradition has been an important aspect of self-identity among the collecting classes, whatever they have actually made of it, and so it must also do so in a critique of collecting practice.

The definition of 'Europe' emerges within this context as a series of self-fulfilling arguments. These centre on a broadly similar 'heroic' prehistory across Europe susceptible to interpretation along Homeric lines, and a range of shared authors writing in Greek and Latin, beginning with Homer. Christendom follows as the successor to the classical world, defined in opposition to Islam and sharing a Latin culture which endured into the eighteenth century. Thereafter is seen a common Enlightenment, a common focus on imperialist nation states, and a common disillusion as the second millennium AD closes. Outsiders have been variously defined as barbarians, non-citizens, pagans and natives, and as being unenlightened and underdeveloped, but the core area defined in terms of the perceived intellectual tradition of which collecting is a part has remained remarkably stable, historical fluctuations notwithstanding, and concentrates upon north-western Europe and the lands around the northern Mediterranean shore.

Within all this, how can 'collecting' and 'collection' be viewed usefully as an aid to the critique through personal testimony of particular material social practices? Here we have to recognise that collecting is a complex business and that a difficult path has to be taken between 'collecting' as narrowly defined in recent decades, and in relation to recent generations (see Pearce, 1995: 39–56 for a summary), and much broader 'accumulation' which contemporaries would not have seen as 'collections' in any meaningful way (although successors might). The view taken in the last three volumes of this series is that 'collectors' are left to be self-defining on the understanding that they will define themselves, of course, according to their perception of their relationship to the European tradition just discussed. The first volume takes a wider view, for reasons which are discussed in its Introduction.

The contemporary interest in collecting practices, referred to earlier, needs the core reference material which is essential to its study, and the present series addresses this need. This formative material is extremely difficult to access because it is widely scattered, exists only patchily in specialist libraries and archives, and sometimes requires translating, usually from Greek or Latin, into English. The editors have endeavoured to bring the most interesting material together, translate it if necessary, and present each piece with an introduction, explanatory notes and bibliographical references. All choice is subjective, and not all will agree with the choices made here; and the editors themselves are aware of much interesting material which has had to be omitted. But we hope that enough is offered to provide material for discussion and to provoke future review of notions about collecting practices in the European tradition.

Susan Pearce, General Editor
August 1999

Acknowledgements

Many people have helped to bring this book into being. Susan Pearce would particularly like to thank the librarians at the Society of Antiquaries, the British Library, and the Bodleian Library. Alexandra Bounia would offer her thanks especially to the State Scholarship Foundation of Greece and the Public Benefit Foundation, and Maria Kassimati, for financial support received during work on her PhD thesis (University of Leicester, Department of Museum Studies) upon which her chapters are based.

We are both grateful to Rachel Lynch, Cathrin Vaughan and others at Ashgate Publishing who have given us invaluable support, and our best thanks go to our families and friends for encouragement and support. All errors and omissions are, of course, our own responsibility.

Every effort has been made to trace all the copyright holders, but if any have been inadvertently overlooked the publishers will be pleased to make the necessary arrangement at the first opportunity.

List of abbreviations

ad Attic.	Marcus Tullius Cicero, *Ad Atticum*
ad Famil.	Marchus Tullius Cicero, *Ad Familiares*
ANRW	*Aufsteig und Niedergang der Römische Welt*
BCH	*Bulletin de Correspondence Héllenique*, Paris
HN	Pliny the Elder, *Historia Naturalis* (Natural History)
Hom	*Homer*
Il	*Iliad*
JDAI	*Jahrbuch des Deutschen Archäologischen Instituts*, Berlin, de Gruyter
MEFR	*Melanges d'Archólogie et d'Histoire de l'École Français de Rome*, Paris, de Boccard
Od	*Odyssey*
RE	*Paulys Real-Encyclopädie der Classischen Altentumwissenschaft*, G. Wissowa et al. (eds), Stuttgart, 1893–
TAPhS	*Transactions of the American Philosophical Society*, Philadelphia, Independence Square

Introduction

Ancient Voices is the first volume in a four-part series designed to offer views of collecting practices in Europe over the long term through the recorded voices of the collectors themselves and their contemporary commentators, where possible. *Ancient Voices* draws upon writings that relate to the accumulation of material objects from as early as British prehistory, perhaps around 1600 BC, through archaic Greece, through the classical and medieval centuries, to around AD 1500: in all a time-span of some three millenniums, and a cultural span embracing prehistoric communities, the notion of the city-state, a world empire, Christian kingdoms and the earliest phases of what is usually called modern society. Such diversity requires discussion, and its inclusion within the collecting theme requires justification.

The point was made in the Preface that collecting is not a simple activity, and in that discussion were linked ideas about the operation of tradition and its relationship to 'Europe', all of which are particularly pertinent to *Ancient Voices* and need to be taken up here. Collecting can be described as both an accumulation of objects and an act of cosmological interpretation carried out in the practice of the accumulation. In this sense, therefore, every gathering of material goods is a collection, and in one sense carries the same weight of cultural significance. But in the complex world of actual historical human practice, this is not what we see. Certain kinds of accumulation are given cultural precedence within the given community and in broad terms, these kinds seem to embrace two characteristics. Firstly, they are of goods deemed precious, as a result of their rarity, the amount of social capital embodied within them through the technical or artistic effort and skill which they represent, and the quality of specialised or arcane knowledge which their 'proper' manipulation requires (or often, all of these). Secondly, in notions closely bound up with these allotted values, such accumulations are given a broad community and individual significance which sustains identity in its cosmological relationships.

This last point invites elaboration. 'Identity' depends upon an ability to discern a particular crux where time and space intersect, and to say 'we' are what this intersection is; the time-span involved is frequently considerable since the notion of 'us' is itself usually long term. The temporal–spatial crossing is then given a cosmological setting through the generation of cultural discussions which validate, reflect and encourage social practice and appropriate systems of understanding and legitimisation. A number of ways in which the collecting together of particular objects has been a part of this creating and defining process in the European tradition offer themselves to view. Collecting forms part of affirming the significance of the mighty dead, as a memorialising activity, whether the accumulation remains open to view or hidden. It acts as a social symbol through which relationships can be created between person and person, person and community, and both of these and the divine. It can act as a form of sacrifice in which valuables are surrendered, and the sacred, particularly the sacred place, created. It can be a part of the poetic of good and evil, and it can construct systems of knowledge which inform and support social action. Implicated in all this are a range of sites – grave, temple, church, palace, study, museum – where practice takes place.

The phrase 'the European tradition' has just been used, and was discussed in the Preface. It should be said here that this emphatically does not involve any quasi-mystical belief in a 'European spirit' or any deterministic idea of the defining presence of 'blood', descent, genes or similar pseudo-scientific misinformation. What is meant is the simple proposition that successive generations draw on, and make use of, the experiences of their forebears, and that they do this in a number of ways. The most obvious of these ways is by actual transmission: later generations hear stories from the past, or read books written in the past. The most easily demonstrated way in which this has worked within Europe is that in which the people of the Roman empire read texts written originally in Greek several generations earlier, and were influenced by them; and the people of the fifteenth century AD and onwards read accounts by both the Greeks and the Romans, and were influenced by them. This chain constitutes a generally perceived tradition in collecting practice, and a very important one: it is the reason why classical texts are allotted a considerable space in this volume.

Equally important is the perceived relationship to a past where the line of any actual traceable contact through directly transmitted practices and texts is lacking. Eighteenth-century English gentlemen felt Homer to be important and to illumine emerging evidence of ancient practices in Britain, partly because of superficial similarities between text and appearance and partly because of a shaped mindset which made Homer the arbiter in such matters. These two aspects of significance arc important in the long term of collecting practice.

The idea of continuity is, of course, crucial to our idea of the relationship of the present to the past. 'Continuity' is not at present a favoured way of perceiving the relationship between past and present, following upon the demonstration of the invention of tradition (Hobsbawm and Ranger, 1983) and the destruction, for example, of the cherished notion that aspects of 'folk' or popular culture have a continuity running back into prehistory (Hutton, 1987). Manifestly, each generation makes its own use of sites, customs and ideas that have come to it from the past, and also creates quite new notions; manifestly, also, these older fragments are seen to pass something of their earlier form and content down the line. This is true of all social practice, and collecting is no exception.

It is to enhance understanding of more recent, say post-1500, practices that the decision was taken to include the volume *Ancient Voices* in this series and so allow testimony relating to the kinds of accumulations, and the themes which they represent, made by the generations who lived before the beginning of the early modern period, when European collecting as generally understood makes its appearance; although, of course, the debt of these practitioners to Greek and (especially) Roman predecessors was recognised by them, and has been ever since. Classical collecting drew, as Bounia has shown, on a context of the long term, in which notions of gathered grave goods, sacred treasures, gift exchange and the ethics of possession are very significant.

These social practices informed the archaic and early classical period in Greece, but were also, as far as we can see, likely to have been important in the corresponding pre-imperial Roman period in northern and central Europe. Prehistoric Britain shows us groups of grave goods, accumulations of valuables usually called 'hoards' and materially well-endowed sacred places. These continue to appear through the Roman period inside and outside the empire, and show up again in Germanic, and later Scandinavian, successor states. They are part and parcel of a complex relationship to the spread of Christian institutions, which we see gradually across western Europe, involving grave treasures in the shape of relics, and their richly decorated sites, treasure hoards and what the twentieth century would call 'art objects', all within a moral and social framework. Such palaces of God were easily appropriated as palaces of the ruler, when circumstances so suggested, as they did in the late fourteenth and fifteenth centuries, and offered a context within and against which the different collecting styles of the later sixteenth century could be constructed. Clearly, each generation, institution and individual acted in relation to a very large range of stimulations, and in one sense each accumulation is a unique event aimed at a particular combination of circumstances; but equally clearly, circumstances have similarity, and bear a perceived relationship to what has gone before.

The keen-eyed reader will note that the term 'accumulation' has been preferred over 'collection' in this last discussion. 'Collection' may be a protean notion best left to the subjective judgement of each self-styled 'collector', but it is not likely to have been the way in which prehistoric or medieval Christian communities thought of themselves. But if, as suggested earlier, the practice of collecting involves an act of accumulation linked with an intention to assert a cosmological interpretation, and with the conscious selection of objects which are deemed capable of making these constructions, then groups of grave goods or accumulations of church silver do come within the scope. In a series of this kind, they are the essential prelude to what comes after.

Part 1, 'Voices from the distant past', is organised into two sections. The first, chronologically generally the earlier, presents accounts of the discovery of British prehistoric accumulations: grave goods from early Bronze Age barrows, metalwork from later Bronze Age hoards and accumulations from Iron Age sites. These are given, naturally, through the accounts of their modern finders, rather than the testimony of contemporaries, and they are of significance both as part of the succession of longer-term contexts just described, and as a stimulant to certain kinds of collecting in later modern times (see Volume 2, *Early Voices*).

The second section gives direct testimony from earlier Greek writers of gift-giving practices and cultural beliefs that initiated a series of notions which influenced object valuation and determined the consequent appreciation of object possession and accumulation. The gift exchange tradition as a means of creating and perpetuating social relations with the gods, nature or other humans, at an individual or communal level, gave material culture a prominent role as the bearer of moral value and as a medium of legitimisation and concretisation of events and relations. Following this line of thought, this section of Part 1 consists of paragraphs from ancient sources focusing on the role of material culture in the creation of the social interaction between men (Homer, *Odyssey*) and men and the gods (Herodotus, *Histories*), and illustrates in the most direct manner both the long-term perspective of the collecting practice and discourse, and the roots of the values attributed to material culture in subsequent generations. At the heart of these ideas lie the genealogies attached to valued objects (Homer, *Iliad*), the association of the particular skills required to produce those precious items with divine or supernatural power (Diodoros; Homer, *Iliad, Odyssey*), and the idea that wealth is immediately related to the accumulation of artefacts bearing certain moral and symbolic qualities, and their removal from the world of commodities into a different sphere, that of the mythic *thalamos* (meaning equally a treasury and a tomb) or sanctuary (Herodotus, *Histories*; Homer, *Odyssey*).

'Greek voices' (Part 2) brings together material from Greek and Roman authors which bears witness to the role and importance of material culture and its accumulation, as well as to the intellectual notions and the practices that relate to it in the Greek world. Material culture was linked to notions of evidence and truth, and thus was related to antiquarianism, the inherent interest in the past, which takes shape in the systematic assemblage of artefacts, information and anything else that can bring people closer to the past, to history, but also to accumulated knowledge. In other words, the prestigious genealogy and inalienability of the gift exchange tradition, as parameters that determined the valuation of material culture, were enhanced with the addition of an active interest in the idea and practice of 'archaeology', that is, in a kind of history that relied on material specimens and recognised their role as evidence and proof. The accumulation of relics of the mighty dead, that will find its culmination in the Christian tradition, is at the crossroad of these two notions and expresses the same need for objects to be understood as symbols and reminders of events, personalities and specific actions, as well as sacred talismans that would shape and protect individual and communal identity (Herodotus, *Histories*; Plutarch, *Life of Theseus*). Objects brought from 'outside', or the past, had also an active role to play as transmitters of rites of passage and markers of important events, as well as media through which a transference to a different time and place could be achieved.

The role and importance of the ancient public collections held in sanctuaries is also presented through a selection of sources. Pausanias' *Description of Greece*, Herodas' fourth *Mime*, and also contemporary researchers' work, like that by D. Harris (1995), describe accumulations of artefacts in ancient 'museums'. In the context of the previously presented sources, it becomes obvious that these 'museums' have more than their functional similarity as repositories of artefacts to recommend them as being worthy of a title that refers to contemporary institutions, and that the assemblages of material culture in sanctuaries did more for the definition of notions of sacred and communal than is obvious at first glance. The public practice of collecting is also discussed in the paragraphs that describe the treasuries (Pausanias, *Description of Greece*); these have to be understood as a social, historical and political transformation of the *thalamos* of the Homeric epics, which was endowed with mythical value, and as a physical expression of the idea of the city-state, very much in the spirit of the public museums of the centuries to come.

A selection of ancient sources regarding collecting practice in the classical world would be incomplete without reference to the Alexandrian Museum, which can clarify the character and origin of the institution, illuminate the perception of the museum in subsequent periods and underline the interdependence between philosophical discourse and collecting practice (Strabo, *Geography*; Diogenes Laertius, *Lives of Eminent Philosophers*).

Finally, paragraphs from Plutarch's *Life of Aratus* and Pliny's *Natural History* describe Hellenistic collectors through the eyes of Roman citizens: Aratus of Sicyon and Attalus of Pergamum were the first individual collectors to be recognised as such; through their portraits presented in

Roman sources we realise the mechanisms of transmission, since these were based on contemporary written Hellenistic accounts that the Roman writers used as sources, in more or less the same way we use theirs, in order to create models for themselves and their contemporaries as well as for the generations to follow.

'Roman voices' (Part 3) continues the classical theme. It brings together testimonies relating to collecting practice in the Roman world and includes the first surviving direct communications of a collector. Cicero, in his private correspondence to his friends and agents T. Pomponius Atticus and M. Fabius Gallus, voices a rational Roman collector's views on the collecting practice and discourse of his era (Cicero, *ad Atticum*; *ad Familiales*). The portrait of other collectors, real or literary, like Asinius Polio, Augustus, Verres, Trimalchio and Euctus, are also drawn in the texts of their contemporaries and they serve to illustrate both the appropriation of Greek material culture and collecting notions of the past into Roman collections, and the psychology of the collector as this was perceived by his contemporaries (Petronius, *Satyricon*; Pliny, *Natural History*; Suetonius, *Augustus*; Cicero, *Verrine Orations*; and Martial, *Epigrams*). Passion for artefacts that often reached irrationality and madness – fetishism – but also the acquaintance with Greek art and the development of art theory and criticism, defined the collecting practice (Plutarch, *Aemilius Paullus*; Livy; Quintilian, *Institution Oratoria*; Martial, *Epigrams*; and Pliny, *Natural History*).

Ancient sources are also particularly explicit in their discussion of the collecting institutions of the Roman world – the mechanisms of the art market with its agents, antiquarians, fakers and the exaggerated prices; the sites of display for the assemblages, in the public or the private domain; art tourism and the first appearances of the official terminology regarding the care of collections; these are presented through a selection of texts (Martial, *Epigrams*; Cicero, *Verrine Orations*; Pliny, *Natural History*; Philostratus, *Imagines*; Josephus, *Jewish War*; Suetonius, *Vitellius*; and Pausanias, *Description of Greece*.).

Part 3 is completed with reference to women who had developed an interest in the accumulation of artefacts (Martial, *Epigrams*). In addition, the influence Roman collections had on subsequent generations is highlighted through a few references regarding a broader definition of collecting to include 'textual' collections, as well as a special mention of Pliny whose role as a major source for the collectors of subsequent periods and as an archetype collector cannot be overstressed. The themes in these two parts are treated at a length commensurate with their importance both at the time and to later readers of the works.

'Early medieval voices' (Part 4), concentrates upon testimonies about collecting practice from the fourth century to around 1150. The mingling of both themes is explicit in the account of the discoveries of fourth-century silverware, the kind of part cult service, part prestige gathering which falls within the broader remit of the collecting theme. The theme is pursued in the material relating to the relic collections in Britain and in Constantinople, and in the art object production and accumulation at the Abbey of St Denis, Paris. The pieces from Anglo-Saxon poetry, *The Ruin* and *Beowulf*, show the significant pleasure taken in treasure simultaneously for its own sake and for the social bonding which it represents; and *Beowulf* gives us accounts of treasure hoards buried in graves, the treasure guarded by the dragon, and that taken with Beowulf to his own barrow. The same themes are picked up in the *Nibelungsaga* and in the *Lay of Angantyr* where, in particular, the focus on the magic sword Tyrfing gives in intense poetic form an idea of the fetishistic power accorded to particular objects. The piece from *The Dream of Maxen Wledig* is included to represent the contemporary world of Celtic material imagination, temperamentally not too dissimilar from that of the Germanic world. The excerpt from Master Gregory's description of his visit to Rome (see Chapter 63) gives testimony to the link which, throughout these centuries and their mixed culture, contemporaries never ceased to feel between themselves and the material remains of the classical world.

High medieval voices up to 1500 are pursued in Part 5. The theme of collecting material from the ancient world runs through many of these pieces, beginning with that describing the activities of Henry of Blois and continuing with the pieces relating to the collecting activities of the Medicis, Cosimo, Piero and Lorenzo. A complementary group of pieces describes the treasure accumulations of contemporary northern Europe through the excerpt from the *Nibelungenlied*, which carries the account of the great treasure into its later manifestation, and those from Canterbury, Exeter and in the possession of William of Wykham, Bishop of Winchester. *Pearl* shows the psychological and symbolic significance of the material, and the text from around 1200 shows the craftsmanship which was involved.

In an almost uncanny way, the cultural multiplicity of these themes are fused into a consistent view, and a consistent collecting practice, in Suger's autobiographical account of his activities at the royal French Abbey of St Denis, Paris (which, as we show in Part 4, was a major art producer in the earlier medieval period). Suger quite consciously looked back to the cosmological aesthetic of the late classical world for his inspiration and as a result gathered gem-studded gold-work to enhance the relics of his church and its altars and ceremonies, cherished antiquities like Dagobert's throne, and hardstone vessels from the ancient classical world. Here at one specific time and site, we can see the themes already mentioned in action through collecting practice. Suger collects to enhance the metaphorical presence of the mighty dead represented by their bones; his accumulation creates relationships between God, the abbey and the feudal lords who presented material, which renders time, place and content sacred; and it constructs a poetic of material knowledge.

We may not be taking too great a liberty if we suppose that in his abbey, his deliberate accumulation of particular riches, and his supporting mystical material philosophy, Suger speaks not just for himself but for his own and succeeding generations. These generations perhaps included the Medici and those elsewhere in Europe who modelled their collecting activities upon them. When we read of Piero looking 'at his jewels and precious stones, of which he has a marvellous quantity of great value, some engraved in various ways, some not. He takes great pleasure and delight in looking at those, and in discussing their various powers and excellencies', we do not seem to be so far from Suger's 'Thus when – out of my delight in the beauty of the House of God – the loveliness of the many-coloured gems has called me away from external cares.' And both remind us of the *Ruin* poet's warriors who 'gazed on wrought gemstones, on gold, on silver, on wealth held and hoarded, on light-filled amber', and of the Roman passion for murrhine crystal vessels, described by Pliny.

The parts have been divided between the two contributors. Bounia was responsible for the Greek material in Part 1, and for Parts 2 and 3; Pearce for the British material in Part 1 and for Parts 4 and 5. This Introduction is a joint production. The arrangement of bibliographical references has given us much thought. Eventually, it was decided to give references to ancient Greek and Latin authors by chapter and line in their own works at the head of each excerpt, following normal usage, and to give the reference to the edition in the section headed 'Source'. Elsewhere, reference in the 'Source' is made by publication and page number. In general, in earlier English texts, spelling and grammar have been left as in the original, but occasionally, for the sake of clarity, some small amendments have been made.

Susan Pearce and Alexandra Bounia

Part I
Voices from the Distant Past

1

British Bronze Age burial mounds discussed by Richard Colt Hoare, William Borlase and Edward Cunnington

The prehistoric burial mounds – mostly Bronze Age – in Britain began to be of interest to educated men from the middle decades of the eighteenth century. The framework of interpretation brought to their excavation is made clear in the musings of Sir William Borlase, published in 1769. Explicit reference is made to Homer through classical stories about Alexander of Macedon and to the 'Druids', a favourite piece of eighteenth-century antiquarian fantasy also with its roots in the classical writers (Piggott, 1968).

Colt Hoare's account is the primary record of the discovery of the richest Bronze Age burial mound so far found (or perhaps likely to be found) in Britain, called the 'Bush Barrow' because it had a prominent bush growing out of its mound. Bush Barrow is one component of a group of some twenty-five Bronze Age barrows erected around 1600 BC and Neolithic mortuary structures built around a thousand years earlier; Stonehenge is about 700 metres away to the north. The whole complex represents one of the most important ritual centres in early prehistoric Britain.

Bush Barrow is an earth mound about 3 metres high, which originally covered the body of a male burial clothed, with a lozenge-shaped plate of sheet gold on his chest, gold belt fittings, and three bronze daggers all in wooden, leather-lined sheaths and one with a handle decorated with thousands of tiny gold pins. There was also a bronze axe-head and what has usually been interpreted as a mace-of-office, comprising a stone mace-head and a wooden shaft fitted with bone rings.

Sir Richard Colt Hoare (1758–1838), the son of a wealthy banker, was interested in classical studies and a connoisseur of the arts, and also strongly affected by the Romantic sympathies of his generation which drew him to travel the more rugged parts of Wales. In 1803 he formed a partnership with William Cunnington (1754–1810), a local wool merchant, which was to see the exploration of many Wiltshire archaeological sites and the production of a history of Wiltshire based on their joint researches. The Introduction to the first volume, published in 1810, proclaimed: 'We speak from facts, not theory', a novel notion for the day. The

pair opened some 465 barrows altogether, not all of which produced grave goods.

William Borlase (1695–1772) was the prime antiquary of Cornwall. He was a clergyman who clashed with John Wesley in 1744
and 1745, and corresponded with men like Alexander Pope. He
published *Cornish Antiquities* in 1754 and *Antiquities of Cornwall*
in 1769.

Edward Cunnington, William's grandson, continued the excavating tradition in Dorset in the 1880s, and in 1882 he opened the
Clandon Barrow, on the north-western end of the chalk ridge
crowned with the multi-period earthworks of Hod Hill and Maiden
Castle. The discoveries included a grave group comprising ceramics, a lozenge-shaped gold plate, a shale mace-head with gold
studs, a cup carved from a lump of amber, and a dagger. Bush
Barrow and Clandon Barrow are members of a well-recognised
complex of barrows which contained rich grave goods all broadly
of the same kind, notably sheet-gold ornaments, bronze daggers,
amber beads often made up into elaborate necklaces, beads and
cups made of carved shale from Kimmeridge, Dorset, faience
(blue-glazed pottery) beads probably from Mycenean Greece and
a range of ceramics. Such barrows are concentrated on the southern British chalklands of Wiltshire and Dorset, but they also occur
in east Devon, Cornwall, Sussex and East Anglia.

The interpretation of these barrows, together with their grave
goods and their contemporary environs over the last two centuries, has informed and exemplified the development of archaeological thinking. In a classic paper of 1938 Stuart Piggot defined
them as the critical component of his Wessex culture, and so as the
burial mounds of kings who controlled the lucrative trade in gold,
amber, tin and faience which linked Ireland, Cornwall, the Baltic
coasts (sources of amber) and Greece. More recently, archaeological interest has concentrated upon the implications of such 'high
status' burials for local patterns of dominance, land control and
the social mechanisms of exchange.

However, the idea of the great chief buried with his collected
wealth as an appropriate social expression of communal deposition has proved powerful and long enduring. It is seen as a fundamental expression of accumulation, both in the reality of Bronze
Age Europe and in how it has been interpreted since the eighteenth century.

SIR RICHARD COLT HOARE

This tumulus was formerly fenced round and planted with trees and its
exterior at present bears a very rough appearance from being covered

with furze and heath. The first attempts made by Mr Cunningham on this barrow proved unsuccessful, as also those of some farmers, who tried their skill digging into it.

Our researches were renewed in September 1808 and we were amply repaid for our perseverance and former disappointment. On reaching the floor of the barrow, we discovered the skeleton of a stout and tall man lying from south to north: the extreme length of his thigh was 20 inches. About 18 inches south of the head, we found several brass rivets[1] intermixed with wood, and some thin bits of brass nearly decomposed. These articles covered a space of 12 inches or more; it is probable, therefore, that they were the mouldered remains of a shield.

Near the shoulders lay a fine axe, the lower end of which owes its great preservation to having been originally inserted within a handle of wood. Near the right arm was a dagger of brass and a spearhead of the same metal, full thirteen inches long and the largest we have ever found, though not so neat in its pattern as some others of an inferior size which have been engraved in our work. These were accompanied by a curious article of gold, which I conceive, had originally decorated the case of the dagger. The handle of wood belonging to this instrument exceeds anything we have yet seen, both in design and execution, and could not be surpassed (if indeed equalled) by the most noble workman of modern times. The viewer will immediately recognise the British zigzag, or the modern Vandyke pattern, which was formed with a labour and exactness almost unaccountable by thousands of gold rivets, smaller than the smallest pin.

The head of the handle, though exhibiting a variety of pattern, was also found by the same kind of studdings. So very minute indeed were these pins that our labourers had thrown thousands of them out with their shovel and scattered them in every direction, before, with the necessary aid of a magnifying glass we could discover what they were; but fortunately enough remained attached to the wood to enable us to decipher the pattern. Beneath the fingers of the right hand lay a lance-head of brass, but so much corroded that it broke in pieces on moving. Immediately over the breast of the skeleton was a large plate of gold in the form of a lozenge and measuring 7 inches by 6. It was fixed to a thin piece of wood, over the edges of which the gold was tapped: it is perforated at top and bottom, for the purpose, probably, of fastening it to the dress in a breast-plate. The even surface of this noble ornament is relieved by indented lines, cheques, or zigzags, following the shape of the outline, and forming lozenge within lozenge, diminishing gradually towards the centre. We next discovered on the right side of the skeleton, a very curious perforated stone, some wrought articles of bone, many small rings of the same material and another article of gold. The stone is made out of a fossil mass of tubulana, and polished; rather of an egg form, or as a farrier who was present observed, resembling the top of a large gimlet. It had a wooden handle, which was fixed into the perforations in the centre, and encircled by a neat ornament of brass, part of which still adheres to the stone. As this stone bears no marks of wear or attrition, I can hardly consider it to have been used as a domestic implement, and from the circumstances of its being composed of a mass of sea worms, or little serpents, I think we may not be too fanciful in considering it an article of consequence. We know, by history, that much importance was attached by the ancients to the serpent and I have before had occasion to mention the veneration with which the *glain hadroeth* was esteemed by the Britons; and my classical readers will recollect the fanciful story related by Pliny on this subject, who says that the Druid's Egg was formed by the scum of a vast multitude of serpents twisted and conjoined up together. This stone, therefore, which contains a mass of serpularia or little serpents, might have been held in great veneration by the Britons who it considered of sufficient importance to merit a place amongst the many rich and valuable relics deposited in this tumulus with the body of the deceased.

Source

Bush Barrow: The Ancient History of Wiltshire, Sir Richard Colt Hoare, Vol. 1 (1812), 203–4

SIR WILLIAM BORLASE

By the contents of all Barrows which have been examined elsewhere as well as in this island, it appears that the principal cause of their erection was to enclose either the Ashes, or the Bodies (unburnt), of the dead: however, the Sepulchres of the Ancients being always looked upon with a kind of veneration, they became afterwards applied to the solemnization of their highest Rites of Religion and Festivity. No sooner was Alexander arrived upon the Plains before Troy, but he performed Sacrifices and other usual Rites at the *Tumulus* of Achilles; and this is recorded of him not as any thing new, or instituted by him; we are therefore only to consider him here, as complying with the already established customs of his country. Again, as the Druids burnt, and afterwards buried their dead, there is no doubt but they had Barrows for their Sepulchres as well as other nations, and this was the original use of them, but they were afterwards otherwise applied; for, on the Stone Barrows, the Druids kindled their annual fires, especially where there is a large flat Stone on the top. Where the Earth-Barrows are inclosed, or shaped by a Circle of Stone erect, they may safely be persumed to have served at Alters for Sacrifice. These Heaps were also, probably, at times, places of Inauguration, the Chieftain elect standing on the top exposed to view, and the Druid officiating close to the edge below. On the same Hillocks (likely) judgement was frequently pronounced, and the most important decisions made, as from a sacred eminence; and where these were not at hand, something of like kind was erected, for the Judge to stand or sit upon, and give forth his Decrees with proper advantage.

Source

Borlase, Sir W., *Antiquities of Cornwall*, 1769: 222

EDWARD CUNNINGTON'S *NARRATIVE* RELATING TO THE CLANDON BARROW

This remarkably fine barrow[2] is situated on a commanding position on a ridge of sand, gravel and clay, capping the chalk at the eastern end of Martinstown, and about a quarter of a mile west of Maiden Castle (actually it is half a mile north west of the extreme defences of the prehistoric hill town). It is a handsome cone, with very steep sides and forms a prominent object for miles around. The diameter is 68 feet, height of centre 18½ feet. It is composed entirely of layers – put in with some regularity – of the sands, clay and gravel …

At a further depth of four feet under the above interments[3] – or seven feet from the surface – a cairn of flints was found of nine inches to a foot in thickness and eight feet in diameter. Almost on the edge of the south side of this, and on the flints, was a bronze dagger … which was unfortunately broken; this had been left in its wooden sheath, small fragments of which were visible, and also a small bronze ring attached to it for attachment …

On top of the cairn and pressing close to a flint, the form of which it had partly taken, was a fine diamond-shaped ornament of thin beaten gold … the greater diameter six inches, the lesser 4½ inches …

Near to the piece of gold, and also upon the flints, was a handsome jet[4] ornament that may have been the head of a sceptre. At its base is a cocket with marks round showing where a handle had been fixed. The shape is elliptical, the sides being slightly flattened, with two gold bosses on each, and another boss on the top. These bosses are ⅝th of an inch diameter, and fitted accurately into sockets. The length of this unique object is three inches, two inches broad and an inch and a half in thickness ...

Scattered amongst the flints and spread over a surface of two feet were the fragments of an amber cup ...

Below the cairn – which rested on a bed of fine white clay, were the broken pieces of an incense cup of dark brown pottery ... This cup had been broken and the parts scattered on the clay, before the flints were placed there.

At six feet from the centre surface and a foot from the flints, a badly baked urn was found. It was crushed perfectly flat upon a thin stratum of ashes and small flints ... It was finely ornamented.

There were several bands of black ashes throughout the barrow, sometimes mixed with worked flints; a good thumb scraper was found at ten feet depth.

Source

'Clandon Barrow' Edward Cunnington's manuscript in Dorset County Museum, Dorchester, published in part in Drew, C.D., 'Two Bronze Age Barrows', *Proceedings of the Dorset Natural History and Archaeological Society* 58, 1937: 18–25

Notes

1   The grave goods are in Devizes Museum, Wiltshire. All the non-gold work is bronze, not brass.
2   The grave goods are in Dorset Museum, Dorchester, Dorset. It should be noted that any actual burial associated with these finds was not located.
3   Above the rich early Bronze Age burial, later burials had been inserted into the mound – a Bronze Age cremation in a funerary urn, and two inhumations in stone-lined graves, possibly Roman.
4   In fact, Kimmeridge shale, not jet.

References

Annable and Simpson, 1964
Grinsell, 1959
Marsdon, 1974
Megaw and Simpson, 1979
Piggot, 1938
Piggot, 1968

2

Excavations in the Derbyshire Peak District by Thomas Bateman

Thomas Bateman (1821–61) was brought up by his grandfather, Thomas Bateman of Middleton Hall, High Sheriff of Derbyshire, and inherited his large estates in 1847. He had a deep fondness for archaeological research, and dug into over 360 burial mounds in Yorkshire, Derbyshire and Staffordshire. In many ways, he represents the northern England antiquarian tradition, which ran parallel to that of Dorset and Wiltshire, and his *Ten Years Diggings* gives an account of his activities.

Like others, Bateman was irresistibly drawn to the burial mounds in the vicinity of Arbor Low, a major Neolithic henge monument of circular bank and ditch with, originally, a large central circle of standing stones, near Bakewell in the Derbyshire Peak District. Arbor Low represents very broadly the same kind of ritual focus as did Stonehenge on the Wessex chalk (and Avebury, near Stonehenge).

The two pieces here from *Ten Years Diggings* give accounts of the opening of two barrows near Arbor Low on Middleton Moor, and at Over Haddon near Grindlow. Both yielded female interments accompanied by elaborate necklaces of jet beads: these are often seen as the northern equivalents of the Wessex amber necklaces. Indeed, these monuments altogether have been seen as the 'Peak culture', equivalent to the 'Wessex culture', and to be interpreted in much the same way. Their interpretation has followed a similar sequence and, like the Wessex material, they have informed concepts of collecting practice.

ARBOR LOW AND OVER HADDON

About fifty yards South-east of the last, is another barrow of very small size, both as to diameter and height; so inconsiderable indeed are its dimensions, that it was quite overlooked in 1824. Fortunately, the contents, with the exception of one skeleton that lay near the surface, had been enclosed in a cist, sunk a few inches beneath the level of the soil. As in the companion barrow, the skeleton near the top was dismembered by the plough, so that it afforded nothing worthy of notice – the original interment, however, which lay rather deeper, in a kind of rude cist or enclosure, formed by ten shapeless masses of limestone, amply repaid our labour. The persons thus interred consisted of a female in the prime of life, and a child of about four years of age; the former had been placed on the floor of the grave on her left side, with the knees drawn up; the child was placed above her, and rather behind her shoulders: they were surrounded and covered with innumerable bones of the water-vole, or rat, and near the woman was a cow's tooth, an article uniformly found with the more ancient interments. Round her neck was a necklace of variously shaped beads and other trinkets of jet and bone, curiously ornamented, upon the whole resembling those found at Cow Low in 1846, (*Vestiges*, p. 92),[1] but differing from them in many details. The various pieces of this compound ornament are 420 in number, which unusual quantity is accounted for by the fact of 348 of the beads being thin lamanæ only; 54 are of cylindrical form, and the 18 remaining pieces are conical studs and perforated plates, the latter in some cases ornamented with punctured patterns. Altogether, the necklace is the most elaborate production of the pre-metallic period that I have seen. The skull, in perfect preservation, is beautiful in its proportions, and has been selected to appear in the *Crania Britannica*, as the type of the ancient British female. The femur measures 15¼ inches. The engraving represents the arrangement of the cist.[2] ...

On the 30th of April a barrow near Over Haddon, in land called Gridlow, was examined as completely as the meeting of three walls on its summit would allow. It had been much mutilated; but fortunately the primitive interments lay too deep to receive injury from the labours of those in search of stone, by whom an important interment of secondary date had been destroyed. The original deposit had been made on the rock a little below the natural surface, and about 5 feet from the top of the mound; it comprised three skeletons, laid in the usual contracted position, two of which were females; with them were one or two rude instruments of flint, and a fine collection of jet ornaments, 73 in number, which form a very handsome necklace. Of these 26 are cylindrical beads, 39 are conical studs, pierced at the back by two holes meeting at an angle in the centre; and the remaining 8 are flat dividing places, ornamented in the front with a punctured chevron pattern, superficially drilled in the jet; 7 of them are laterally performated with three holes, to admit of their being connected by a triple row of the cylindrical beads, whilst the 8th, which is of bone, ornamented in the same style, has nine holes at one side, which diminish to three on the other by being bored obliquely.[2] Above these bodies, which were covered with stone, the mound was of unmixed earth, very compact and clayey, and between stones and earth were many pieces of calcined bone, and numerous splinters of the leg bones of large animals, some of which are likely to have been used as points for weapons.

Source

Bateman, T., 1852, *Ten Years Diggings*, Sheffield: 24–6, 46–8

Notes

1   *Vestiges* refers to Bateman's previous work, *Vestiges of the Antiquities of Derbyshire*, 1848.
2   Finds in City Museum, Sheffield.

References

Ashbee, 1960
Marsden, 1974
Megaw and Simpson, 1979

3

Verses on barrow excavation by Stephen Isaacson

It is worth making the point that Victorian antiquarian activity produced a good deal of occasional material, some, like this verse, memorable for its awfulness, but interesting because of the tone and detail which it captures at a time when ideas of the scope of prehistory and its significance were first penetrating the intellectual scene.

This poem was written by the Reverend Stephen Isaacson, a companion of Thomas Bateman on some of his excavations. It was penned on the occasion of the first archaeological conference in the world, held by the newly-formed British Archaeological Association at Canterbury, Kent in 1844. One of the days of the meeting was devoted to barrow-digging on Breach Downs, near Canterbury, and it is to this expedition that the verses refer.

BARROW-DIGGING ON BREACH DOWNS

My Dear brother Bob,

This is the scud, that took place in the mud,
While we sat and looked on from the carriage:
Such a dash was not seen, such a splash has not been,
My dear Bob, since the day of my marriage.

Fine ladies so soiled, as onward they toiled,
While Professors so grave grubbed away;
Would have made you declare, had you only been there,
It was ten times as good as a play.

There were clergy in cloaks, cutting all kinds of jokes,
(For many were far from their homes:)
There were 'cutters' and 'pasters' and some sketch-book wasters,
All intending to make weighty tomes.

Such draggling of skirts! such giggling of flirts,
As you see in a storm in Hyde Park;

With no end of umbrellas, to shelter the Fellows,
Who seemed bent upon digging til dark.

The 'Buckland' Professor,[1] a very great messer,
In clay, and in rubble, and chalk:
Jumped into a grave, some relick to save.
And there held a pretty long talk.

Sir William Betham, of course too was with 'em,
It's nothing without 'Ulster King',[2]
How he handled the thigh-bones, and other queer dry bones,
Sometimes shouting out – 'No such thing!'

Then the chuckles o'er buckles, as down on their knuckles,
They pick up little odd bits of brass;
The clowns standing round, asking what they had found,
If coins? and they thought they would pass.

So there we sat still, half a mile from the mill,
And a 'right merrie' trio we were:
And when to the Bourne, all horses they turn,
Why we were the first to be there.

Shall I tell you for why? we saw by the sky
There would be no change in the weather;
So instead of staying last, we chose to ride fast,
And not all come to luncheon together.

The best of good feeding, with true courtly breeding,
Was prepared for us all at Bourne Park;[3]
Had the party been weeded, to say truth it needed,
We could gladly have staid there 'till dark.

But all things must end, and so, my dear friend,
Did this very enjoyable day;
Should kind fate, my dear brother, grant me such another,
May you not be miles far away.

Source

Marsden, B., 1984, *Pioneers of Prehistory*, Ormskirk and Northridge, Hesketh:
    29.

Notes

1 'Professors' included William Buckland, Professor of Geology at Oxford. He excavated material relating to early man at the Kent's Cavern site, Torquay, Devon, and was a famous anti-Darwinian.
2 Sir William Betham was Ulster King-at-Arms, and a well-known antiquary.
3 Bourne Park was the home of Lord Albert Denison Conyngham, President of the British Archaeological Association.

References

Marsden, 1984

4

Descriptions of the finding of Bronze Age hoards

In the later Bronze Age (roughly 1450–700 BC) elaborate barrow burials with rich grave goods dropped out of fashion. Instead, and perhaps as the contemporary equivalent, communities in Britain and across much of northern Europe deposited groups of bronze pieces, sometimes by burial and sometimes by throwing into water. The bronzes involved are axes ('celts'), spearheads, rapiers and swords, personal ornaments and smaller pieces: the balance of types in these depositions differs across time and place. Sometimes gold objects were placed with bronze (as here at Lanant) and sometimes the depositions are wholly of gold. All these groups are conventionally called 'hoards', but this conceals a mixture of characters. Some seem to be the sites of workshops, and others the rubbish of domestic occupation. But many were clearly very valuable and were deposited with ceremony; there is now general agreement that these are 'ritual' offerings, dedicated to the gods and constituting conspicuous consumption of community wealth linked with notions of 'treasure' concealed for ever in a sacred place.

Such hoards must have turned up from time to time since their deposition stopped abruptly at the beginning of the Iron Age, but the first record of such a find is that of John Leland quoted in the Borlase and Hitchen pieces given here. From the later eighteenth century they begin to be noticed and recorded as part of the burgeoning interest in antiquities, and as agriculture and development have become steadily 'heavier' since the 1760s, so the numbers of hoards coming to light has grown. Their concentrated study since the 1960s has done much to develop and refine ideas about the role of material culture in societies, and the concepts which underlie accumulating, hoarding and collecting practices.

MATERIAL FOUND AT CARN BREA, CORNWALL

In the year 1744, in the side of Karn-brê[1] hill, were dug up several hollow instruments of brass, of different sizes, called Celts.[2]

With these instruments were found several Roman Coins, six of which came into my hands; one of ANTONINVS AVG. Nº 2. uncertain. Nº 3.

15

DIVO CONSTANTIO PIO; Reverse MEMORIA FELEX. N° 4. defaced.
N° 5. SEVERVS ALEXANDER. N° 6. defaced.

At present let the Celts be the subject of our enquiry, what nation we
shall ascribe them to, and to what use that nation applied them. As they
are found here in Cornwall in company with Roman Coins, one would be
apt to imagine that they were of Roman original. Upon much less grounds
are they asserted to be Roman by the learned Dr. Plot, who, finding one
of like kind, engraved in the Museum Moscardi, immediately concludes
all the Celts found at the several places were mentioned to be Roman
(though no Coins of that nation were found with them), and determines
also the Barrows where they were found to have been erected by that
people.

Mr. Hearne[3] follows Dr. Plot, in attributing them to the Romans:
others take them to be British.

First, then, I do not take them to be purely Roman, foreign, or of
Italian invention and workmanship.

They are made of Brass, which the Romans of Italy would not have
done after Julius Cesar's time, when the superior hardness of iron was so
well understood by that cultivated people, and so easily to be had from
any of their conquered provinces.

They do not appear in the complete collection of arms on the Trajan,
or Antonine Pillar, which, if they had been Roman instruments, they
certainly would have done.

There are but very few in the cabinets of the curious in Rome, Naples,
and the other cities of Italy, as I am informed by a gentleman who has
examined them with equal penetration and diligence (and has been so
kind as to favour me with several informations relating to that subject),
and 'where they occur, they are looked upon, by all the Italian Virtuos as
Transalpine Antiquities, and not to have belonged to the predecessors'.

In the great discoveries which have of late years been made among the
ruins of Herculaneum,[4] where weapons, tools, and utensils for every
occurrence in life, have been found, none of these instruments have been
met with, as far as yet appears.

Spon[5] in his Miscellanea mentions none of them. 'They occur not in
the Museum Romanum, published by Mons. de la Chausse, not in the
Museum Kercherianum published by Bonani.' In the 'voluminous collection of Montfaucon, there are none engraved or mentioned'. So far this
learned Gentleman.

Now if these instruments had been of foreign original, and by the
Romans introduced into Britain, they would have been frequently found
in Italy, and very numerous in the collections of the curious, and could
never have escaped the authors above-mentioned. I am therefore apt to
believe that they are not to be ascribed in general to the Romans, nor used

by the Roman legions in Italy and the East; but that they were probably made and used by the provincial Romans of Britain, and by the Britains themselves when they had improved the arts under their Roman masters.

They are found here at Karn-brê, and have been found at Aldborough (the ancient Isurium) in Yorkshire, in company with many Roman Coins, the reason of which seems to be this, when the Romans had thought fit to admit the natives of their conquered provinces into their armies (the very legions themselves being, at last, occasionally recruited out of such provinces), it is not to be doubted but the Britans were allowed to carry the weapons of war, which they had been trained up to, and were become easy and habitual to them. And as we do not find these weapons of general use among the Eastern Romans, we may conclude, that the Romans suffered the British discipline, as to this particular, to prevail here in this province; and finding the Britains expert in the use of these arms, and the arms really of service against the Picts, Scots, and rebellious Britains, not only indulged and encouraged the Britans in the use of them, but fell into the use of them themselves. In short, most of them seem to me too correct and shapely for the Britains before the Julian conquest; and yet the Romans do not appear to have used them beyond the Alps; I imagine, therefore, that they were originally of British, Gaulish, or Northern, invention and fabrick, and afterwards used by the provincial Romans, as well as Britans. Let us consider, in the next place, that they are frequently found in all parts of Britain.

Leland[6] ... tells us, that a few years before his being in Cornwall, there were found spear-heads, battle-axes, and swords made of copper, near the Mount, in the parish of St. Hillary, where, by the spear-heads, he certainly meant those which we (from Begerus, &c.) now call Celts. Camden[7] says, they were found not long before in Wales, and in Germany. Mr Thoresby[8] gives an account of some found in Yorkshire near Bramham-Moor, in 1709. 'Several of them have been found in a stone quarry in the same country, many of which had hafts exactly fitted to them. In May, 1735, were found above 100 on Easterley-Moor, twelve Miles N.W. of York.

Source

Borlase, Sir W., 1769, *Antiquities of Cornwall*, London: 281–3

ACCOUNT OF ANTIQUITIES DISCOVERED IN CORNWALL, BY THE REV. MALACHY HITCHINS[9]

Read Dec. 9, 1802.

Sir   *St. Hilary, Cornwall, June 5*, 1802

Since I did myself the honor of sending you a short account of three Roman Urns, and a newly-discovered *cromlêh*, a farmer who lives in the parish of Lanant,[10] just four miles directly north of St. Michael's Mount, happening to be employed in digging up earth for manure, in the ditch of one of his fields, found a place where the ground was loose to more than an usual depth; which tempting him to search for the cause, at two feet under the surface he met with ashes; many celts some entire and others broken; several pieces of copper swords; and heavy lumps of fine copper evidently brought thither to fusion, as there is every appearance that this was a military foundery.[11] In the bottom of one of the largest and most perfect of the celts, were found some small bars of gold, none of them larger than a straw, and one of them about three tenths of an inch wide, but very thin; the whole was as bright as if it had been lately deposited, and weighed about an ounce, as the farmer told me; but as he was apprehensive that the lord of the manor might claim the whole if he knew its value, it is probable that the bullion was more than he would allow, especially as he wished to decline a minute discussion of this subject, and the person who purchased it was equally evasive. It is the disposition of most farmers to turn every thing, of which they know not the use, into money as soon as possible; and accordingly the finder of these curiosities immediately carried them to St. Ives, and sold them to a brasier for sixpence a pound, but for the gold he had its proper value. It does appear that the celts, &c. which fell into the farmer's hands weighted about fourteen or fifteen pounds, but some articles were carried off by his neighbours. As soon as I heard of this discovery I went to the spot, and observed that as the loose earth continues to run out under the field, to the same depth as in the ditch, it is probably that the whole foundery is not yet explored, and that many more articles may still be found by digging farther: an experiment which, at my persuasion, would have then been made, had not the farmer's illness prevented it, and which is still postponed by the question of the right of search between his landlord and him. I have got possession of two complete celts, one 4½ and the other 3½ inches long, in which latter the gold was found, some broken pieces of copper swards, two or three other articles whose use I cannot conjecture, and a lump of fine copper.

Though celts are by no means scarce, yet as an Antiquary may possibly find the other things more rare, and I am anxious to snatch every occasion of testifying my gratitude to you for many and important favours, I have packed them up in a small box and forwarded them to you; and if you will condescend to take them into your possession, they will by that circumstance acquire much more importance than they have intrinsically. It is remarkable that there is not the smallest vestige, or materials of a building on the spot, nor any whole or broken crucibles, and the bank-hedge near which these antiquities were found, was made within the last century.

Happening to mention this discovery at our last Easter vestry, a farmer of this parish, (St. Hilary), told me that about eighteen months since, having carried the earth of the ditch of his field, he found some military weapons made of copper, consisting, as I found by inquiries, of celts, spear-heads, many broken pieces of copper swords, and several lumps of that metal, weighting altogether about eighty pounds. All these he immediately melted adown for domestic purposes, reserving only one of the spear-heads, which, with the exception of a little injury at the point, is in great perfection, and which I have sent you in the box with the articles found at Lanant. Though these weapons were dug up in this parish, and within one mile of my house, I should never have heard of it in all probability but for the above accident.

This is not the first time that antiquities of the same kind have been discovered in this parish; for Leyland[12] says that a few years before he was in Cornwall, there were found spear-heads, battle-axes, and swords made of copper, near St. Michael's Mount, in the parish of St. Hilary. By the spear-heads, says Dr. Borlase, he *certainly* meant those which we now call celts. It seems to me, however, extremely probable that the spear-heads were of the same kind as the one which the farmer preserved, and which somewhat resembles a modern boarding-pike; for those weapons, by their having holes in the sockets for fixing them on the hafts by pins, by their raper length, and sharp points and sides, were much more likely to be called spear-heads than celts can be, which are not universally acknowledged to be weapons of war. Besides, as spear-heads were found here mixed with celts, it seems likely they could not be used for the same purpose, *i.e.* pushing at the enemy as with modern bayonets: for it must be allowed that the celts would require much more offensive violence to penetrate the human body than the spear-heads, which, by their construction, were evidently designed for stabbing.

These spear-heads, celts, pieces of swords, and lumps of copper, of which last some pieces weighed 12 or 14*lb.* each, were crammed into a space less than a cubic foot, and lay very near the surface just between the earth and clay, not wrapped up in cloth, like those mentioned by Leland, or any other envelope, and without any remains of decayed wood, which might have been their handles; and as no ashes were found in this place, or other signs of a forge, it is likely these articles were deposited here in haste for a temporary concealment.

The farmer who ignorantly destroyed these curiosities, and who, being also an agent in the mines, is pretty much in the habit of running metals, assured me that the celts were so extremely difficult to be melted, that he thinks they must have been hardened by some art at present unknown. If this be true, query whether the small bars of gold, found in the bottom of one of the celts at Lanant, might not have been put there for fusion?

I have the honor to be,
With great Respect,
Sir,
Your much obliged, and very humble Servant,
MALACHY HITCHINS.

Source

Hitchins, Rev. M., 1806, 'Account of Antiquities discovered in Cornwall, the Rev. Malachy Hitchins, in a letter to the Rt. Hon Sir Joseph Banks, Bart KB PRS and RSA', *Archaeologia* 15: 118–21

ABERDEEN JOURNAL, WEDNESDAY 29 MARCH 1843

INTERESTING RELICS. About three weeks ago some woodcutters in pursuit of rabbits on the hill of Knockie in Glentanner, accidentally discovered under a cairn an ancient burial place covered by a large flat stone. On removing this, they found the following articles. 1. Two bronze vessels capable of holding about two thirds of a pint, of neat workmanship, cast in rather an elegant shape, and with a handle on one side. 2. Seventeen spear or axe heads of bronze known among antiquaries by the name of Celts. 3. From thirty to forty bronze bracelets, of various sizes but mostly, it would seem, designed for the wrist. 4. Four bronze pieces, two of them richly gilt, consisting of three rings, each about one inch in diameter. Joined together in a line, slightly curved, as to be worn on the shoulder or body. 5. Six bronze rings, of good workmanship, of different sizes. 6. A circular piece of bronze, probably part of the mounting of a weapon.

In one of the cups there was a small quantity of resinous matter, and in the other what the workmen described as 'something like a piece of parchment' but which crumbled to pieces on being handled.

The whole of these interesting relics are in admirable preservation, and are evidently of Roman manufacture, and to belong, at the latest, to the middle of the fourth century. We trust the Noble Lord of the Manor, the Marquis of Huntly will take care to have them deposited in some public museum. The lovers of antiquities are in the meantime under great obligations to the Minister of Aboyne and Glentanner, the Rev. Robert Milne Miller for his exertions in rescuing many of the articles from the hands of the workmen.

Source

Aberdeen Journal, Wednesday 29 March 1843

Notes

1 'Karn-brê' is the prominent west Cornwall hill now known as Carn Brea. It was the site of extensive occupation in the Neolithic period (roughly 4000– 200 BC) and the Iron Age (roughly 700 BC–AD 50).

2 The 'celts' are late Bronze Age socketed axes, roughly 900–700 BC; the Roman coins found are third and fourth centuries AD. They were found together because Carn Brea is a multi-period site. Borlase's discussion shows the difficulties faced in the eighteenth century in understanding the relative dating of antiquities.

3 Thomas Hearne (1678–1735). Born in Berkshire, educated at Oxford, be- came Assistant Keeper of the Bodleian Library (1699) and subsequently Second Keeper (1712). He was deprived of his post for refusing to take the oaths of loyalty in 1716, and stayed in Oxford, editing and publishing important medieval texts.

4 Note the reference to Herculaneum, and see Vol. 2 in this series.

5 Jacob Spon (1647–85) of Lyons, traveller and antiquity, wrote of the antiq- uities of Lyons, of contemporary collections and of his travels in Italy, Greece and the Levant with George Wheeler. The references are to famous collections gathered by Monsieur de la Chauffe and the Jesuit Athenasius Kircher.

6 John Leland (1506–52) was born in London and educated at Cambridge. He became Librarian and Chaplain to Henry VIII and in 1533 was commis- sioned as King's Antiquary to search for manuscripts and relics. In 1536– 42 he went on an antiquarian tour of England and Wales, but became insane in 1550. His *Itinerary* was not published until 1710–12 and his *Collections* not until 1715 (both by Thomas Hearne). His work was used by Camden. This is believed to be the first reference to a find of Bronze Age metalwork.

7 William Camden (1551–1623), born in London, educated at Oxford. He travelled, accumulating material for his *Britannia*, first published in 1586. He was a master (1575) and Head of Westminster School, and founded the Oxford Chair of Ancient History.

8 Ralph Thoresby was born in 1658, the son of a Leeds cloth merchant. He

had experience of northern Europe, and made a major collection of coins and medals, prints and material of all kinds; by 1682 the museum in his home in Kirkgate was attracting attention, and he published its catalogue in 1713. He died in 1725, and his collection was allowed to decay.

9   This extract shows how communications about finds were made to the learned world by way of pieces read to meetings of the Society of Antiquaries of London and then published in their journal, *Archaeologia*, for Sir John Banks – see Vol. 2 in this series.

10 Lanant, St Hilary and St Michael's Mount are all in west Cornwall.

11 The bronze fragments detailed are still in the collection of the Society of Antiquaries.

12 This reference to Leland is the same as that mentioned above, note 6, and the Borlase reference is to the piece printed above.

13 The pieces came into possession of Colin Milne Miller, Robert's son, and eventually turned up in Exeter, Devon. (See Pearce 1970–71 and 1976–77.)

References

Bradley, 1990
Chope Pearse, 1967
Pearce, 1970–71
Pearce, 1976–77

5

Information on the Iron Age burial at Hunmanby, Yorkshire, by Thomas Sheppard

Thomas Sheppard (1876–1945) was appointed curator of the Municipal Museum, Hull in 1901; it had been the Museum of the Hull Literary and Philosophical Society until acquired by the City Corporation. Sheppard was one of the most vigorous of the new generation of curators who believed that education was at the heart of the museum's activities, that displays should be as accessible as possible, and that the collections should be both systematic and mostly from the locality, in this case the East Riding of Yorkshire.

Sheppard was himself one of the great museum collectors, and was the prime mover in securing the Mortimer Collection for public ownership in Hull museums. This collection, formed by the two Mortimer brothers, comprised some 60,000 items of local archaeology – many from local Bronze Age burial mounds – and 6,000 geological specimens. Sadly, Sheppard's final years were overcast by the events of the Second World War, which saw his 'Old Time' Street Museum destroyed in the 1941 air raids and the main Municipal Museum gutted by incendiary bombs in 1943, although by this time the Mortimer Collection had been moved from display.

This text records his examination of a fourth-century BC Iron Age chariot burial which appeared in a brick pit at Hunmanby. This burial belongs to a small east Yorkshire group of similar sites usually called 'Arras-style' burials, after a site at Arras, northern France, which shows similar characteristics. This similarity has been used to argue that the men buried in the Yorkshire chariot graves came originally (or their immediate ancestors did) from northern France, but other explanations for the similarities, based on cross-Channel links or separate war-like developments, are possible. It is, however, worth noting that classical sources tell us the Iron Age tribe in the Arras region was the Parisii, and that of Yorkshire the Parisi.

The important point here is that this Iron Age burial, among a large number of others in the Iron Age, documents the reappearance of elaborate graves endowed with larger or smaller accumulations of goods. Throughout the Iron Age, the ideas of 'treasure' deposited either as 'hoards' or in graves operates as a significant

23

social practice, a tradition which continues into the Romano-British world.

HUNMANBY

In May last, during the process of excavating clay for brick-making in a pit close to Hunmanby station, a landslip occurred which exposed some articles of bronze. The writer was acquainted with the circumstances, and immediately went to Hunmanby, where, with the assistance of Mr. C.G. Danford, of Reighton, and of Mr. Parker, the owner of the pit, excavation were made, resulting in the discovery of a British chariot-burial.[1] ...

The objects exposed by the recent landslip were a bronze bridle-bit, and fragments of a thin bronze plate.

Attention was first paid to the slipped mass of gravel. This was carefully examined, and yielded the iron hoop of a chariot wheel, though it was in several fragments. The hoop is slightly over an inch in width, but on account of its oxidised state it is not possible to ascertain the exact original thickness of the iron. The rim appears to have been turned inwards on each side. Sand and small pebbles have adhered to the tyre. From the specimens obtained the diameter of the wheel was calculated to have been nearly three feet. Portions of the iron hoops for the naves were also secured. These appeared to be of thicker material, and, if complete, would be six or seven inches across. Obvious traces of wood were found adhering to the iron of both the large and small hoops, but nothing was present to indicate how many spokes existed, nor, indeed, was there evidence of spokes at all. One or two curved pieces of iron were also found.

After being satisfied that there were no further relics amongst the slipped material, attention was devoted to the grave, which was well shown in section at the top of the pit, the disturbed portion being readily distinguished from the natural bedded gravel at its sides, particularly as a thin layer or 'pan' of iron lined the grave. This 'pan' owes its existence to the disintegration of iron, of which metal quite a large quantity must have occurred amongst the objects interred.

The burial was situated under a slight mound, or tumulus, now almost levelled as a result of agricultural operations, though some of the workmen remembered it when it was much more conspicuous than it is to-day. The grave was basin-shaped, and the sides curved inwards. It was 11 feet 6 inches across the top, and 3 feet 6 inches deep (measured from the original land level) in the middle. The floor of the excavation was not horizontal, but was five or six inches deeper at one end than at the other. The infilling consisted largely of sand, with occasional sandstone, etc., pebbles. This material, partly from the quantity of iron it contained, and partly no doubt from the decayed organic material, was exceedingly compact and difficult to work. Towards the bottom of the grave was a quantity of greyish material, with the peculiar 'greasy' feeling so characteristic in places of this nature.

On carefully examining the section, it was seen that traces of bronze occurred. Some of this material was in very thin plates, and too far decayed to bear touching, and some was in the form of a beading or tube cut horizontally, about a quarter of an inch wide. After several hours' work it was seen that lying on the bottom of the grave was a large shield of wood, apparently oak, ornamented on the upper surface with exceedingly thin plates of bronze, and with a border formed of more substantial material – a strip of bronze, about one-sixteenth of an inch in thickness, and three-quarters of an inch in width. This had been carefully hammered over into a U-section, into which the edge of the wood shield was clearly fitted. This bronze strip was fastened to the wood by means of small bronze rivets, about a quarter of an inch long, exactly the thickness and shape of an ordinary household pin-head. Unfortunately the greater portion of this shield had fallen with the landslip, and with the exception of a few pieces of bronze, forming the border, not any of it was recovered; nor is this to be wondered at, as even in that portion examined in position both the wood and the thin ornamental plates were so fragile and decayed, that they would not bear touching. As much as could be possibly moved was taken away, though this was only accomplished by also removing the soil upon which it rested …

Across one end of the shield were the remains of a flattened tube of thin bronze, of which little more than the cast remained – the metal having almost entirely disappeared. This was traced for about six inches, and may have been the remains of the thin end of a bronze scabbard, or of a spear – most probably the latter, as no other signs of a sword were visible.

Near the edge of the shield, and a few inches about it, were two curved pieces of it of doubtful use – possibly part of the chariot – as well as various other pieces of that metal. Amongst the latter were two rivet-like pieces of iron (*i.e.* small bars with 'heads' at the ends) with the wood still adhering to the sides, evidently used in connection with the construction of the chariot. These and many other evidences of the vehicle itself having been buried, are of some importance, as according to some authorities a 'chariot-burial' sometimes means that only the wheels and horse-trappings were buried with the warrior.

As might be expected from the nature of the subsoil, bones were very few indeed. Immediately below the tyre of the wheel presently to be described, however, were a fragment of bone and parts of two teeth of a horse, in an advanced state of decay, but apparently good evidence of the animal having been buried with the chariot.

Perhaps one of the most interesting finds, however, was the iron tyre of the second wheel, the upper portion of which was found in position about a foot from the bottom of the grave. It was soon found that the wheel had collapsed, the lower portion being flattened out on the bottom of the excavation. The position of the iron demonstrated that the wheel, and presumably the chariot also, had been buried in its normal standing position, and that as the wood decayed the tyre gradually subsided under the weight of the earth above. Had the wheels alone been buried, even in a standing position, the soil would gradually have taken the place of the decaying wood, and the tyre would have been found complete. Between the two crushed portions of this iron rim were found the remains of the smaller ring of iron which surrounded the nave of the wheel.

The bridle-bit of bronze[1] found in the first instance ... is very similar in type to the specimen from Arras, now in the York Museum, which is figured and described by the Rev. Edward William Stillingfleet, in the 'Account of the Opening of Some barrows on the Wolds of Yorkshire'. The Hunmanby bridle-bit, however, is rather larger, and is more delicate in design. The two rings forming the bit are made of bronze, they are 2⅞ inches in diameter, and the hoop-shaped piece is 2½ inches in length.

There is also a thin lenticular piece of plain bronze, measuring about 3 inches by 2½ inches, which is polished on the convex side. At its edge there still remains a rivet, in position, from which it would appear that it has been fastened to something. The use of this is doubtful; it is possibly a portion of a bronze hand-mirror, metal mirrors having been found with chariot-burials of this period elsewhere. The precise original position of this object cannot be ascertained, as, together with many smaller fragments, it was found in the slipped earth. From the same material also a portion of a large bronze ring ... was secured. This at first was thought to be part of a second bit (as bits generally occur in pairs in chariot-burials), but from the way it thickens towards its broken extremities it has evidently been for some other purpose. Where broken there are traces of iron, which have the appearance of being part of something to which the ring was attached. A smaller ring of bronze thickened in two places, was found in the grave near the tyre. It is probably part of the harness.

Source

Sheppard, T., 1907, 'Note on a British Chariot-Burial at Hunmanby in East Yorkshire', *Archaeological Journal* 19: 483–97

Notes

1 Other east Yorkshire sites like Hunmanby have been found at Dove's Graves, Driffield, East Burn, Cowlam, Pexton Moor, Huntow and Sawdon.

References

Cunliffe, 1974
Schadla-Hall, 1989

6

Iron Age Material from Bulbury, Dorset, described by Edward Cunnington

Many of the most important finds of objects of all prehistoric (and later) periods have been made by chance through digging for other purposes. This has meant that much contextual detail is lost, and the finds consequently difficult to assess. Cunnington describes the Bulbury[1] group as a 'hoard', a term which implies they were deliberately concealed together for a specific purpose, which may or may not have included recovery. Later writers have seen some of these earlier finds as not 'hoards' in any real sense, but as the debris of settlement activity, particularly of craft-working.

The Bulbury material is a case in point. Iron Age hoards of ornamental metalwork, such as the bronze animal figures here, certainly exist; Iron Age hoards of so-called 'iron currency bars', gold ornaments, and coins are also well recognised. All of these may well have ritual significance, and the Bulbury animals could well share this character. On the other hand, the presence at Bulbury of the blacksmith's tools, and the other relatively large pieces of iron, look more like the remains of a smithy workshop. Only a detailed study of the local context could have thrown light on these questions, and this is now irretrievably lost.

Nevertheless, it is clear that Iron Age communities in Britain retained a social need to gather together valuables for those purposes of social process which can broadly and collectively be called ritual. Such accumulations were sometimes buried, sometimes thrown into water, and sometimes formed an important part of specially important graves.

THE BULBURY GROUP

On a Hoard of Bronze, Iron, and other Objects found in Belbury Camp, Dorset.
Communicated by EDWARD CUNNINGTON, *Esq. of Dorchester.*

Read March 30, 1882.

I have the honour of exhibiting to the Society of Antiquaries, through Mr. Joshua James Foster, of Dorchester, some objects of bronze, iron, glass, and earthenware lately found together in Belbury Camp, near Higher Lychett, Poole, Dorset.

This camp is nearly circular, with a south aspect, the ground gradually sloping for about 700 feet to a small stream. Its rampart on the north side is the best preserved, showing a height of 10 feet above the external ditch; that on the east is in process of destruction by the plough. Its length and breadth are each about 11 or 12 chains, making an inside area of rather more than 10 acres. The entrances east and west are guarded by the vallum being brought inside about 82 feet. The centres of north and south are open to the north for a road and to the south for the water supply. The breadth of the vallum was 41 feet in its present condition.[2] The objects and a large quantity of wrought iron were all found together in the western side from 2 feet to 3 feet underground whilst draining the camp.

The antiquities discovered were as follows:–

Two bronze cast figures about 4 inches long with bull's head and horns.

Two small bronze ornaments pierced with holes for fastening on wood, and ornamented on the sides and top.

Two large bronze rings, 3 inches in diameter, with small rings encircling them for attachment.

Three smaller bronze rings.

Handle of an iron dagger with bronze fittings.

Pieces of bronze with iron ribs for strengthening it.

An anchor 4 feet 6 inches long, 27½ inches from point to point of the fluke, the main stem varying from 2 to 3 inches in breadth, the links of the chain close to anchor 5 inches in diameter, the rest of the links about 2 inches.

Two glass beads 1 inch in diameter, and six of the same kind ½ inch in diameter.

Several fragments of bronze.

A bar of iron 3 feet long, and 1 inch by ¾ in thickness.

Large nails, 6 or 7 inches long, 'as thick as a thumb' …

A large sledge hammer, 6 inches long, 2½ inches square, weight 7½ lbs.

A smaller hammer.

An iron hatchet.

A long iron with two feet, exactly similar to andiron.

A piece of fine bronze chain or armilla.

Two or three rounded flat pieces of iron, which may be timber-clamps.

Half of a good quern of a very hard sandstone.

Fragments of black well-burnt pottery.

This hoard was found in the autumn of 1881. Having heard of the discovery, I paid a visit to the old woman who was reported to possess several of the objects. On inquiring of her for them, she hold me that she 'hadn't a' got 'em'. On my asking what had become of them, she said 'Well, there! I was obliged to send 'em to my poor boy, for he was ter'ble bad, and did sort o' pine for 'em; and a' thought if a' could have thic there little dog, and nail un up over the door, a' would be better'. I then went to the son's house, where I duly found the animal nailed over the door. Afterwards I learned that a quantity of beads, a duplicate of the animal, and some pieces of rusty iron, had been discovered at the same time and place, but had been dispersed. My search for these was successful, and its results appear in this communication.[3]

Source

Cunnington, E., 1884, 'On a hoard of Bronze Iron and Other Objects found in Belbury Camp, Dorset', *Archaeologia* 48: 115–17

Notes

1   In Cunnington's paper the site is referred to as 'Belbury', but in subsequent publications it is called 'Bulbury'.
2   Bulbury camp is a typical small, single-bank enclosure of the type perhaps constructed throughout the Iron Age (roughly 700 BC – AD 50).
3   For Edward Cunnington, see Part 1, Chapter 1 in this volume.

References

Cunliffe, 1978
Cunliffe, 1972
FitzPatrick, 1984
Wait, 1985

7

The gift exchange tradition described by Herodotus

'Lifting objects away from the world of common commodities into a world of special significance' is a fundamental characteristic of the collecting process (Pearce, 1995: 27). This notion has its root in archaic ideas about objects serving to create and perpetuate social relationships with other people or the gods, as well as in the idea of the 'sacred' as it emerged in the early European languages, and links with the oath–ordeal paradigm, and kinship relations. Gift exchange in particular, as a means of creating social relationships, helps us to understand the role of collecting within the whole social fabric. The emotional values connected with gifts are embraced in modernist capitalist societies by collections (Pearce, 1995: 406–7).

Gift exchange can be described as 'an exchange of inalienable things between transactors who are in a state of reciprocal dependence' (phrased as such in Gregory, 1982: 19).[1] It follows that whereas commodity exchange establishes a relationship between the objects exchanged, gift exchange establishes a relationship between the subjects. The transactors, though, instead of aiming to 'pay off' their debts, try to preserve them, and acquire as many gift-debtors as possible, rather than maximum material profit (Morris, 1986: 2).

Gods and the spirits of the dead, being the real owners of the world's wealth, are the first groups with whom men must make contacts (Mauss, 1970: 13). Giving is one way of keeping contact with the divine, and becomes a kind of investment 'which makes symbolic capital accrue and establishes very real ties of power and dependence' (Burkert, 1987: 15–16). Recompense is conceived in terms of honour and reinforcement of the network of obligations, as well as certain material gain in the form of success and victory over enemies.

The paragraph that follows is one among many that could be chosen to illustrate the tradition of exchange with the divine. Written by Herodotus, in the fifth century BC, it refers to events that had taken place long before (Gyges was the first ruler of the Mermnad dynasty – he ruled from c. 685 to c. 657 BC) and relate to an attempt by the Lydian kings to establish a relationship of indebtedness with the Greek sanctuary at Delphi.

31

HERODOTUS, *HISTORIES*, 1.14

Thus did the Mermnadae rob the Heraclidae of the sovereignty and take it for themselves. Having gained it, Gyges sent not a few offerings to Delphi: there are very many silver offerings of his there: and besides the silver, he dedicated great store of gold: among which six golden bowls are the offerings chiefly worthy of record. These weigh 30[2] talents and stand in the treasury[3] of the Corinthians: though in very truth it is the treasury not of the Corinthian people but of Cypselus son of Eetion. This Gyges then was the first foreigner (of our knowledge) who placed offerings at Delphi after the king of Phrygia, Midas son of Gordias. For Midas too made an offering, to wit, the royal seat whereon he sat to give judgment, and a marvellous seat it is; it is set in the same place as the bowls of Gyges. This gold and the silver offered by Gyges is called by the Delphians 'Gygian' after its dedicator.

Source

Godley, A.D. 1946, *Herodotus*, Loeb Classical Library in 4 volumes, Vol. 1, Books 1 and 2, London and Cambridge, Mass., Heinemann and Harvard University Press: 17–18

Notes

1 'Inalienable' are the objects that cannot be separated from their owner, even if they are given away; they carry part of their owner's identity with them. A more detailed discussion of the notion of 'inalienable' will be presented in Chapter 10 in this volume.
2 A 'talent' was used as a weight measurement; it ranged from 26 to about 38 kilograms in the different Greek regional weight standards (Pollitt, 1990: 206).
3 The treasuries were small temple-like buildings offered to sanctuaries by, or in the name of, city-states to commemorate an event or to celebrate a victory. It is interesting to note here the distinction made by Herodotus about the 'real' dedicator of the treasury, that is, the tyrant of Corinth instead of the people of the city. See Parts 1 and 2 in this book for a discussion of the treasuries, and a relation between collectors and tyrants.

References

Burkert, 1987

Gregory, 1982
Linders and Nordquist, 1987
Mauss, 1970
Morris, 1986
Pearce, 1995a
Pollitt, 1990

8

Gift exchange as social relationship in *The Odyssey*

The gift exchange system was the basis of all social interaction in the Homeric epics and it operated among strangers and friends, men and gods (see Finley, 1979; Langdon, 1987; 109; and von Reden, 1994). Although the Homeric epics are surrounded by many methodological problems, and the date of their composition as well as the society which they illustrate have been the subjects of debate (for example, Finley, 1979; Snodgrass, 1974; and Morris, 1986), Homeric poetry presents a world-view which might not correspond to a particular historical period. It does, though, provide a reliable picture of the world of Bronze Age and archaic Greece. Heroic or aristocratic life of that time was accompanied by an important circulation of prestige goods. Gift giving was part of the network of competitive honorific activity. One measure of man's true worth was how much he could give away in treasure. Heroes boasted of the gifts they had received and of those they had given as signs of their prowess. Metal objects, chariots, horses and women[1] were all objects that changed hands as a result of war or other social circumstances. Their 'participation' in those events added to their intrinsic value, constituted their importance and gave them the status of 'honourable gifts of imperishable fame'.

The objects exchanged would carry the identity of their previous owners with them and would bestow their status and value to their new owner. They would serve as memorials, vehicles of memory (μνῆμα) for those who would receive the gift, a notion that related to the inalienability of gifts as bearers of individual and communal identity (for example *Iliad*, 23. 619; *Odyssey*, 15. 126–7; 21. 38–41).

The passage that follows is part of the dialogue between Telemachus, the son of Odysseus, and the goddess Athena, who had taken the form of Mentes, a foreign king from Taphos and a guest in the palace of Ithaca. The gift exchange would take place in the context of hospitality.

HOMER, *ODYSSEY*, 1. 306–18

Telemachus: Stranger, you say these things out of a friendly heart, like a father to his son, and I shall never forget them. But come now and stay on, although you are anxious to be on your way: after bathing and enjoying yourself, you will return to your ship with a gift, rejoicing in your heart, a very fine and precious gift, which shall be an heirloom from me, such as dear friends give to friends. Athena, the grey-eyed goddess, answered: 'Do not detain me, as I am eager to be on my way. The gift, which your heart bids you give me, you will offer it to me on my return to take home. Choose a very beautiful one, and you will get an adequate one in return.'

Source

Austin, M.M. and Vidal-Naquet, P., 1977, *Economic and Social History of Ancient Greece: An Introduction*, Berkeley, University of California Press: 199

Notes

1   On the role of women as property and in the Homeric gift exchange tradition see von Reden, 1994: 49–55.

References

Finley, 1979
Langdon, 1987
Linders and Nordquist, 1987
Morris, 1986
Snodgrass, 1974
von Reden, 1994

9

Gifts to men, in *The Odyssey*

Those objects which were qualified as prestige items are, on the one hand, preserved in the palace treasury, and on the other are 'used', in the sense that they take part in events that constitute the life of heroes, they circulate. It was precisely their circulation in violent or peaceful events that gave them a prestige which took them to another dimension. It was the will to circulate and become vehicles of memories and of myths that gave these objects their value. In other words, the objects were also considered to be in a position to legitimise and materialise events and relations.

Objects that had been through this network of exchanges and had been acquired as a result of a social relation with either a human or a god, were obviously fortified with moral value, which could be transferred from the owner to the object and vice versa. The reverse was also true, so that when the objects were products of unfair, incomplete or non-noble transactions, their accumulation was equated to an illicit and punishable act.[1]

HOMER, *ODYSSEY*, 4. 121–37

While he was thinking over these matters in his mind and heart, Helen came out of her fragrant high-roofed bedroom, looking like Artemis of the golden shafts. Adraste, coming with her, set a well-made chair for her, and Alcippe brought a rug of soft wool, and Phylo brought a silver basket which Alcandre had given her, the wife of Polybos, who lived in Egyptian Thebes, where very many possessions lie in the houses. He had given Menelaos two silver baths, a pair of tripods, and ten talents of gold. Apart from that his wife had bestowed fine gifts on Helen: she had handed her a golden distaff, a basket on wheels made of silver, with a finish of gold along its rims. It was this that her maid Phylo brought and set beside her, stuffed full of elaborate thread, and lying across the top was the distaff with dark purple wool. She sat down on the seat, and there was a footstool beneath her feet. At once she began speaking to her husband, asking about everything.

Source

Dawe, R.D., 1993, *The Odyssey: translation and analysis*, Lewes, Book Guild: 167–8

Notes

1 The method of acquisition of material culture remains of vital importance and determines the acceptance or the rejection of the collection in subsequent periods as well. See, for instance, Cicero's views on the collection of Verres and the method of its acquisition in Part 3 in this volume.

References

Bounia, 1998

10

The prestigious genealogy of objects in *The Iliad*

Inalienability is a paramount characteristic of gift exchange (Mauss, 1970: 9–10, 18, 24). It means that 'the objects are never completely separated from the men who exchange them; the communion and alliance they establish are well-nigh indissoluble' (Mauss, 1970: 31). The possession of an inalienable object authenticates the authority of its owner and affects his other transactions. The ability 'to keep' that object empowers the ability to attract other important gifts. In other words, 'things exchanged are about things kept' (Weiner, 1992: 10).

The inalienable possessions as sources of difference and hierarchy, and as retaining for the future memories of the past, are representations of how social identities are constructed through time. 'The reproduction of kinship is legitimated in each generation through the transmission of inalienable possessions, be they land rights, material objects, or mythic knowledge' (Weiner, 1992: 11).

The anthropomorphic quality of gifts has also to be related to that aspect of inalienability (Mauss, 1970; Gregory, 1982: 20). According to Mauss, the goods transacted were thought to be persons or pertain to a person; in exchanging something one was in effect exchanging part of oneself. The bonds created by things were thus bonds created between people, since they were parts of the people exchanged through things. One man gives away part of his own substance, and receives part of somebody else's nature. This part needs to be absorbed within his own clan/family/owner; it is not inert. In other words, it is inalienable, cannot be separated from its owner, even though it has been given away (Mauss, 1970: 8–10).

A trophy with a history of being the property of gods and heroes obviously shed greater glory on both the donor and recipient than just any object. It endowed them with honorific quality which distinguished the wealth of the heroes from that of other classes and other ages (Finley, 1979). Descendence from a god is a common motif for an object. This meant prestige for the family, which was thus supposed to have divine origin and, consequently, be in special relationship with the divine. Therefore, in this case the emphasis lies on the political aspect of gift exchange, as well as on the competitive character of it (for example *Il.*, 5. 266; 16.381 and 867; 23.277–8, 2.827; 7.146; 18.84; 24.74–5). This was an aspect of the prestigious genealogy, and had to do with the relation with the 'other'; furthermore, this was a way of legitimatisation for the dominant families, and a medium of practising power over people. The linear syntax used to express the change of hands of objects also indicates a long line of prestigious ancestors.

HOMER, *ILIAD*, 2. 100–107

Then among them lord Agamemnon uprose, bearing in his hands the sceptre which Hephaistus had wrought with toil. Hephaistus gave it to king Zeus, son of Cronos, and Zeus gave it to the messenger Argeïphontes; and Hermes, the lord, gave it to Pelops, driver of horses, and Pelops in turn gave it to Atreus, shepherd of the host; and Atreus at his death left it to Thyestes, rich in flocks, and Thyestes again left it to Agamemnon to bear, that so he might be lord of many isles and of all Argos.

Source

Murray, A.T., 1995, *Homer, Iliad*, Loeb Classical Library (originally published 1954), 2nd edition revised by Dimock, G.E., London and Cambridge, Mass., Heinemann and Harvard University Press: 57–9

References

Finley, 1979
Gregory, 1982
Mauss, 1970
Weiner, 1992

11

The role of craftsmen, by Diodorus

The impressive rituals that the heroic society needed to enact, and the distinctions of birth and hierarchy which were at the basis of all interaction in that world, encouraged the development of fine craftsmanship that would produce objects suitable for taking part in these rituals and emphasising them (Pearce, 1995: 46).

Classical Greeks attributed the origins of the arts to people living in areas where Bronze Age craftsmanship had reached a high level. A number of legends attributes the invention of fine art to mysterious people with supranatural capabilities and powers. One such area associated by tradition with the origins of arts, and a centre of Bronze Age craftsmanship, was the island of Rhodes (Pollitt, 1990: 12). It is interesting to note that the craftsmen are admired for the quality of their work, their God-given capabilities and their role in society.

Diodorus Siculus was a Greek historian, born in Sicily, who flourished about 60 BC. He travelled in Egypt and spent some years in Rome. His history, *Bibliotheca Historia*, only survives in part, but is valuable because it quotes other authors, now lost.

DIODORUS, 5.55.1–3

A people known as the Telchines was the first to settle the island called Rhodes ... (Tradition records) that they were the inventors of some of the arts and the introducers of other things that were useful for the life of men. They are said to have been the first to make images of gods, and some of the ancient images are named after them. Among the Lindians, for example, there is a statue referred to as the Telchinian Apollo; among the Ialysians there is a Telchinian Hera and the Nymphs, and among the Kameirians a Telchinian Hera. These men were also wizards and could summon clouds, storms, and hail whenever they wished, and in a like manner they could even bring forth snow ... It is also said that they could change their own shapes, and that they were jealous about giving instruction in their arts.

Source

Pollitt, J.J., 1990, *The Art of Ancient Greece: Sources and Documents*, Cambridge University Press: 12

References

Pearce, 1995a

12

Craftsmen and the gods in *The Iliad* and *The Odyssey*

In the Homeric epics the gods hold a prominent role and are actively involved in the affairs of the people. All human qualities have their origin in the divine power, which has been bestowed upon individuals.

The paragraphs that follow relate to craftsmanship and its divine origins. The first is a description of the workshop of Hephaistus, the protector god of craftsmanship, and it could be seen as a reliable description of the workshop of a successful craftsman. We have to notice the presence of the tripods in it, objects that in Homeric poetry are very prominent gifts: they appear as the first prize in the funeral games of Patroclus, as the guest-gifts taken home by Odysseus, and as the appeasement offered to Achilles by Agamemnon. Participating in the ceremonies of the heroic world, the tripod acquired a direct linkage with their values and social practices, which eventually made it the most appropriate category of object to operate as a transitional medium through which the social rituals of the aristocratic world were transferred to the social organisation as this changed shape in the following periods (Langdon, 1987).

The second paragraph creates a direct link between Bronze Age craftsmanship and the Homeric understanding of the divine world, and attributes the education of humans in the arts to Athena and Hephaistus.

HOMER, *ILIAD* 18.369–79

Silver-footed Thetis[1] came to the house of Hephaistos, an imperishable starry house, outstanding among the immortal houses, wrought all of bronze, which the lame-footed god had made himself. She found him there sweating as he hovered busily around the bellows. He was engaged in making tripods, twenty in all, which were to stand along the wall of his well-constructed hall, and he set gold wheels beneath the stand of each, so that they might, moving by themselves, enter the divine assembly and again come back to the house – a marvellous thing to see. They were complete up to a point, but the skillfully wrought handles had not yet been placed upon them. These he was preparing, and he was also cutting the attaching bands.

HOMER, *ODYSSEY* 6.232–4

[Athena sheds grace on Odysseus in Phaiakia]: ... just as when a man inlays silver with gold, a craftsman, whom Hephaistos and Pallas Athena have taught all manner of skills, and he fashions pleasing works of art.

Source

Pollitt, J.J., 1990, *The Art of Ancient Greece: Sources and Documents*, Cambridge University Press, p. 18

Notes

1 Thetis is the mother of Achilles; she visited Hephaistus' workshop in order to ask him for new armour for her son, after the death of Patroclus.

References

Bounia, 1998
Langdon, 1987
Linders and Nordquist, 1987

13

Competition in material wealth: Herodotus discusses King Croesus

Destruction of wealth is the occasion *par excellence* for the gift exchange tradition. Gregory (1982: 60–61) assumes that the destruction of wealth is the simplest strategy available to an individual who wishes to achieve pre-eminence in a gift society. The most characteristic expression of that is 'potlatch', where men who rival each other in generosity destroy precious objects. This concerns not only them and the objects involved, but also 'their spirits of the dead which take part in the transactions and whose names the men bear; it concerns nature as well' (Mauss, 1970: 12). Mostly this notion concerns what we call 'sacrifice'. 'Sacrificial destruction implies giving something that is to be repaid' (Mauss, 1970: 14). Grave goods[1] and sanctuary offerings therefore form destruction of wealth in this sense (Morris, 1986: 9).

The development of pan-Hellenic sanctuaries after the ninth and eighth centuries BC initiated a transformation in the tradition of gift exchange: instead of destroying the conspicuous gifts to the gods, 'setting them up high for display' became the norm (Burkert, 1987: 49ff). Herodotus records this transition in the paragraph that follows, when he mentions that Croesus, the King of the Lydians[2] both destroyed artefacts in a conspicuous sacrifice, and offered others for display as a visible perpetuation of his generosity and, consequently, power.

The power of the great king of the East is exemplified through the display of his wealth. He could afford to sacrifice huge amounts of both living creatures and artefacts – the list of which sounds very familiar to the students of ancient collections – either by destroying them, or by taking them out of circulation in a conspicuous display. The reasons for this are obvious: to exchange these with the favour of the god, who would thus agree to bestow him his wishes (on sacrifice, see Vernant, 1991a; Detienne and Vernant, 1989; Burkert, 1983; and Hubert and Mauss, 1899).

HERODOTUS, *HISTORIES*, 1. 50–51

After this, he strove to win the favour of the Delphian god with great sacrifices. He offered up three thousand beasts from each kind fit for sacrifice, and he burnt on a great pyre couches covered with gold and silver, golden goblets, and purple cloaks and tunics; by these means he hoped the better to win the aid of the god, to whom he also commanded that every Lydian should sacrifice what he could. When the sacrifice was over, he melted down a vast store of gold and made of it ingots of which the longer sides were of six and the shorter of three palms' length, and the height was one palm. These were an hundred and seventeen in number. Four of them were of refined gold, each weighing two talents and a half; the rest were of gold with silver alloy, each of two talents' weight. He bade also to be made a figure of a lion of refined gold, weighing ten talents. When the temple of Delphi was burnt, this lion fell from the ingots which were the base where one it stood; and now it lies in the treasury of the Corinthians, but weighs only six talents and a half, for the fire melted away three and a half talents.

When these offerings were fully made, Croesus sent them to Delphi, with other gifts besides, namely, two very great bowls, one of gold and one of silver. The golden bowl stood to the right, the silvern to the left, of the temple entrance. These too were removed about the time of the temple's burning, and now the golden bowl, which weighs eight talents and a half, and twelve minae, lies in the treasury of the Clazomenians, and the silver bowl at the corner of the forecourt of the temple. This bowl holds six hundred nine-gallon measures: for the Delphians use it for a mixing-bowl at the feast of the Divine Appearance. It is said by the Delphians to be the work of Theodorus of Samos, and I believe them, for it seems to me to be of no common workmanship. Moreover, Croesus sent four silver casks, which stand in the treasury of the Corinthians, and dedicated two sprinkling-vessels, one of gold, one of silver. The golden vessel bears the inscription 'Given by the Lacedaemonians', who claim it as their offering. But they are wrong, for this, too, is Croesus' gift. The inscription was made by a certain Delphian, whose name I know but will not reveal, out of his desire to please the Lacedaemonians. The figure of a boy, through whose hand the water runs, is indeed a Lacedaemonian gift; but they did not give either of the sprinkling-vessels. Along with these Croesus sent, besides many other offerings of no great mark, certain round basins of silver, and a golden female figure three cubits high, which the Delphians assert to be the statue of the woman who was Croesus' baker. Moreover he dedicated his own wife's necklaces and girdles.

Source

Godley, A.D., *Herodotus*, 1946, in 4 volumes, Vol. 1, Books 1 and 2, Loeb Classical Library, London and Cambridge, Mass., Heinemann and Harvard University Press: 57–9

Notes

1   Other explanations have been offered for the grave goods as well. For example, Rosenblatt et al. (1976: 67–76) suggest that grave goods serve to 'break ties ... and facilitate establishment of new patterns of living' (p. 68). Discussion of the same issue can also be found in Firth (1965: 344–7).
2   Croesus was the last and best-known King of the Lydians; he ruled from 560 to 546 BC.

References

Burkert, 1983
Burkert, 1987
Detienne and Vernant, 1989
Firth, 1965
Hubert and Mauss, 1899
Linders and Nordquist, 1987
Rosenblatt, Walsh and Jackson, 1976
Vernant, 1991

14

Palace treasuries in Homer

In the heroic world of Homer riches are of two kinds: the durable and storable valuables (κειμήλια – *keimeilia*, a word which derives from the verb κεῖμαι, *keimai*, which means 'to rest') and the movable property, that is, slaves, cattle or any kind of livestock (πρόβατα – *provata*, from the verb προβαίνω – to walk, to proceed) (*Od.*, 2.75; Benveniste, 1973; also van Wees, 1992: 244). *Keimeilia keitai* (rest) usually (*Il.*, 6.47; *Od.*, 4.613; 15.101; 21.10) in the *thalamos* (θάλαμος) of the palace. Frequently next to the word *keimeilia* appear the words πολλά και ἐσθλά (*polla ke esthla* – many and good of their kind),[1] a phrase that denotes the abundance and richness of these treasuries, as well as the importance that the possession and keeping of these objects had for the owner as indications of wealth and distinction, as prestige objects that belong to the warrior and indicate his rank and wealth. A common formula when these objects are discussed is that they are made of gold, bronze or iron (*Il.*, 18.289).[2]

The word *thalamos* refers to the treasury of the palace;[3] the same word is also used for the women's quarters.[4] Sometimes the word denotes the young girl's room before her wedding (*Od.*, 7.7), sometimes the nuptial chamber or couch (*Il.*, 18.492; Pindar, *Pythian Odes*, 2.60), whereas the verb θαλαμεύω (*thalameuo*) means to marry (Heliodorus, 4.6). Women are associated with the accumulation and storing of goods, and the men with acquiring them (Vernant, 1983: 149–150). In Xenophon's *Oeconomicus* (7.20–21, 25, 356; 7.33) the model wife is compared to the queen bee who dwells in the hive watching over the honey collected in the honeycombs (also called *thalamos* or *thalame*). Other similar associations regarding the role of women and material culture include the assimilation of the *thalamos* with a woman's lap, or even her stomach (as in Hesiod, who presents the woman as seated inside, storing the riches that the husband brings directly in the depths of her stomach – *Theogony*, 598–9) (Vernant, 1983: 149).[5]

Thalamos also has a series of other meanings revealed in the discussion of mythology (see Gernet, 1981). It is represented as an underground chamber, and the legend of Danaos has preserved its mythical connotations (Sophocles, *Antigone*, 947). The same implications are true for the *thalamos* of Aietes (Pindar, *Pyth.* 4.160), the keeper of the Golden Fleece. For Mimnermus (frg

11.5ff) there is a golden *thalamos* 'in which the rays of the sun repose'. Euripides (frg 781) speaks of a *thalamos* where the king, the alleged father of Phaethon, keeps his gold locked up, and where the body of Phaethon himself (in reality, the son of the Sun) is placed at the tragedy's conclusion. The queen, according to Euripides, has the keys to it. In a parallel fashion, Athena, Zeus' daughter, has the keys to the treasury where Zeus' thunderbolt is kept (Aeschylus, *Eumen.* 826–8). The idea of royal treasury is based on a belief in protective sacra, which are kept in a secret corner, guarded by a mythical king or king-god (Gernet, 1981: 101). The same term is also used for the funeral chapter of the tomb (Scheid-Tissinier, 1994: 48; Vernant, 1983; 148ff; and Rups, 1986).

HOMER, *ODYSSEY*, 21.1–66

But the goddess, flashing-eyed Athene, put it into the heart of the daughter of Icarius, wise Penelope, to set before the suitors in the halls of Odysseus the bow and the gray iron, contest and beginning of death. She climbed the high stairway to her chamber, and took the bent key in her strong hand – a beautiful key of bronze, and on it was a handle of ivory. And she went her way with her handmaids to a storeroom, far remote, where lay the treasures of her husband, bronze, and gold, and iron wrought with toil. And there lay the back-bent bow and the quiver that held the arrows, and many arrows were in it, loaded with groanings – gifts which a friend of Odysseus had given him when he met him once in Lacedaemon: Iphitus, son of Eurytus, a man resembling the gods. The two had met one another in Messene in the house of wise Ortilochus. The truth was that Odysseus had come to collect a debt which the whole people owed him, for the men of Messene had lifted from Ithaca in their benched ships three hundred sheep and the shepherds with them. It was on an embassy in quest of these that Odysseus had come a far journey, while he was but a youth; for his father and the other elders had sent him out. And Iphitus, for his part, had come in search of twelve brood mares, which he had lost, with sturdy mules at the teat; but to him afterwards they brought death and doom, when he came to the stout-hearted son of Zeus, the man Heracles, who well knew deeds of daring; …

It was while asking for these Iphitus met Odysseus, and gave him the bow, which of old great Eurytus carried, and had left at his death to his son in his lofty house. And to Iphitus Odysseus gave a sharp sword and a stout spear, as the beginning of a loving friendship; yet they never knew one another at the table, for before that could happen the son of Zeus had killed Iphitus, son of Eurytus, a man resembling the golds, who gave

Odysseus the bow. The bow noble Odysseus, when going to war, would never take with him on the black ships, but it lay in his halls at home as a memorial of a staunch friend, and he carried it in his own land.

Now when the beautiful woman had come to the storeroom, and had stepped upon the threshold of oak – which in the old days the carpenter had skillfully planed and trued to the line, and fitted doorposts on it, and set on them bright doors – without delay she quickly loosed the thong from the hook and thrust in the key, and with sure aim shot back the bolts. And as a bull bellows when grazing in a meadow, even so bellowed the beautiful doors, struck by the key; and quickly they flew open before her. Then she went up to the high platform, where the chests stood in which fragrant clothes were stored. Reaching up from here she took from its peg the bow, together with the bright case which surrounded it. And there she sat down and laid the case upon her knees and wept aloud, and took out the bow of her husband. But when she had had her fill of weeping and crying, she went her way to the hall, to the company of the lordly suitors, bearing in her hands the back-bent bow and the quiver that held the arrows, and many arrows were in it, loaded with groanings. And by her side her maidens bore a chest, in which lay abundance of iron and bronze, the games of the man her husband. Now when the beautiful women reached the suitors, she stood by the doorpost of the well-built hall, holding before her face her shining veil; and a faithful handmaid stood on either side of her.

Source

Murray, A.T., *Homer, Odyssey*, revised by G.E. Dimock, 2nd edition, 1995 (originally published 1954), Loeb Classical Library, Cambridge, Mass., Heinemann and Harvard University Press: 311–15

Notes

1   It is very interesting to note that one of the translations offered for the word when referring to people is 'morally good'; it would be interesting to associate this with the ideas of the objects being products of noble social interaction, as mentioned earlier.
2   For metalworking in Homer see Gray, 1954.
3   Other descriptions of the *thalamos* in *Il.*, 6.288–95 (Hecabe in Priam's *thalamos*); 24.191–2, 228–35 (Priam fetches precious objects from his *thalamos*); *Od.*, 2.337–55 (Odysseus' *thalamos*); 15.99–119 (the *thalamos* of Menelaus).
4   For instance, *Od.*, 23.41ff. It is interesting to note the role of women, as

wealth and as sacred and connoisseurs' items; this reminds one of more recent collectors, for example Lord Hamilton.

5   Is it from such a kind of associations that passionate collecting, storing and hiding the artefacts of the collection are considered indications of effeminate behaviour? Is it from here that the passionate collector usually appears in the same part of the equation as women?

References

Benveniste, 1973
Gernet, 1981
Gray, 1954
Rups, 1986
Scheid-Tissinier, 1994
van Wees, 1992
Vernant, 1983

Part II
Greek Voices

15

The notion of evidence in material distinctions, by Thucydides

Objects and material possessions form means through which people construct their relationship to their past. People turn to the past for a series of reasons: to reaffirm and validate their present, to give meaning, purpose and value to themselves, to find alternatives to an unsatisfying present, to enrich their lives by acquiring links with events and people prior to themselves, and so on (Lowenthal, 1985: 41). Material culture forms the bridge that joins the intellectual, spatial and temporal gap between people and their past; articles are used as mnemonic tools to create, store and retrieve a sense of past.

Ancient Greeks had a profound appreciation of material culture as evidence and the intellectual trends concerning the past had a predilection toward monuments and objects. The paragraphs that follow introduce the interest that historiographical research encouraged towards material evidence. Although Thucydides does not express the antiquarian historical tradition of the descriptive and analytical approach, he did observe the visible traces in the soil and put them in relation to tradition, in order to analyse them materially (Schnapp, 1996: 51). He used monuments and inscriptions (Hornblower, 1987) in order to argue about the distant past, when his ordinary methods of cross-questioning and autopsy were inappropriate or impossible. Twice in his narrative Thucydides used objects and monuments to reach archaeological conclusions. The best known of these paragraphs is the one concerning the purification of Delos, the first of the two paragraphs that follow.

Thucydides employed a typological and comparative approach in order to analyse these tombs. In this sense, he moved the focus from objects or monuments as signs of power, to objects as elements of history (Schnapp, 1996: 27).

The second paragraph describes the ruins of Mycenae. The historian examines the ruins, compares sources, establishes levels of similarity, and thus reaches conclusions. His method suggests that observations acquire validity only through careful consideration, and that material evidence gets its value through a constant dialectic between imagination, reason, past, present and future perceptions, knowledge and critical ability[1] (see also Schnapp, 1996: 49).

THUCYDIDES, *HISTORY OF THE PELOPONNESIAN WAR*, 1.8.1.

... for Carians inhabited most of the islands, as may be inferred from the fact that, when Delos was purified by the Athenians in this war and the graves of all who had ever died on the island were removed, over half were discovered to be Carians being recognised by the fashion of the armour found buried with them, and by the mode of burial, which is that still in use among them.[2]

THUCYDIDES, *HISTORY OF THE PELOPONNESIAN WAR*, 1.10.1–2.

And because Mycenae was only a small place, or if any particular town of that time seems now to be insignificant, it would not be right for me to treat this as an exact piece of evidence and refuse to believe that the expedition against Troy was as great as the poets have asserted and as tradition still maintains. For if the city of the Lacedaemonians should be deserted, and nothing should be left of it but its temples and the foundations of its other buildings, posterity would, I think, after a long lapse of time be very loath to believe that their power was as great as their renown.

Source

Forster Smith, C. 1951, *Thucydides, History of the Peloponnesian War*, Vol. 1, Loeb Classical Library, London and Cambridge, Mass., Heinemann and Harvard University Press: 13–15 and 18–21

Notes

1   We can compare Herodotus' views about evidence with those of Thucydides': Thucydides, unlike Herodotus who depends on an oral tradition, writes from written sources, and has placed the emphasis on tangible evidence in a way that Herodotus was not prepared to do. Therefore, in his paragraph on Mycenae, Thucydides has to warn his readers about the 'traps' that material evidence *per se* includes. He argues that these have not to be taken at face value, but have to be compared with other information and critically discussed.
2   Contemporary archaeology is well aware that these tombs were Geometric (ninth–eighth centuries BC).

References

Hornblower, 1987
Lowenthal, 1985
Schnapp, 1996

16

The idea of 'archaeology' in Plato

From the middle of the fifth century BC onwards, two distinct types of history can be identified. The first had developed from the Herodotean and Thucydidean tradition, was interested in the recent past and became the basis of political science. The second was represented by the authors of local histories, chronographies, genealogies, erudite dissertations and ethnographical works that were interested in the distant past and followed an analytical and descriptive approach. Historical research in its latter form was also distinguished by the extensive use of lists, inscriptions and monuments (Bounia, 1998a).

Although history acquired its name right from the start, erudition had to wait longer. The most important word describing this sort of enquiry was the term *archaiologia* which firstly appeared in Plato's *Hippias Major*. It was put in the mouth of the sophist Hippias, who in his discussion with Socrates proudly asserts that nobody is indifferent to his services, not even the Spartans; they do not show any interest in the subjects he mainly specialises in (that is, astronomy, geometry, arithmetics, rhetoric or language), but they are interested in the genealogies of heroes and men, traditions about the foundation of cities and lists of eponymous magistrates – all those parts of a science called *archaiologia*. This new word, the creation of the sophist movement – although perhaps not devised by Hippias himself – is not intended to describe a new discipline; rather it is a new term, devised in order to include all those descriptions of origins, of 'antiquity' as a period and the antiquities as objects of knowledge. In this sense, the term reveals an interest in the past which is less determined by the explanation than by the description (Schnapp, 1996: 61; and Momigliano, 1950).

PLATO, *HIPPIAS MAJOR*, 285D

Socrates: Well, just what is it they love to hear about from you, and applaud? Tell me yourself; I can't figure it out.
Hippias: The genealogies of heroes and men, Socrates, and the settlements (how cities were founded in ancient times), and in a word all 'archaiologia' – that's what they most love to hear

about … So because of them I have been forced to learn up on such things and to study them thoroughly.

Socrates: Good lord, Hippias, you're lucky the Spartans don't enjoy it when someone lists our archons from the time of Solon. Otherwise, you would have had a job learning them.

Source

Woodruff, P., 1982, *Plato: Hippias Major*, Oxford, Blackwell: 39

References

Bounia, 1998
Momigliano, 1950
Schnapp, 1996

17

The practice of 'archaeology' in Strabo

In ancient Greece, there was active personal involvement in the creation of the past, in the form of active search for objects, encouraged and mediated sometimes through prophecies and oracles (as we will see in the next section), at other times through the initiation of people. Strabo offers an insight into the latter when he describes the foundation of an Augustan colony in the first century BC on the site of ancient Corinth.

The underlying principle of object valuation remains the same, whether the initiation comes from a 'divine source' or from humans: objects are evidence that can bear information about the past, they are parts of the past that can be touched and owned. The emphasis, though, in this case has been transferred from objects being markers of power, as was the case in the Eastern monarchies, or historical evidence, as in the case of Thucydides, to becoming antiquities in the Augustan age that could be collected and exchanged (Schnapp, 1996: 28). The same attitude is developed toward monuments, which also become objects that could be collected to form part of the inventory of the Roman domination (Elsner, 1994: 241).

STRABO, *GEOGRAPHY*, 8.6.23

Now after Corinth had remained deserted for a long time, it was restored again, because of its favourable position, by the deified Caesar, who colonised it with people that belonged for the most part to the freedmen class. And when these were removing the ruins and at the same time digging open the graves, they found numbers of terra-cotta reliefs, and also many bronze vessels. And since they admired the workmanship they left no grave unransacked; so that, well supplied with such things and disposing of them at a high price, they filled Rome with Corinthian 'mortuaries', for thus they called the things taken from the graves, and in particular the earthenware.[1] Now at the outset the earthenware was very highly prized, like the bronzes of Corinthian workmanship, but later they ceased to care much for them, since the supply of earthen vessels failed and most of them were not even well executed. The city of the Corinthians, then, was always great and wealthy, and it was well equipped with men skilled both in the affairs of state and in the craftsman's arts; for both here and in Sicyon the arts of painting and modelling and all such arts of the craftsman flourished most. The city had territory, however, that was not very fertile, but rifted and rough; and from this fact all have called Corinth 'beetling', and use the proverb. 'Corinth is both beetle-browed and full of hollows'.

Source

Jones, H.L., 1954, *Strabo, Geography*, Vol. 4, Loeb Classical Library, London and Cambridge, Mass., Heinemann and Harvard University Press: 201–3

Note

1   Corinthian bronzeware was also famous in antiquity (see, for example, Pliny, *HN*, 34.1; Petronius, 50.2; Cicero, *ad Atticum*, 2.1.11; Martial 9.59; 14.172; 177; and Emanuele, 1989, where there is also a complete list of ancient references to Corinthian bronze).

References

Elsner, 1994
Emanuele, 1989
Schnapp, 1996

18

The relics of the mighty dead as described by Herodotus and Plutarch

Although the Greeks and the Romans did not have any sense of archaeological curiosity, they developed methods of active involvement in the acquisition of tangible proofs and material tokens of the past (as we also saw in the previous entry). These are important because they emphasise the tendency to pursue and appreciate objects, not merely for their role as historical sources in the epistemological sense, but mainly as symbols and reminders of an event, a personality or a specific action, and as sacred talismans that would protect individuals and communities. The paragraphs that follow are not indicative of the use of archaeological methodology, but of a thinking that related material remains with the past: glorious heroes of the past can be touched, literally and metaphorically, when their relics are unearthed, and they can prove the divine provenance, or divine will; therefore, they deserve as such to be preserved and honoured. This is also a notion that refers to antiquarianism and collecting.

Schnapp (1996: 56) relates these approaches to ideas about the sacred, and argues that they imply an immediate connection to the objects collected in sanctuaries. He attributes these to the social role of the sanctuary, that has its origins in the tradition of 'presents' which is so familiar to Homer. The objects that heroes used have acquired a long history and the list of their proprietors is inseparable from their intrinsic quality. In Greece, where social distinction depended upon genealogy, the exchange of objects was part of a complex system of giving among heroes, kings and nobles. Thus, a genealogy of objects emerges, as important as the genealogy of people.

The first paragraph records the active involvement of the Spartans in the retrieval of the bones of Orestes, after the guidance of the oracle at Delphi. The possession of the relics would, and did, enable Sparta to overcome its enemies and establish its power in the Peloponnese. Boedecker (1993) and Huxley (1979) both agree that the possession of the bones, although it did not provide some kind of general right to hegemony over their neighbours, offered to the Spartans 'the power to defeat Tegea' (Boedecker, 1993: 167).

The second paragraph refers to the retrieval of the bones of Theseus from the island of Scyros, where the hero died, according to Greek mythology, and their transference to Athens, where they were received with appropriate honours and explicit delight deriving from the association of the relics with notion of sanctity and divine approval.

HERODOTUS, *HISTORIES*, 67–68

In this former war with Tegea the Spartans had continually the worst of it, but by the time of Croesus, under their kings Anaxandrides and Ariston, they had got the upper hand. This is the story of their success: after a long series of reverses in the war they sent to Delphi and asked of which god they should beg favour in order to ensure their conquest of Tegea, and the Priestess promised them victory if they brought home the bones of Orestes, Agamnemon's son. Unable to find the tomb of Orestes, they sent again to inquire where the body lay, and the messengers received this answer ...

They searched everywhere, but all in vain until Lichas, who was one of the Spartan special agents called 'Agathoergi', or 'good-service men', solved the riddle ... Taking advantage of the better relations which existed at this time between the two towns, he went to Tegea and entered a forge where he watched some iron being hammered out, a process which caused him great surprise. The smith, seeing his astonishment, paused in his work and said: 'Well, my friend, your surprise at seeing me work in iron would be nothing to what you'd have felt, if you had seen what I saw. I wanted to make a well in the yard here, and as I was digging I came on a huge coffin – ten feet long! I couldn't believe that men were ever bigger than they are to-day, so I opened it – and there was the corpse, as big as the coffin![1] I measured it, and then shoveled the earth back.' Lichas turned over in his mind the smith's account of his discovery, and came to the conclusion that the oracle was fulfilled and that this was the body of Orestes ... Then he dug up the grave, collected the bones and took them away to Sparta; and ever since that day the Lacedaemonians in any trial of strength had by far the better of it. They had now subdued the greater part of the Peloponnese.

Source

de Sélincourt, Aubrey, 1972, *Herodotus*, revised by A.R. Burn, Harmondsworth, Penguin Classics (originally published 1954): 66–7.

PLUTARCH, *LIFE OF THESEUS*, 36

And after the Median wars, in the archonship of Phaedo, when the Athenians were consulting the oracle at Delphi, they were told by the Pythian priestess to take up the bones of Theseus, give them honourable burial at Athens, and guard them there. But it was difficult to find the grave and take up the bones, because of the inhospitable and savage nature of the Dolopians who then inhabited the island. However, Cimon took the island, as I have related in his Life, and being ambitious to discover the grave of Theseus, saw an eagle in a place where there was a semblance of a mound, pecking, as they say, and tearing up the ground with his talons. By some divine ordering he comprehended the meaning of this and dug there, and there was found a coffin of a man of extraordinary size, a bronze spear lying by its side, and a sword.[2] When these relics were brought home on his trireme by Cimon, the Athenians were delighted, and received them with splendid processions and sacrifices, as though Theseus himself were returning to his city.

Source

Perrin, Bernadotte, 1914, *Plutarch's lives: Theseus*, Loeb's Classical Library, London, Heinemann: 82–5.

Notes

1 Ancient Greeks imagined that the size of their ancestors was equal to their importance, that is, much larger than their own.
2 This is a quite common description of an ancient burial: the hero is buried with his weapons, here a bronze spear and a sword, in the context of the exchange of gifts with the dead (as discussed in Part 1) and the fetishisation of artefacts (as well will discuss in detail in Part 3).

References

Boedecker, 1993
Dougherty and Kurke, 1993
Huxley, 1979
Schnapp, 1996

19

The role and decoration of temples: Olympia

The role of sanctuaries as repositories of treasure has been well identified. 'Museum' is a term often attributed to ancient sanctuaries (Wernicke, 1894: 103; Kent Hill, 1944: 353; Wace, 1969: 204; Alsop, 1982: 197), but the attribution refers, more often than not, to the functional aspect of being repositories of *objects d'art* (at least as they are categorised by contemporary scholars) and arms (Snodgrass, 1980: 63). Nevertheless, there is a more profound relationship between ancient sanctuaries and museums. They are both historical (in the long term) manifestations of the idea of the communal shrine, where communal treasure is 'set aside' as a means to create relationships with the 'sacred' and thus reinforce and legitimise the community's own judgements about aesthetics, knowledge and history. In other words, they are both repositories of collections.

Pausanias' description of the sanctuary of Olympia includes a detailed account of the contents of the temple of Hera, an early sixth-century building, whose role and function in the sanctuary has been the subject of scholarly debate (for example Wernicke, 1894; Kent Hill, 1944; Arafat, 1995). Pausanias suggests that the temple held more than twenty statues, whose date ranged from the early sixth century to his own day, as well as a number of other items, like the discus of Iphitus, where the Olympic truce was written, and the chest of Kypselos, the tyrant of Corinth, dedicated by his family, presumably during their period of power (that is, until c. 582 BC).

The hypothesis that the temple did not have a cult role by the time Pausanias visited it in c. AD 173, and that the increased demand for storage space and for catering for the needs of cultural tourism (which became so popular during the imperial period) led to a change of role for the building (Arafat, 1995), does not alter the importance Pausanias' testimony has for the collecting discourse. Even if the temple of Hera was not the centre of cult any more, it did have a sacred character, since the visitors were expected to admire there a collection of works of art and objects of historical (in the broadest sense of the term) interest, which were appreciated not only in aesthetic, artistic or art historical terms, but also as sacred symbols of the individual and communal identities, deposited in a sacred repository.

PAUSANIAS, *ELIS* 1, 16.1–20.8

It remains after this for me to describe the temple of Hera and the noteworthy objects contained in it. The Elean account says that it was the people of Scillus, one of the cities in Triphylia, who built the temple about eight years after Oxylus came to the throne of Elis. The style of the temple is Doric, and pillars stand all round it. In the rear chamber one of the two pillars is of oak. The length of the temple is one hundred and sixty-nine feet, the breadth sixty-three feet, and height not short of fifty feet. Who the architect was they do not relate ...

These things, then, are as I have already described. In the temple of Hera is an image of Zeus, and the image of Hera is sitting on a throne with Zeus standing by her, bearded and with a helmet on his head. They are crude works of art.[1] The figures of Seasons next to them, seated upon thrones, were made by the Aeginetan Smilis. Beside them stands an image of Themis, as being mother of the Seasons. It is the work of Dorycleidas, a Lacedaemonian by birth and a disciple of Dipoenus and Scyllis. The Hesperides, five in number, were made by Theocles, who like Dorycleidas was a Lacedaemonian, the son of Gegylus; he too, they say, was a student under Scyllis and Dipoenus. The Athena wearing a helmet and carrying a spear and shield is, it is said, a work of Medon, a Lacedaemonian, brother of Dorycleidas and a pupil of the same master. Then the Maid and Demeter sit opposite each other, while Apollo and Artemis stand opposite each other. Here too have been dedicated Leto, Fortune, Dionysus and a winged Victory. I cannot say who the artists were, but these figures too are in my opinion very ancient. The figures I have enumerated are of ivory and gold, but at a later date other images were dedicated in the Heraeum, including a marble Hermes carrying the baby Dionysus, a work of Praxiteles, and a bronze Aphrodite made by Cleon of Sicyon. The master of this Cleon, called Antiphanes, was a pupil of Periclytus, who himself was a pupil of Polycleitus of Argos. A nude gilded child is seated before Aphrodite, a work fashioned by Boëthus of Calchedon. There were also brought hither from what is called the Philippeum other images of gold and ivory, Eurydice the wife of Aridaeus and Olympias the wife of Philip.

There is also a chest made of cedar, with figures on it, some of ivory, some of gold, others carved out of the cedar-wood itself. It was in this chest that Cypselus, the tyrant of Corinth, was hidden by his mother when the Bacchidae were anxious to discover him after his birth. In gratitude for the saving of Cypselus, his descendants, Cypselids as they are called, dedicated the chests at Olympia. The Corinthians of that age called chests *kypselai*, and from this word, they say, the child received his name of Cypselus. On most of the figures on the chest there are inscriptions, written in the ancient characters ...

There are here other offerings also: a couch of no great size and for the most part adorned with ivory; the quoit of Iphitus; a table on which are set out the crowns for the victors. The couch is said to have been a toy of Hippodameia. The quoit of Iphitus has inscribed upon it the truce which the Eleans proclaim at the Olympic festivals; the inscription is not written in a straight line, but the letters run in a circle round the quoit. The table is made of ivory and gold, and is the work of Colotes. Colotes is said to have been a native of Heracleia, but specialists in the history of sculpture maintain that he was a Parian, a pupil of Pasiteles, who himself was a pupil of ... There are figures of Hera, Zeus, the Mother of the gods, Hermes, and Apollo with Artemis. Behind is the disposition of the games. On one side are Asclepius and Health, one of his daughters; Ares too and Contest by his side; on the other are Pluto, Dionysus, Persephone and nymphs, one of them carrying a ball. As to the key [Pluto holds a key] they say that what is called Hades has been locked up by Pluto, and that nobody will return back again therefrom.

I must not omit the story told by Aristarchus, the guide to the sights at Olympia.[2] He said that in his day the roof of the Heraeum had fallen into decay. When the Eleans were repairing it, the corpse of a foot-soldier with wounds was discovered between the roof supporting the tiles and the ornamented ceiling. This soldier took part in the battle in the Altis between the Eleans and the Lacedaemonians.[3] The Eleans in fact climbed to defend themselves on to all high places alike, including the sanctuaries of the gods. At any rate this soldier seemed to us to have crept under her after growing faint with his wounds, and so died. Lying in a completely sheltered spot the corpse would suffer harm neither from the heat of summer nor from the frost of winter. Aristarchus said further that they carried the corpse outside the Altis and buried him in the earth along with his armour.

Source

Jones, W.H.S. and Ormerod, H.A. 1926, *Pausanias, Description of Greece*, Loeb Classical Library, London and New York, Heinemann: 471–99

Notes

1 This has to be understood as an indication of the early date of the works.
2 The presence of guides in sanctuaries is also attested elsewhere; see the discussion in Pausanias' *Description of Greece*, 3.9.
3 c. 400 BC.

References

Alsop, 1982
Arafat, 1995
Kent Hill, 1944
Snodgrass, 1980
Wace, 1969
Wernicke, 1894

20

The role and decoration of temples: the Parthenon

The list of treasures that follows comes from a detailed study of the inventories of the Athenian Acropolis contacted by D. Harris (1995). More specifically, this is the list of objects held in the 'Parthenon', that is, the west cella of the temple devoted to Athena, the protrectress goddess of Athens. The chamber had four ionic columns, and was not open to the public. No cult statue was kept in the room – it was merely a storage area of Athena's treasure in the fifth century BC. The only visitors in the room would be the priests and treasurers.

The term 'Parthenon' refers to the whole temple; nevertheless, it seems that in the fifth century there was a clear distinction between the parts of the temple, and the term 'Parthenon' was saved for part of the building, the western part of the cella, Athena's private bedroom, in a way (the term itself used to denote the bedroom of the unmarried girl).

The treasures are a mixture of arms and weapons, jewellery, furniture, wreaths and vessels. The names of the dedicators do not survive, although some objects from Lesbos may have been war booty from the campaign in 428/7 BC, and the Persian daggers relics of the Persian wars or some other activity against the Persians in the fifth century (Harris, 1995: 81–2).

The list supports our argument about the role of temples as repositories of relics of the past and other treasures dedicated by individuals and cities to honour the gods in the form of conspicuous consumption, but also to safeguard their past for the future. The material aspect of these possessions was also taken into account, since the exact reference to the value of the objects serves not only to guarantee the honesty of the treasurers and keepers, but also to underline the objects' material worth.

INVENTORY OF THE PARTHENON

Arms and Weapons
    6 Persian daggers overlaid with gold …
    1 Persian dagger overlaid with gold; unweighed …
    A gold-plated helmet …

3 bronze helmets ...
A bronze Illyrian helmet, from Lesbos ...
14 breast-plates ...
16 breast-plates ...
31 brazen shields ...
Six shields with blazons ...
33 shields with blazons ...
33 shields with blazons, of these three are inscribed ...
33 shields with blazons, of these five are not inscribed ...
Shields with blazons ...
33 shields with blazons, of these three are inscribed ...
13 shields, gilt wood ...
14 shields, gilt wood ...
15 shields, gilt wood ...
1 shield with blazon, from Lesbos ...
2 shields, gilt wood ...
A bronze light shield ...
Light shield overlaid with gold, complete ...

Baskets and Containers
2 gilt-wood baskets
A gilt-wood box

Coins
A gold tetradrachm; weight of this: 7 drachms 2½ obols ...
Two gold pieces ...
Unmarked gold; weight of this: 1 dr., 4 obols ...
Unmarked gold; weight of this: 7 dr. ...
Unmarked gold ...

Figurines and Statues
A gilt kore on a base
A gorgoneion, gilt monster-figures
Horse, griffin, griffin's promote, large griffin, lion's head, flowery chain, snake, all these gilt
Golden wheat: 12 stalks
A mask, silver-gilt; weight of this: 116 dr.

Furniture
7 Chian couches
10 Milesian couches: 3 in need of repair
4 stools
13 feet for couches, overlaid with silver

9 campstools
Ten campstools
An ivory-inlaid table
6 thrones

Jewellery
An onyx having a gold ring; unweighed
Eight gilt seals and two stone griffins; weight of these: 40+ dr.
2 chains and a golden olive branch; weight of these: 35 dr. 3 ob.
Wide collars set with stones attached to a leather band, five in number, weight of these: 55 dr.
100+ earrings ...
Two gold earrings set with stones; weight of these: 21 dr.
A gold belt
The smaller gold necklace set with stones, having 20 rosettes
The larger gold necklace set with stones, having 20 rosettes and 1 ram's head: weight of these: 30 dr.

Musical Instruments
The gilded ivory aulos-case from Methymna
A gilt lyre
3 ivory lyres
4 ivory lyres
4 wooden lyres
5 wooden lyres

Tools
9 sabres
4 swords
Five swords
Two nail, silver gilt: weight of these: 184 dr.

Vessels
... silver phialai; weight of these 723+dr.
138 silver phialai, a silver drinking-horn; weight of these: 2 talents 3307 dr.
8 silver phialai; weight of these: 807 dr.
5 gold phialai; weight of these: 782 dr.
Two silver phialai; two silver goblets; weight of these: 580 dr.
4 silver phialai, 2 silver containers, a silver horse; weight of these: 900 dr.
A gold *karchesion* [goblet] having a silver base, sacred to Herakles in Elaious; weight of this: 138 dr.

An incense-burner, gilt wood
4 silver Chalkidian drinking-cups; eight of these: 124 dr.
3 silver Lesbian cups; weight of these: 370 dr.

Wreaths
A gold wreath; weight of this: 60 dr.
A gold wreath; weight of this: 18 dr. 3 ob.
A gold wreath, weight of this: 29 dr.
A gold wreath of Athena Nike; weight of this: 29 dr.
A gold wreath; weight of this: 33 dr.
A gold wreath of Athena Nike; weight of this: 33 dr.

Source

Harris, D., 1995, *The Treasures of the Parthenon and Erechteion*, Oxford University Press: 83–103

References

Harris, 1995

21

Temple visiting, described by Herodas

The description of another sanctuary, that of Asclepius on the island of Kos,[1] comes through the testimony of two women who had gone to the temple to pay their respects, offer a sacrifice and admire the statues and paintings that decorated it. This is the fourth of Herodas' *Mimes*. Very little information on Herodas is available; from references in his work we reach a date for his life around the period of King Ptolemy Euergetes (246–261 BC). The *Mimes* are poetic compositions devoted to a variety of subjects, among which is the one described in the following paragraph,

HERODAS, *MIMES*, IV

Ky.[2]   Hail to thee, Lord Paieon, ruler of Tricca, who hast got as thine habitation sweet Kos and Epidauros, hail to Koronis thy mother withal and Apollo; hail to her whom thou touchest with thy right hand, Hygieia, and those to whom belong these honoured shrines, Panake and Epio and Ieso; hail ye twain which did sack the house and walls of Leomedon healers of savage sicknesses, Podaleirios and Machaon, and what gods and goddesses soever dwell by thine hearth, Father Paieon; come hither with your blessings and accept the aftercourse of this cock whom I sacrifice, herald of the walls of my house. For we draw no bounteous nor ready spring; else might we, perchance, with an ox or stuffed pig of much fatness and no humble cock, be paying the price of cure from diseases that thou didst wipe away, Lord, by laying on us thy gentle hands. Set the tablet, Kokkale, on the right of Hygieia.[3]

Ko.   La! Kynno dear, what beautiful statues! What craftsman was it who worked this stone, and who dedicated it?

Ky.   The sons of Praxiteles – only look at the letters on the base, and Euthies, son of Prexon, dedicated it.[4]

Ko.   May Paieon bless them and Euthies for their beautiful works. See, dear, the girl yonder looking up at the apple; wouldn't you think she will swoon away suddenly, if she does not get it? Oh, and yon

71

old man, Kynno. Ah, in the Fates' name, see how the boy is strangling the goose. Why, one would say the sculpture would talk, that is if it were not stone when one gets close. La! in time men will be able even to put life into stones. Yet, only look, Kynno, at the gait of this statue of Batale daughter of Myttes. Anyone who has not seen Batale, may look at this image and be satisfied without the woman herself.[5]

Ky.   Come along, dear, and I will show you a beautiful thing such as you have never seen in all your life. Kydilla, go and call the sacristan. It's you I am speaking to, you who are gaping up and down! La! not an atom of notice does she take of what I am saying, but stands and stares at me for all the world like a crab! Go, I tell you again, and call the sacristan. You glutton, there is not a patch of ground, holy or profane, that would praise you as an honest girl – everywhere alike your value is the same. Kydilla, I call this god to witness, that you are setting my wrath aflame, little as I wish my passion to rise. I repeat, I call him to witness that the day will come when you shall have cause to scratch your filthy noodle.

Ko.   Don't take everything to heart so, Kynno: she is a slave, and a slave's ears are oppressed with dullness.

Ky.   But it is day-time and the crush is getting greater, so stop there! For the door is thrown open and there is access to the sacristy.

Ko.   Only look, dear Kynno, what works are those there! See these, you would say, were chiselled by Athene herself – all hail, Lady![6] Look, this naked boy, he will bleed, will he not, if I scratch him, Kynno; for the flesh seems to pulse warmly as it lies on him in the picture,[7] and the silver toasting-iron, if Myllos or Pataikiskos, son of Lamprion,[8] see it, won't their eyes start from their sockets when they suppose it real silver!
And the ox and its leader, and the girl in attendance, and this hook-nosed and this snub-nosed fellow, have they not all of them the look of light and life? If I did not think it would be unbecoming for a woman, I should have screamed for fear the ox would do me a hurt: he is looking so sideways at me with one eye.

Ky.   Yes, dear, the hands of Apelles of Ephesus are true in all his paintings, and you cannot say that he looked with favour on one thing and fought shy of another: no, whatever came into his fancy, he was ready and eager to essay off-hand, and if any gaze on him or his works save from a just point of view, may he be hung up by the foot at the fuller's!

S. Your sacrifice is entirely favourable, ladies, with still better things in store; no one has appeased Paieon in greater sort than you. Glory, glory to thee, Paieon, mayst thou look with favour for fair offerings on these, and all that be their husbands or near of kin. Glory, glory, Paieon. Amen, Amen.

Ky. Amen, Almighty, and may we come again in full health once more bringing larger offerings, and our husbands and children with us. Kokkale, remember to carve the leg of the fowl off carefully, and give it to the sacristan, and put the mess into the mouth of the snake reverently, and souse the meat-offering. The rest we will eat at home; and remember to take it away.

S. Ho there! give me some of the holy bread; for the loss of this is more serious to holy men than the loss of our portion.

Source

Knox, A.D. (ed.), 1922, *Herodas: The Mimes and Fragments*, with notes by Walter Headlam, Cambridge University Press: 166–73

Notes

1 Usually the temple where the scene takes place is identified with that of Asklepius on Kos; nevertheless, Cunningham (1971: 128) suggests that although it is beyond doubt a temple of Asclepius, there is no particular reason to locate it on Kos.
2 The characters that take part in this *Mime* are two women: the one that makes the sacrifice is called Kynno, the other's name has been the subject of dispute. Cunningham (1971: 127) suggests that she is called Phile, and the name Kokkale, which also appears refers to a slave. Kokkale, though, is usually taken to be the name of the second woman, and this is the version that Knox embraces in the following translation. There were also two slave women (Kydilla and Kokkale [?]), and the attendant of the temple who briefly advises of the success of the sacrifice.
3 The two women visit the temple of Asclepius, the god of medicine; in their opening prayer they refer to the god, his family and associated deities that relate to matters of health and the cure of disease: Hygieia (health), Ieso

('healing one'), Panake ('remedy of all'), Epio ('gentle one') are all Asclepius' daughters.

4 The name of both the artist and the dedicator are mentioned. The statue was probably inside the temple; it was the work of the sons of Praxiteles, namely Kephisodotos and Timarchos, whose collaboration is attested elsewhere as well (for example Plutarch, *Moralia*, 843 e–f).

5 Naturalism is the main artistic criterion for the two women. Although it is widely supposed that the two women's views are expressions of the poet's own, the naivety and the unsophisticated appreciation of naturalness and excellence could well illustrate the views of uneducated and poor people.

6 The goddess Athena was protector of the arts; according to mythology she was a skilled artist herself, and the one who had instructed men and women to produce works of art.

7 This is a description of one painting by Apelles: it depicts a sacrifice, a boy in front of a fire, an ox who is going to be sacrificed and the attendants surrounding them (Cunningham, 1971: 140).

8 Myllos and Pataikiskos were an interesting pair: the former silly enough to think that the silver was real, the latter a well-known rogue prepared to steal the treasure of a temple (Knox, 1922: 202–3; Cunningham, 1971: 140).

References

Knox, 1922
Cunningham, 1971

22

Exotic objects as rites of passage

Athenaeus in his *Deipnosophists*, completed not long after AD 228, quotes a series of lengthy and elaborate descriptions of a festival pavilion built by Ptolemy II Philadelphos probably in 276 BC, and a procession which was part of the same festival. He took his descriptions from the writer Kallixeinos of Rhodes (mid-second century BC) who wrote a book on the city of Alexandria. These are important for a number of reasons: first, because they present an example of the grandeur and luxury of the kings of the East that impressed the Romans; second, because they provide an example of the sources from which many Roman practices derived. For the purpose of this work, we should note the theatrical settings to display works of art, the interest in architectural fantasy and use of objects to transfer to a different time and place, as well as the role of material culture in celebrations that indicate a rite of passage (religious ceremonies) (Pollitt, 1990: 34).

ATHENAEUS, *DEIPNOSOPHISTS*, 5. 201B–202F

After these, in the procession, marched two hunters carrying gilded hunting-spears. Dogs were also led along, numbering two thousand four hundred, some Indian, the other Hyrcanian or Molossian or of other breeds. Next came one hundred and fifty men carrying trees on which were suspended all sorts of animals and birds. Then were brought, in cages, parrots, peacocks, guinea-fowls, and birds from the Phasis and others from Aethiopia, in great quantities.

After he[1] has spoken of very many other things, and enumerated many droves of animals he adds: 'One hundred and thirty Aethiopian sheep, three hundred Arabian, twenty Euboean; also twenty-six Indian oxen entirely white, eight Aethiopian, one large white she-bear, fourteen leopards, sixteen panthers, four lynxes, three panther-cubs, one giraffe, one Aethiopian rhinoceros. Next in a four-wheeled cart was Dionysus at the altar of Rhea, having found refuge there while being pursued by Hera; he had on a gold crown, and Priapus stood at his side, with a gold ivy-crown. The statue of Hera had a gold diadem. Then there were statues of Alexander and Ptolemy, crowned with ivy-crowns made of gold. The statue of Goodness which stood beside Ptolemy had a gold olive-crown.

Priapus stood beside them also wearing an ivy-crown made of gold. The city of Corinth standing beside Ptolemy, was crowned with a gold band.

Beside all these figures were placed a stand for cups, full of gold vessels, and a gold mixing-bowl of fifty gallons capacity. Following this cart were women who wore very rich robes and ornaments; they bore the names of cities, some from Ionia, while all the rest were the Greek cities which occupied Asia and the islands and has been under the rule of the Persians; they all wore gold crowns. In other carts, also, were carried a Bacchic wand of gold, one hundred and thirty-five feet long, and a silver spear ninety feet long; in another was a gold phallus one hundred and eighty feet long, painted in various colours and bound with fillets of gold; it had at the extremity a gold star, the perimeter of which was nine feet.'

Many and varied though the things are which have been mentioned as belonging to these processions, yet I[1] have selected for mention only those things which contained gold and silver. For there were numerous articles worth mentioning, and quantities of wild beasts and horses, and twenty-four huge lions. There were other carts besides, which carried images of kings and of gods as well, many of them. After them marched a choral band of six hundred men; among them three hundred harp-players performed together, carrying harps gilded all over, and wearing gold crowns. After them two thousand bulls, all of the same colour and with gilded horns, came by, having gold stars on their foreheads, wreaths between the horns, and necklaces and aegises on their breasts; all these were of gold. And after this came marching in the carnival a division in honour of Zeus and one of other gods in great number, and following all one devoted to Alexander, whose effigy in gold was borne, Victory and Athena on either side, in a chariot drawn by live elephants. In the procession also were many thrones constructed of ivory and gold; on one of these lay a gold diadem, on another a gilded horn, on still another a gold crown, and one another a horn of solid gold. Upon the throne of Ptolemy Soter lay a crown made of ten thousand gold coins. In the procession also were three hundred and fifty gold censers, and gilded altars wreathed with gold crowns; on one of these, four gold torches fifteen feet long were affixed. And two gilded braziers were also carried in the procession, of which one was eighteen feet in circumference and sixty in height, the other measured twenty-two and a half feet. There were also nine Delphic tripods of gold of six feet each, eight more of nine feet, another of forty-five feet; on this were figures in gold seven and a half feet high, and a vine-wreath of gold encircled it. There went by also seven gilded palm-threes twelve feet high and a gilded herald's staff sixty-seven and a half feet long, a gilded thunderbolt sixty feet long, also a gilded temple measuring sixty feet all round; there was a double horn in addition, twelve feet high. A very large number of gilded figures were in the procession, the most of which were eighteen feet high; and there were figures of wild beasts of extraordinary size, and eagles thirty feet high.

Three thousand two hundred gold crowns were shown in the procession, and there was another mystic crown of gold one hundred and twenty feet in circumference, adorned with precious stones; this was hung round the portal of Berenice's shrine; there was similarly a gold aegis. And there were also very many gold diadems in the procession, carried by girls richly dressed; one diadem was three feet high, and it had a perimeter of twenty-four feet. There was paraded also a gold breast-plate eighteen feet in length, and another of silver, twenty-seven feet, with gold thunderbolts on it fifteen feet long, and an oak crown of gold studded with jewels. Twenty gold shields, sixty-four suits of armour in gold, two pairs of gold greaves four and a half feet long, twelve gold hods, saucer-shaped cups in very great number, thirty wine-pitchers, ten large ointment-holders, twelve water-jars, fifty bread-platters, various tables, five stands of gold vessels, a horn of solid gold forty-five feet long. And these articles of gold were exclusive of those carried by in the division of Dionysus. Further, there were four hundred cartloads of silver vessels, twenty of gold vessels, and eight hundred of spices. After all these marched the cavalry and infantry forces, all wonderfully armed.

Source

Gulick, Charles Burton, 1927, *Athenaeus, Deipnosophists*, in 6 volumes, Vol. I., London and New York: Loeb Classical Library, Heinemann and G.P. Putnam's Sons: 411–17.

Notes

1   These pronouns refer to Athenaeus or Masurius, the character that describes the procession.

References

Pollitt, 1983

23

Treasuries and the city-state:
the testimony of Pausanias

The princely *thalamos* that Homer has described was gradually replaced by other forms of the same notion, communal treasuries in the new centres of Hellenism and power.[1]

A mixture of art and historical material was arranged in and around the buildings of the sanctuaries, devoted (donated) by people who wanted to commemorate their deeds and their names, and thus legitimise the social hierarchy that supported them and was supported by them. The construction in pan-Hellenic sanctuaries in the eighth century BC onwards of large monuments is related to a process of institutionalisation of religion empowered by the creation of city-states (see de Polignac, 1995; also Morgan, 1990: 5). Sanctuaries, therefore, became the arenas where practices and ideologies of the aristocratic world were transferred, as a result of changing circumstances. The holdings of the sanctuaries came to represent frozen wealth, to be admired but not consumed; a kind of conspicuous consumption, expected to be 'repaid' in terms of status, legitimacy, proof of class and of claims to rule and to domination (see also Pearce, 1995: 90; Burkert, 1987: 49).

Snodgrass (1980) analyses the deposits of bronze goods in important sanctuaries from the eleventh century to the eighth century, and reports a considerable increase in bronze dedications which coincided, as Morris's research suggests, with a decline in grave goods in many areas, where the city-state was gaining precedence, around 700 BC (Morris, 1992). Morris further argues that this transition, which is evident in the archaeological record, is a clear example of change from gifts-to-men to gifts-to-gods, in the context of destruction of wealth. He associates this with the need of aristocratic competition to be represented as having a wider communal value at a time of great social stress, that is, as the result of a profound structural change in society, empowered by the creation of the *poleis* (Morris, 1986). The arguments that Morris offered to support his thesis are two: firstly, the word *agalma* which from being a term denoting the 'precious' in the gift exchange tradition of the Homeric society (see Gernet, 1981), is transferred in the context of sanctuaries to mean the offering in general from the fifth century onwards (and gradually in modern Greek simply the statue); secondly, the inscriptions found in abundance in sanctuaries made sure that the donors' names would be commemorated, serving, that is, the need to impress and to compete, but also to assure the return of the gift.

Indeed, these are not the only arguments that can be put forward to support this thesis. The buildings of treasuries within the sanctuary enclosures make the same point and even elaborate it; we can argue that treasuries are expressions of the tradition of gift exchange, insofar as they are also associated with mythic values and concerns. Treasuries monumentalise the transition from gifts-to-men to gifts-to-gods and bear both the socio-political set of values of gift exchange, as well as the mythic parameters of value, that is, qualities that people cannot comprehend and thus attribute to mythic or religious spheres.

The political motivation behind the building of treasuries is more or less evident and falls within the generally accepted role of the sanctuaries as arenas for competition. According to the sources, treasuries were mainly dedicated as spoils of war (Strabo, *Geography*, 9.3.7–8), to commemorate a victory or to display a city's prosperity, as in the case of the Siphnian treasury at Delphi. Another reason was the display of piety to the gods. As monuments erected to celebrate the wealth, achievement and civic pride of individual states, they were striking and innovative artistic creations, lavishly decorated, that could not be matched by the buildings related to the sanctuary as collective entities (Morgan, 1990: 18).

The treasuries were small-scale, temple-like buildings, with a porch and an inner room of similar width behind. Most had porches consisting of two (usually Doric) columns between the forward continuations of the side walls. In Delphi, we have examples of more elaborate buildings, like the Siphnian treasury, which had two Caryatids at the entrance.

PAUSANIAS, *DESCRIPTION OF GREECE*, 6, *ELIS*, 2. 19.1–10

1. There is a terrace made of conglomerate stone in the Altis to the north of Heraeum, and at the back of it extends Mount Cronius. On this terrace are the treasuries, just as at Delphi some of the Greeks have made treasuries for Apollo.

2. At Olympia there is a treasury called the treasury of the Sicyonians, an offering of Myron, tyrant of Sicyon. Myron built it after he had gained a victory in the chariot-race in the thirty-third Olympiad. In the treasury he made two chambers, one in the Doric, the other in the Ionic style. I saw that they were made of bronze, but whether the bronze is Tartessian bronze, as the Eleans say, I do not know.

3.   They say that Tartessus is a river in the land of the Iberians, which
     empties itself into the sea by two mouths, and that there is a city of
     the same name situated between the mouths of the river. The river,
     which is the greatest in Iberia, and is moreover tidal, received in
     later times the name of Baetis. But some think that Carpia, a city of
     the Iberians, was anciently called Tartessus. On the lesser of the
     chambers at Olympia there are inscriptions, mentioning that the
     weight of the bronze is five hundred talents, and that the treasury
     was dedicated by Myron and the people of Sicyon. In this treasury
     are kept three quoits, which are employed in the pentathlum. There
     is also a bronze-plated shield, curiously painted on its inner side,
     and along with the shield there are a helmet and greaves. An
     inscription on the arms states that they are a first-fruit offering
     presented to Zeus by the Myanians. Different conjectures have
     been made as to who these Myanians were. I recollected that
     Thucydides in his history mentions various cities of the Locrians
     who border on Phocis, and amongst others in the city of the
     Myanians. In my opinion, then, the Myanians referred to on the
     shield are the same as the Myanians in Locris. The inscription on
     the shield runs a little awry, which is to be explained by the
     antiquity of the votive offering. Here are also deposited other
     notable things: the sword of Pelops with a golden hilt; the horn of
     Amalthea made of ivory, and offering of that Miltiades, son of
     Cimon, who was the first of his family to reign in the Thracian
     Chersonese. In the horn is an inscription in old Attic letters:

>   I was dedicated as an offering to Olympian Zeus by the men
>   of the Chersonese after they had taken the stronghold of
>   Aratus: their leader was Miltiades.

     There is also a boxwood image of Apollo with the head gilt: the
     inscription says that it was dedicated by the Locrians who dwell
     near Cape Zephyrium, and that it was made by Patrocles of Crotona,
     son of Catillus.

4.   Next to the treasury of the Sicyonians is the treasury of the
     Carthaginians, a work of Pothaeus, Antiphilus, and Megacles. In it
     are dedicated a colossal image of Zeus and three linen corselets. It
     is an offering of Gelo and the Syracusans for a victory over the
     Phoenicians either by sea or land.

5.   The third and fourth of the treasuries are offerings of the
     Epidamnians ... It contains a representation of Atlas upholding the
     firmament, and another of Hercules and the apple-tree of the
     Hesperides, with the serpent coiled about the tree. These also are

of cedar-wood, and are works of Theocles, son of Hegylus: the inscription on the firmament states that he made them with the help of his son. The Hesperides were by the Eleans, but were still to be seen in my time at the Heraeum. The treasury was made for the Epidamnians by Pyrrhus and his sons Lacrates and Hermon.

6. The Sybarites also built a treasury next to that of the Byzantines. Those who have made a study of Italy and its cities say that the city of Lupiae, situated between Brundusium and Hydrus, is the ancient Sybaris with a changed name. The roadstead is artificial, a work of the Emperor Hadrian.

7. Beside the treasury of the Sybarites is a treasury of the Libyans of Cyrene: it contains statues of Roman emperors. Selinus, in Sicily, was destroyed by the Carthaginians in war, but before this calamity befell them the people of Selinus dedicated a treasury to Zeus at Olympia. It contains an image of Dionysus, whereof the face, feet, and hands are made of ivory.

8. In the treasury of the Metapontines, which adjoins that of the Selinuntians, there is a figure of Endymion, also of ivory, except the drapery. I do not know what was the occasion of the destruction of Metapontum, but in my time nothing was left of it save the theatre and the circuit wall.

9. The people of Megara, near Attica, built a treasury, and dedicated offerings in it, consisting of small cedar-wood figures inlaid with gold, and representing Hercules' fight with Achelous. Here are represented Zeus, Dejanira, Achelous, and Hercules, and Ares who is helping Achelous. Also there was formerly an image of Athena, because she was an ally of Hercules; but this image now stands beside the Hesperides in the Heraeum. In the gable of the treasury is wrought in relief the war of the giants and the gods, and above the gable is a shield with an inscription stating that the treasury was dedicated by the Megarians from the spoils of the Corinthians. I believe that this victory was won by the Megarians when Phorbas was archon for life at Athens; for in those days the annual archonships were not yet instituted at Athens, and the Eleans had not yet begun to record the Olympiads. The Argives are said to have helped the Megarians against the Corinthians. The treasury in Olympia was made by the Megarians years after the battle, but they must have had the votive offerings from of old, since they were made by the Lacedaemonian Dontas, a pupil of Dipoenus and Scyllis.

10. The last of the treasuries is beside the stadium: the inscription states that the treasury and the images in it were dedicated by the people of Gela. However, there are images in it no longer.

PAUSANIAS, *DESCRIPTION OF GREECE*, 10, *PHOCIS*, 11.1–2, 4

1. Near the offering of the Tarentines is a treasury of the Sicyonians; but neither in this nor in any other of the treasuries are there treasures to be seen.[2] The Cnidians brought images to Delphi, to wit, an image of Triopas, founder of Cnidus, standing beside a horse, an image of Latona, and images of Apollo and Artemis shooting arrows at Tityus, who is represented wounded in various places. These images stand beside the treasury of the Sicyonians.

2. The Siphians also made a treasury for the following reason: – there were gold mines in the island of Siphnus, and the god bade them bring a tithe of the profits of Delphi; so they built the treasury and brought the tithe. But when out of avarice they ceased to bring the tribute, the sea flooded and buried the mines.

    ...

4. The treasury of the Thebans was built with the spoils of war, and so was the treasury of the Athenians. The Theban treasury was built with the spoils of the battle of Leuctra, the Athenian treasury with the spoils taken from the army which landed at Marathon under the command of Datis. But I do not know whether the Cnidians built their treasury to commemorate a victory or to display their wealth. The Cleonaeans, like the Athenians, suffered from the pestilence, and, in obedience to an oracle from Delphi, sacrificed a he-goat to the rising sun. So, finding that the plague was stayed, they sent a bronze he-goat to Apollo. The Potideans in Thrace and the Syracusans have also treasuries: the latter was built from the spoils taken in the great overthrow of the Athenians; the former was erected out of reverence for the god.

PAUSANIAS, *DESCRIPTION OF GREECE*, 10, *PHOCIS*, 13. 3–4

3. The Dorians of Corinth also built a treasury, and the gold from Lydia used to be kept there. The image of Hercules is an offering of the Thebans, sent by them at the time when they waged the Sacred War, as it is called, with the Phocians. There are also bronze images dedicated by the Phocians when they had routed the Thessalian cavalry in the second encounter. The Phliasians brought to Delphi a bronze Zeus, and along with it an image of Aegina.

4. There is a bronze Apollo, an offering from Mantinea in Arcadia: it stands not far from the treasury of the Corinthians.

Source

Pausanias, *Description of Greece*, 1898, trans. with a commentary by J.G. Frazer in 6 volumes: Vol. 1, London: MacMillan.

Notes

1   See, on *thalamos*, Chapter 14 in this volume.
2   On the fate of the offerings in the sanctuary of Delphi, see Ehrhardt, 1966.

References

Burkert, 1987
Ehrhardt, 1966
Linders and Nordquist, 1987
Morgan, 1990
Morris, 1986
Morris, 1992
Pearce, 1995a
de Polignac, 1995
Snodgrass, 1980

24

The *mouseion* in Aristotle's Lyceum

The term *mouseion* – 'museum' – refers to a shrine devoted to the Muses[1]. This was a common tradition in the Greek world (see, for instance Pausanias, 9.27ff), where they were cult centres with occasionally a funeral association (Fraser, 1972: 313). More often, though, they had literary connections and they formed the focus of circles for the study of literature and especially of the Homeric epics. The exact arrangement of those 'museums' is not clear, and the presence of an actual temple is highly doubtful.

The Muses played a particularly important role in the philosophical schools of Plato and Aristotle. In Plato's Academy there was an altar devoted to the Muses (Pausanias, 1.30.2) and the Academy was organised as a *thiasos*, a group of people associated with the religious purpose of serving the Muses. In Aristotle's Lyceum there was a Museum (*mouseion*), probably a small temple; Theophrastus was concerned about it and left instructions to his successors to finish its rebuilding, and to make sure that a bust of Aristotle was installed in it, together with all the other offerings that were there before the destruction. The Alexandrian Museum was, after all, an intellectual construction of the Peripatetics. It has been argued that since the very first 'museums' were mainly open-air sanctuaries discernible as such only because of the offerings that decorated them (Roux, 1954: 45), the transition to the Renaissance and modern museums was much facilitated, since the term was used to denote not primarily a temple, but mainly a collection of works of art and relics set aside in a sacred garden or grove consecrated by the presence of the divine Muses (Bounia, 1998).

In any case, this Greek type influenced the arrangement of the Roman gardens, where intellectuals and upper-class Romans used to enjoy their role and importance as successors of their famous Greek predecessors. The objects these amateurs displayed in their gardens assimilated the arrangement in the Greek μουσεῖα, by hosting statues, portraits of famous personages, and so on.

The text that follows is part of the will of Theophrastus as preserved by Diogenes Laertius, where the philosopher's interest in the Museum of the Lyceum is expressed.

DIOGENES LAERTIUS, *LIVES OF EMINENT PHILOSOPHERS*, 5. 51–3

I have also come across his will, couched in the following terms:

'All will be well; but in case anything should happen, I make these dispositions. I give and bequeath all my property at home[2] to Melantes and Pancreon, the sons of Leon. It is my wish that out of the trust funds at the disposal of Hipparchus[3] the following appropriations should be made. First, they should be applied to finish the rebuilding of the Museum with the statues of the goddesses, and to add any improvements which seem practicable to beautify them.[4] Secondly, to replace in the temple the bust of Aristotle with the rest of the dedicated offerings which formerly were in the temple. Next, to rebuild the small cloister adjoining the Museum at least as handsomely as before, and to replace in the lower cloister the tablets containing maps of the countries traversed by explorers. Further, to repair the altar so that it may be perfect and elegant. It is also my wish that the statue of Nicomachus should be completed of life size. The price agreed upon for the making of the statue itself has been paid to Praxiteles, but the rest of the cost should be defrayed from the source above mentioned. The statue should be set up in whatever place seems desirable to the executors entrusted with carrying out my other testamentary dispositions. Let all that concerns the temple and the offerings set up be arranged in this manner. The estate at Stagira belonging to me I give and bequeath to Callinus. The whole of my library I give to Neleus. The garden and the walk and the houses adjoining the garden, all and sundry, I give and bequeath to such of my friends hereinafter named as may wish to study literature and philosophy there in common, since it is not possible for all men to be always in residence, on condition that no one alienates the property or devotes it to his private use, but so that they hold it like a temple in joint possession and live, as is right and proper, on terms of familiarity and friendship. Let the community consist of Hipparchus, Neleus, Strato, Callinus, Demotimus, Demaratus, Callisthenes, Melantes, Pancreon, Nicippus. Aristotle, the son of Metrodorus and Pythias, shall also have the right to study and associate with them if he so desire.'

Source

Hicks, R.D., 1925, *Diogenes Laertius, Lives of Eminent Philosophers*, Loeb Classical Library, in 2 vols, Vol. 1, London and New York: Heinemann and G.P. Putnam's Sons: 503–5

Notes

1   For a very detailed presentation of the ancient sources referring to the Greek
    mouseia, and the genealogy of the museum in the ancient world, see
    Oberhummer, 1933.
2   Theophrastus was a native of Eresus.
3   Hipparchus was acting as a trustee for Theophrastus, but also for the school;
    this in the eyes of the law was a religious establishment, like the museum in
    Alexandria (see Hicks, 1925: 502, note b).
4   It seems that the museum had suffered from recent political disturbances in
    Athens. Hicks (1925: 502–3, note c) mentions that these might have been the
    second siege of Athens by Demetrius Poliorcetes (296–294 BC), or the revolt
    of Athens from Macedonia (289–287 BC).

References

Fraser, 1972
Oberhummer, 1933
Roux, 1954

25

The Museum of Alexandria

The Museum of Alexandria was established as a combined centre of religious and literary activities. It was founded most probably by Ptolemy Soter, under the influence of the Peripatetic philosopher Demetrius Poliorcetes, who became a tyrant of Athens (317–307 BC) and after he was expelled from the city fled to Egypt. He became an adviser of the King, who was more than willing to follow the Aristotelian tradition of learning.

It had been a custom for those involved in literary pursuits to ask for the support of the Muses; the term 'museum' therefore refers to resorts dear to the Muses, where art and letters enjoyed favour (Couat, 1931). Indeed, the museum in Alexandria was organised as a kind of college, where scholars pursued their studies under the patronage of the court and the protection of the Muses.

Strabo provides a picture of the establishments of the museum: they were part of the royal quarter, its members formed a society for religious purposes and they were presided over by a priest. The members of the museum enjoyed exception from taxes, and they were free to pursue their studies, their philosophical discussion and teaching arrangements. The modern connotation of the museum as an establishment for the storage of material culture would be unfamiliar to ancient Alexandrians, although the seeds of what we would call collecting activities must have been there. The buildings of the museum were surrounded by courtyards and porticoes, which would probably have had a decoration of statues and portraits of philosophers. Animals and plants must have been among the items that interested the scientifically oriented scholars, and would have formed part of their collections. In addition, the museum was soon to be accompanied by a library, that is, a collection of books and a setting for portrait assemblages (see Fraser, 1972).

STRABO, *GEOGRAPHY*, 17.1.8

The shape of the area of the city is like a chlamys;[1] the long sides of it are those that are washed by the two waters, having a diameter of about thirty stadia, and the short sides are the isthmuses, each being seven or eight stadia wide and pinched in on one side by the sea and on the other by the lake. The city as a whole is intersected by streets practicable for horse-riding and chariot-driving, and by two that are very broad, extending to more than a plethrum in breadth, which cut one another into two sections and at right angles. And the city contains most beautiful public precincts and also the royal palaces, which constitute one-fourth or even one-third of the whole circuit of the city; for just as each of the kings, from love of splendour, was wont to add some adornment to the public monuments, so also he would invest himself at his own expense with a residence, in addition to those already built, so that now, to quote the words of the poet,[2] 'there is building upon building'. All, however, are connected with one another and the harbour, even those that lie outside the harbour. The Museum is also a part of the royal palaces; it has a public walk, an Exedra with seats, and a large house,[3] in which is the common mess-hall of the men of learning who share the Museum. This group of men not only hold property in common, but also have a priest in charge of the Museum, who formerly was appointed by the kings, but is now appointed by Caesar.

Source

Jones, Horace Leonard, 1954, *Strabo, Geography*, Loeb Classical Library, Vol. 4, London and Cambridge, Mass., Heinemann and Harvard University Press: 33–5

Notes

1   Strabo describes a part of Alexandria.
2   Naturally, the poet is Homer, when he refers to the palace of Odysseus, *Od.* 17.266.
3   The translator and commentator of the text points out that a similar reference to the buildings which are appropriate for philosophers and rhetoricians is made by Vitruvius (*De Architectura*, 5.11.2): 'Spacious exedras within three porticoes with seats, where philosophers, rhetoricians and all others who take delight in studies can engage in disputation.' He also mentions that Suidas seems to understand the exedra as a building distinct from the museum, but also associated to it: 'They live near the Museum and the Exedra' (Jones, 1954: 34, note 3). See also the references made by Cicero when describing the objects he desires for the decoration of his villa to his friend Atticus.

References

Couat, 1931
Fraser, 1972

26

Hellenistic collectors: Aratus of Sicyon

Plutarch in his biography of Aratus, a Sicyonian general who became the leader of the Achaean League in the mid-third century BC, sketches the portrait of a connoisseur and collector of works of art. He relies on the Memoirs of Aratus, a work now lost, and on the antiquarian Polemo of Ilium (fl. c. 200 BC), who wrote on the Sicyonian group of painters (Porter, 1937) in order to recount an incident which is indicative of the power of works of art when collectors are involved. Aratus gained the support of King Ptolemy III (Euergetes) of Egypt by sending to him works of art by the famous Sicyonian artists Pamphilus and Melanthus, both well-acknowledged painters of their era (Pliny, *HN*, 35.75; 35.80). These gained the King's admiration – he was also a connoisseur and a collector of books, since we know that he bought and transferred to Alexandria the official texts of the plays of Aeschylus, Sophocles and Euripides from the city of Athens (Fraser, 1972: 325/480, note 147; Alsop, 1982) – and the King thus provided the much-needed support.

PLUTARCH, *LIVES* – ARATUS, 12. 5–13. 1–4.

From Caria, after a long time, he made his way across to Egypt, and found the king both naturally well disposed towards him, and much gratified because Aratus had sent him drawings and paintings from Greece. In these matters Aratus had a refined judgement, and was continually collecting and acquiring works of artistic skill and excellence, especially those of Pamphilus[1] and Melanthus.[2] These he would send to Ptolemy.

For the fame of Sicyon's refined and beautiful paintings was still in full bloom, and they alone were thought to have a beauty that was indestructible.[3] Therefore even the great Apelles, when he was already admired, came to Sicyon and gave a talent that he might be admitted into the society of its artists, desiring to share their fame rather than their art. Hence it was that Aratus, although he at once destroyed the other portraits of the tyrants when he had given the city its freedom, deliberated a long time about that of Aristratus (who flourished in the time of Philip of Macedon). For it was the work of Melanthus and all his pupils, and Aristratus was painted standing by a chariot in which was a Victory;

Apelles also had a hand in the painting, as we are told by Polemon the Topographer. And the work was a marvellous one, so that Aratus was moved by the artistic skill therein; but afterwards, such was his hatred of the tyrants, that he ordered it to be removed and destroyed. Accordingly, the painter Nealces, who was a friend of Aratus, interceded with him for the picture, as we are told, and with tears, and when he could not persuade him, said that war should be waged against the tyrants, but not against the treasures of the tyrants. 'Let us therefore leave the chariot and the Victory, but Aristratus himself I will undertake to remove from the picture'. Aratus therefore yielded, and Nealces erased the figure of Aristratus, and in its place painted a palm-tree merely, not daring to introduce anything else. We are told, however, that the feet of the erased figure of Aristratus were left by an oversight beneath the chariot.

In consequence of this love of Art Aratus was already beloved by the king, and in personal intercourse grew yet more upon him, and received for his city a gift of a hundred and fifty talents. Forty of these Aratus took with him at once and sailed to Peloponesus; the rest the king divided into instalments, and sent them to him afterwards one by one.

Source

Perrin, Bernadotte, 1954, *Plutarch's Lives*, Vol. II, Loeb Classical Library, London and Cambridge, Mass., Heinemann and Harvard University Press: 27–31

Notes

1   Pamphilus (mid-fourth century BC) introduced the teaching of drawing into schools in Greece, and developed the technique of encaustic painting in wax (Pliny, *HN*, 35.76.123).
2   Melanthus was a pupil of Pamphilus.
3   The Sicyonian school of painters flourished between the end of the Peloponnesian War and the death of Alexander the Great.

References

Alsop, 1982
Fraser, 1972

Hellenistic collectors: Attalus of Pergamum

King Attalus I of Pergamum is usually considered the first art collector of the ancient world (Hansen, 1971). Even those who do not share this view, and attribute the beginning of art collecting to the kings of Egypt (Alsop, 1982: 190), agree that the man was one of the first Greek monarchs who actually pursued antiques and works of art and assembled a rich collection, which was further enriched by his successors. Attalus was the first of a dynasty of collectors which ended when after the death of Attalus III in 133 BC, his whole kingdom was bequeathed to Rome and the Roman Senate.

Ancient sources, and Pliny in particular, preserve many stories about Attalus' interest in collections and works of art. Since there was more than one person bearing the same name, though, it is quite difficult to know which one of the Pergamene monarchs is mentioned in each case. We know that Attalus I bought Aegina from the Aetolian League, and carried off from the island a number of works of art, including a bronze statue of Apollo by Onatus[1], a statue by Theron[2], and a bronze figure of a horse (Pausanias, 6.14.11; 8.42.7; *Anthologia Palatina*, 9.238; Hansen, 1971: 316). From the Euboean city of Oreus he carried off a group of works by Silanion of Athens[3]. We also know that the Pergamene collection included a group of Cephisodotus, the son of Praxiteles, (Pliny, *HN*, 36.24), a painting of Ajax by Apollodorus of Athens (Pliny, *HN*, 35.60), and the group of the Graces by Bupalus[4], which Pausanias mentions as existing in Attalus' 'chambers' (9.35.6)[5]. Pliny also mentions King Attalus when he refers to passionate and irrational collectors, as for instance in the paragraph that follows, where Attalus is considered not only indirectly responsible for the intrusion of luxury in Roman society (for the same reason Attalus III is more directly accused in 33.147), but also so irrational that he was prepared to pay an enormous amount of money for the purchase of works of art (a similar accusation in 7.126).

PLINY, *HISTORIA NATURALIS*, 35.8.24.

This high esteem attached officially to foreign paintings at Rome originated from Lucius Mummius who from his victory received the surname of Achaicus. At the sale of booty captured King Attalus bought for 600,000 denarii a picture of Father Liber or Dionysus by Aristides, but the price surprised Mummius, who suspecting there must be some merit in the picture of which he was himself unaware had the picture called back, in spite of Attalus's strong protests, and placed it in the Shrine of Ceres: the first instance, I believe, of a foreign picture becoming state-property at Rome.[6]

Source

Rackham, H., 1952, *Pliny, Natural History* (libri 33 –35), Vol. 9, Loeb Classical Library London and Cambridge, Mass., Heinemann and Harvard University Press: 276–9

Notes

1 Onatus of Aegina was a sculptor of the fifth century BC.
2 Theron was active in the third century BC.
3 Silanion of Athens was active during the fourth century BC. Also, see Hansen, 1971: 316–17.
4 This refers to an archaic group by the sixth-century sculptor Bupalus.
5 For a discussion of Pergamene collecting, see Fränkel, 1891; Howard, 1986; Alsop, 1982: 192–3.
6 With regard to this story: firstly, there was no auction of pictures; Mummius took to Rome the most valuable and handed over the rest to Philopoemen; and secondly, Attalus was not present at Corinth, where this scene occurred. (For another description of the scene, see Pausanias, 7.16.1,8; Strabo, 8.4. 23–381.)

References

Alsop, 1982
Fränkel, 1891
Hansen, 1971
Howard, 1986

Part III
Roman Voices

28

Roman acquaintance with Greek art, discussed by Plutarch and Livy

The conquest of foreign lands brought to Rome a large number of works of art and artefacts that had been removed as a right of war. Plundering the land of the defeated enemy had been a long-standing practice, as Pausanias argues in his discussion of Augustus' removal of objects from Greece (*Description of Greece*, 8.46.1–3). Based on the ancient religious tradition of *evocatio* – an invitation to the gods and goddesses protecting an ancient city to transfer their protection to the victor, which was initiated by the actual transfer of the statues of the divine – the Romans made their conquests the starting point for a long-lasting acquaintance with Greek art (Chevallier, 1991).

During the second Punic war, in 211 BC,[1] the Roman General Marcellus captured Syracuse and brought back a multitude of statues and paintings to decorate the city of Rome. This became the beginning of a long line of generals who celebrated their victories by long processions displaying the works of art and the wealth they had removed from the conquered people. Among the most well-known cases are L. Scipio, who defeated Antiochus in Asia, in 190 BC; Marcus Fulvius Nobilior who occupied Ambracia in 189 BC and returned with hundreds of bronze and marble statues (Livy, 32, 54); and L. Mummius, who was responsible for the sack of Corinth in 146 BC (Pape, 1975).

Although the artistic taste of those generals is highly doubted by the ancient sources – indeed, Mummius was considered completely ignorant in matters of art and there are a number of anecdotes about his lack of taste[2] – there is no doubt that the captured works of art became the foundation of both public and private collections in Rome and initiated an interest in the acquisition of objects.

The long processions celebrating victories, 'triumphs', also became the first temporary exhibitions held in the city of Rome. The texts that follow describe the triumphs held in 194 BC by Flamininus, who celebrated the defeat of Philip V of Macedonia,[3] and in 168 BC by Aemilius Paullus, who celebrated the defeat and capture of King Perseus.

LIVY, 34.52

When he had thus completed the organisation of Thessaly, he marched through Epirus to Oricum, whence he planned to set sail. From Oricum all his troops were conveyed across to Brundisium. Thence they proceeded all the way through Italy to Rome in a virtual triumph, the captured articles forming as long a column as the troops which marched ahead of him. When they arrived in Rome, Quinctius was granted an audience with the senate outside the city for the narration of his achievements, and a well-deserved triumph was voted by the eager senators. The triumph lasted three days. On the first day the procession displayed the arms, weapons, and statues of bronze and marble, more of which had been captured from Philip than received from the cities of Greece; and on the second day the gold and silver, wrought, unwrought, and minted. Of unwroughted silver he had forty-three thousand two hundred and seventy pounds; of wrought silver there were many vases of all varieties, most of them embossed and some of remarkable workmanship; there were besides many fashioned from bronze, and in addition ten shields of silver. Of minted silver there were eighty-four thousand Attic coins called 'tetrachma', and the weight of silver in them is about equivalent to three denarii each. There were three thousand seven hundred and fourteen pounds of gold, one shield made completely of gold, and fourteen thousand five hundred and fourteen gold coins with the image of Philip upon them. On the third day one hundred and fourteen golden crowns, gifts from the cities, were carried past; the victims were in the procession, and in front of the chariot there were many noble prisoners and hostages, among whom were Demetrius, the son of King Philip, and the Spartan Armenes, son of the tyrant Nabis. After them Quinctius himself entered the city. Following the chariot were throngs of soldiers, since the whole army had been brought back from the province. Each of these received in the distribution two hundred and fifty asses for the infantry, twice that amount for the centurions, and thrice for the cavalry. A striking sight in the procession was furnished by the prisoners who had been released from slavery, following with shaven heads.[4]

Source

Sage, Evan T., 1953, Vol. 9 (Books 31–34), *Livy*, Loeb Classical Library, London and Cambridge, Mass., Heinemann and Harvard University Press: 551

PLUTARCH, AEMILIUS PAULLUS, 32–33

This speech, they tell us, so rebuffed the soldiery and changed their minds that the triumph was voted to Aemilius by all the tribes. And it was conducted, they say, after the following fashion. The people erected scaffoldings in the theatres for equestrian contests, which they call circuses, and round the forum, occupied the other parts of the city which afforded a view of the procession, and witnessed the spectacle arrayed in white garments. Every temple was open and filled with garlands and incense, while numerous servitors and lictors restrained the thronging and scurrying crowds and kept the streets open and clear. Three days were assigned for the triumphal procession. The first barely sufficed for the exhibition of the captured statues, paintings, and colossal figures, which were carried on two hundred and fifty chariots. On the second, the finest and richest of the Macedonian arms were borne along in many waggons. The arms themselves glittered with freshly polished bronze and steel, and were carefully and artfully arranged to look exactly as though they had been piled together in heaps and at random, helmets lying upon shields and breast-plates upon greaves, while Cretan targets and Thracian wicker shields and quivers were mixed up with horses' bridles, and through them projected naked swords and long Macedonian spears planted among them, all the arms being so loosely packed that they smote against each other as they were borne along and gave out a harsh and dreadful sound, and the sight of them, even though they were spoils of a conquered enemy, was not without its terrors. After the waggons laden with armour there followed three thousand men carrying coined silver in seven hundred and fifty vessels, each of which contained three talents and was borne by four men, while still other men carried mixing-bowls of silver, drinking horns, bowls and cups, all well arranged for show and excelling in size and in the depth of their carved ornaments.

On the third day, as soon as it was morning, trumpeters led the way, sounding out no marching or processional strain, but such a one as the Romans used to rouse themselves to battle. After these there were led along a hundred and twenty stall-fed oxen with gilded horns, bedecked with fillets and garlands. Those who led these victims to the sacrifice were young men wearing aprons with handsome borders, and boys attended them carrying gold and silver vessels of libation. Next, after these, came the carriers of the coined gold, which, like the silver, was portioned out into vessels containing three talents; and the number of these vessels was eighty lacking three. After these followed the bearers of the consecrated bowl, which Aemilius had caused to be made of ten talents of gold and adorned with precious stones, and then those who displayed the bowls known as Antigonids and Seleucids and Theracleian, together with all the gold plate of Perseus's table. These were followed by the chariot of Perseus, which bore his arms, and his diadem lying upon his arms.

Source

Perrin, Bernadotte, 1918, *Plutarch's Lives: Aemilius Paullus*, Vol. 6, Loeb Classical Library, London, Heinemann: 441–5

Notes

1 The Second Punic War (between Rome and the Carthaginians under the leadership of Hannibal) lasted from 218 to 201 BC. The cities of Syracuse and Capua revolted, but were brought back into line in 211 BC.

2 Velleius Paterculus, for instance, describes Mummius' ignorance in these words: 'Mummius was so uncultivated that when, after the capture of Corinth he was contracting for the transportation to Italy of pictures and statues by the hands of the greatest artists, he gave instructions that the contractors should be warned that if they lost them, they would have to replace them by new ones.' (L.xiii.4, trans. by Shipley, 1924).

3 King Philip V of Macedonia joined Hannibal and attacked Illyria. This led to three Macedonian wars (214–205, 200–196, 172–167 BC) and the gradual control of Greece by the Romans.

4 Shaven heads were a mark of slavery, from which they had been rescued.

References

Chevallier, 1991
Pape, 1975
Pollitt, 1983
Shipley, 1924

29

The development of art history and criticism in the Roman world

The relation between ancient art criticism and history and art collecting has been discussed in detail by Alsop (1982) and recently by Tanner (1995). They both claim that the development of a certain critical view of art has implications on art collecting. Alsop (1982), in particular, has argued that art collecting at a very early stage preceded art history; this led to an appreciation of old masters.Then art criticism and history were created, which in turn led to art collecting in a more systematic way.

Pollitt (1974) distinguished four main traditions of art criticism in the ancient classical world. Firstly, the professional artists' tradition which concerns itself primarily with form and design, and makes its appearance as early as the sixth century BC. Secondly, the philosophical tradition, which focuses on moral and epistemological issues regarding the works of art, the artists and the beholders. This appears in the middle of the fifth century BC and continues as an active tradition until late antiquity. Third is the tradition that relates to literary criticism, being concerned with issues of style and the analogy between rhetoric and the visual arts. The development of this line of thought must be credited mainly to the Hellenistic period. Fourthly and finally is the popular art tradition, which dwells on the marvelous and magical properties of art and underlies all the other categories of thought throughout their history.

In Roman literature there are two main histories of art, albeit very brief – those by Quintillian (*Institutio Oratoria*, 12.10.1–10), and by Cicero (*Brutus*, 70). They both subscribe to the tradition of rhetorical and literary criticism, in other words they use the history of the visual arts in Greece as an analogy for the development of rhetorical style (Pollitt, 1974: 60). Rhetoric, similarly to sculpture and painting, is seen as following a transition from simple and primitive forms to perfection and grandeur (naturalism), a quality that in artistic terms finds its culmination in the art of Pheidias, the fifth-century Athenian sculptor. Both Quintilian and Cicero rely on earlier sources, namely to Xenocrates, Antigonus of Carystus, and possibly other less well-known Hellenistic rhetoricians, artists and writers.[1]

The interest in the artists of the ancient Greek past, the critical appreciation of their techniques, along with the distinguished role they held in setting the artistic canon not only on issues of visual arts but also on matters of rhetoric, account for much of the Roman interest in the acquisition of certain *objets d' art*, even if they were copies. In addition, these views account for the formation of a certain intellectual rationale towards collections, that is, the belief that those who can appreciate art and follow the critical tradition regarding its appreciation, have access to education and the cultural capital of the elite.

QUINTILIAN, *INSTITUTIO ORATORIA*, 12.10.1–10

[The works produced by any art] differ greatly from one another; for they differ not only by species – as statue differs from statue, picture from picture, and action from action – but also in genus – as statues in the Etruscan style differ from Greek statues, and the Asiatic style of rhetoric differs from the Attic. Moreover just as these different genera of works of which I speak have authors, so too do they have devotees; and the result is that there has not yet been a perfect practitioner of any art, not only because some qualities are more eminent in one artist than in another, but also because one form is never pleasing to everybody; this is partly because of the circumstances of times and places, and partly because of the judgment and point of view of each person.

The first artists whose works should be inspected not only for the sake of their antiquity [but also for their artistic merit] are said to have been those famous painters Polygnotos and Aglaophon, whose simplicity of color has still such zealous advocates that these almost primitive works, which are like the primordial beginnings of the great art of the future, are preferred to the works of artists who came after them – a judgment prompted, in my opinion, by the urge to appear as a connoisseur.[2] Afterwards Zeuxis and Parrhasios – who were not very far removed from one another in time [for they both were active around the time of the Peloponnesian War, since a conversation of Socrates with Parrhasios is to be found in Xenophon] – contributed much to the art of painting. Of the two, the first discovered the calculation [*ratio*] of lights and shades, while the second is reputed to have concentrated on subtlety of line. For Zeuxis gave more emphasis to the limbs of the body; he thought that this made his art grander and more august, and in this respect, they think, he followed Homer who likes to use the most mighty form in every case, even in the case of a woman. Parrhasios, on the other hand, drew all types of outlines so well that they call him the 'proposer of laws', since other artists follow the representations of gods and heroes that have been handed down by him as if there were some sort of necessity to do so. The art of painting flourished primarily, however, from around the time of Philip down to the successors of Alexander, although [different artists were distinguished] for various points of excellence [*virtutes*]. Thus Protogenes was outstanding for laborious care, Pamphilos and Melanthios for theoretical knowledge, Antiphilos for ease of execution, Theon of Samos for imaginary visions which they call *phantasias*,[3] and Apelles for ingenuity and grace [*ingenium et gratia*], the last of which, he himself boasted, was best revealed in his own art.[4] What makes Euphranor worthy of admiration is that while he was classed among the foremost men in other fields of study, he was also gifted with marvellous skill in both painting and sculpture.

The same differences exist among the sculptors. For Kallon and Hegesias made works that are rather hard and close to the Etruscan style; Kalamis made works that were less rigid and Myron made his even softer than those artists spoken of so far. Precision and appropriateness appears above all in the art of Polykleitos, to whom the victor's branch is awarded by many critics, although, lest no fault be found in him, they hold that he lacked weightiness [*pondus*]. For while he gave to the human form an appropriateness which surpassed the ordinary,[5] he seems not to have expressed the impressiveness of the gods. On the contrary it is said that he shied away from representing the more mature age level and did not dare to undertake anything more challenging than smooth cheeks.[6] But those qualities in which Polykleitos was lacking are attributed to Pheidias and Alkamenes. Pheidias, however, is credited with being more skillful at making images of gods than of men, and in working in ivory he is thought to be far beyond any rival and would be so even if he had made nothing besides his Athena in Athens and his Olympian Zeus in Elis, the beauty of which seems to have added something to traditional religion; to such an extent is the majesty of the work equal to the majesty of the god. They affirm that Lysippos and Praxiteles were most successful in achieving realism. Demetrios, however, is criticized because he was too realistic and was hence more fond of verisimilitude than of beauty.

Source

Pollitt, J.J., 1990, *The Art of Ancient Greece: Sources and Documents*, Cambridge University Press: 221–3

Notes

1   For Xenocrates, Antigonus and the other sources on art history and criticism of Quintillian, Cicero and Pliny, see Schweitzer, 1932; Jex-Blake and Sellers, 1896.

2   There is here a clear hint for art collectors and connoisseurs in the ancient Roman world, whose views had been influenced by art history.
3   *Phantasia* as a technical artistic term is of Stoic origin; it signifies the mental process of 'imagination', along with its effects (Pollitt, 1974: 205). For *phantasia* see Watson, 1988; 1994.
4   All these notions, 'execution', *'facilitas'*, *'phantasias'*, *'ingenium et gratia'* are technical words that refer to certain qualities which were appreciated by ancient historians and critics. For a detailed discussion, see Pollitt, 1974.
5   This means that his forms were ideal, more proportioned than living people are.
6   Young beardless boys.

References

Alsop, 1982
Jex-Blake and Sellers, 1896
Pollitt, 1974
Schweitzer, 1932
Tanner, 1995
Watson, 1988
Watson, 1994

30

Petronius' Trimalchio: an ignorant connoisseur

Satyricon is an ironic, self-reflective work, balancing between satire and novel. It was written by T. Petronius Niger, Nero's 'arbiter of elegance', whom Tacitus (*Annals*, 16.18) describes as a connoisseur, 'the finished artist of extravagance' (Jackson, 1951). The work's composition dates to Nero's reign, between AD 66 to AD 65,[1] and its dramatic setting, possibly, slightly earlier.[2] Unfortunately, only part of what must have been a very lengthy work now survives.

The central part of the extant work is called *Cena Trimalchionis* and is a critical description of a pretentious dinner party. Thus, it is indebted to Greek descriptions of feasting and the symposium (for example Plato's and Xenophon's *Symposia* were the setting for philosophical discussion) (Coffey, 1989: 187–8), but also on the Roman satiric tradition, where the host characteristically appears as a boorish figure condescending to his intellectually superior guests and humiliating his freedmen by serving them with inferior food and wine. Trimalchio, the host of the banquet, is a rich synthesis of the traditional portrayal of the unrefined, arrogant master and the contemporary freedman of substantial wealth – that is, between the vulgar man in Theophrastus and Horace, and the vulgar man of Petronius' own observation; in short, Trimalchio is a combination of the literary and the observed (Walsh, 1970).[3] From his synthesis, Petronius created a portrait underlining three features that particularly offended him in his contemporary society: the vulgar abuse of wealth, evident in both the boorish behaviour at the dinner and the contemptuous treatment of the slaves, the pretentious claims to learning, and the dominating superstition. These criticisms make it possible to see that Petronius proclaims the opposites of the above: in other words, social refinement, literary taste and a rational attitude toward life and death (Walsh, 1974: 187; also in Walsh, 1996: xxvii–xxxiii).

Paragraphs 50–52 are the most explicit both in terms of Trimalchio's collecting habits and of Petronius' response to it. Trimalchio claims that he is the sole owner of real Corinthian bronzeware. Encolpius, one of the other protagonists of the work, thinks this is just another boast of wealth, but it turns out to be a pun: Trimalchio's dishes are made by a man named Corinthius. Trimalchio is very concerned not to be thought 'ignorant', so he caps with this a hilariously scrambled account of the origin of Corinthian ware. In his attempt he mixes the cities of Ilium and Corinth, the sack of Corinth with the seizure of Spain by Hannibal, Hannibal with Mummius.

Trimalchio continues in the same line with his confession that he prefers glass, but he does not collect it because it is very cheap. The assertion is complemented by a cautionary tale of the danger of too much knowledge – a man who knows how to make malleable glass dies because of this knowledge. Various versions of this anecdote were current in antiquity.[4] In this case, the tale along with Trimalchio's confession serve to emphasize the interdependency of Trimalchio's setting of values with intrinsic merit. Material which is cheap in financial terms is not appreciated, the only value is gold. Petronius' personal point about the existence of other values besides the ones Trimalchio can discern seems present at once.

Paragraph 52 is Trimalchio's clear admission that he has a 'great passion for silver' (*studiosus sum*). He admits the ownership of cups engraved with mythological scenes, like that of Cassandra killing her sons. Bactrian imitations of such Greek silver cups in fact survive (see Horsfall, 1989 with references; also Ville, 1964). Naturally, it was not Cassandra who killed her sons (52.1) but Medea. As for the bowl that Minos – or Mummius (the reading depends on the MSS)[5] – left to his patron and he bequeathed to Trimalchio, it also bears engravings that again confuse incidents of Greek mythology. The error here concerns three unrelated events of the Greek mythology, Daedalus, Niobe and the Trojan Horse, which are brought together in Trimalchio's mind – the man who owns two libraries. However, more than his mythology is confused.[6] His praise for the realism of the 'Cassandra cups' fits in with a disturbing sense of naive realism. There is here a fundamental 'confusion of the modalities of life and death' (Arrowsmith, 1966: 311), mediated through realistic art – which is in turn satirized (Slater, 1990: 67–8). Trimalchio also owns silver goblets decorated with the fights of Hermeros and Petraites.[7]

The concluding remark summarizes both the literal and the metaphorical notions of the paragraph. All the above collector's items are beyond anything else 'evidence of learning', and as such cannot be sold at any price. The hilarious mixture described above, though, undermines the importance of such a statement. Trimalchio thinks that these are evidence of his learning, but in fact they are quite the opposite. He possesses neither the literary-mythological, nor the art-critical knowledge to understand, and thus Trimalchio represents the antitype of the true connoisseur.

Petronius' irony lies exactly in this naivety, or ignorance of ignorance, which purports to know, and does know, the symbol and the symbolism, but ignores the meaning of the latter. In

Trimalchio's case, obviously, what collecting stands for – knowledge, culture, education – is clear; and so is the medium for such a
symbolism: objects (lavish, expensive, engraved ...). But the true
meaning of the symbolism escapes him.

Trimalchio has an obsessive relationship with his objects. He
prizes them for their costliness, which depends on the intrinsically
valuable material; he also appreciates their 'meaning': that is,
their mythological scenes. They are bearers of prestige and knowledge: they bring alive the possibility of having their owner included in a social and intellectual cultural elite. Undoubtedly,
Petronius recognises the fact that Trimalchio and his like can and
do recognise the possibilities offered to them by the objects. But
exactly because this is so, while not being all, Petronius criticises
him. The author of *Satyricon* could not have been the man who
would distance himself from the futilities of life. The accounts by
both Tacitus and Pliny argue for the contrary. In Pliny's account
(*HN*, 37.20), Petronius breaks his favourite murrhine cup to 'spite
Nero', not to let him have it on his table. In Tacitus' version he
breaks his signet ring, so that his personal validity dies with him.
A man so immediately and passionately associated with material
culture could not have considered it disreputable for somebody
else to relate to it as well. The emphasis is placed elsewhere.
Trimalchio follows a road well lit by his predecessors. Collecting
Corinthian ware was by then a common practice. Similarly common were the 'qualities' that such a collection carried with it:
distinction, wealth, worthiness, knowledge, education. This is the
identity that he hopes to shape for himself and share.

PETRONIUS, *SATYRICON*, 50–52

The cook got back his shirt, and seized a knife. Then with shaking hand
he slit the pig's belly on each side. At once the slits widened with the
pressure of the weight inside, and sausages and black puddings came
tumbling out.

The slaves clapped their hands at this trick, and cried in unison:
'Three cheers for Gaius!' The cook too was rewarded with a drink and a
silver crown; he was handed a goblet on a tray of Corinthian ware.
Agamemnon took a closer look at the tray, whereupon Trimalchio re-
marked: 'I am the only person to possess genuine Corinthian ware'. I
anticipated that his words would match his general extravagance, and that
he would claim that he imported vessels from Corinth. But he went one
better. 'Perhaps', he said 'you are wondering why I am the sole possessor
of genuine Corinthian. It's because the bronze-smith from whom I purchase is called Corinthus. How can any ware be Corinthian, if one doesn't

have a Corinthus to supply it? But in case you think I am an ignoramus, I'm perfectly aware how Corinthian bronze originated. At the capture of Troy, that rascally slimy lizard Hannibal piled all the statues of bronze, gold and silver on a pyre, and set fire to them; all the various elements merged into an alloy of bronze. Craftsmen then removed lumps of this amalgam and made plates, dishes and statuettes out of them. This is how Corinthian ware originated, from this *mélange* of metal which is neither one thing nor the other. Pardon me for saying so, but I myself prefer glassware; at any rate no smell comes off it. I'd prefer it to gold if it didn't get broken, but as things are it's cheap stuff.

'There was a craftsman who made a glass goblet which was unbreakable. He was accordingly ushered with his gift into Caesar's presence. He got Caesar to hand it back to him, and he let it drop on the paved floor. Caesar could not have been more startled. However, the craftsman picked up the goblet from the ground; it was dented like a bronze vessel. He then produced a little hammer from his clothing, and without fuss restored the goblet good as new. After this demonstration he thought that he was on top of the world, especially when the emperor asked: "Does anyone else know about this technique of glass-making?" Now hear the outcome. When the craftsman said no, Caesar ordered him to be beheaded, for of course if the secret had leaked out, gold would be as cheap as dirt.

'I'm quite keen on silver. I have something like a hundred three-gallon bumpers ... with the motif of Cassandra killing her sons; the boys are lying there so vividly dead that you'd think they were alive! I have a bowl which king Minos bequeathed to my patron; on it Daedalus is enclosing Niobe in the Trojan horse. I've also got in relief on goblets all of solid silver the fights of Hermeros and Petraites. I wouldn't sell these evidence of my learning at any price.'

Just as he was recounting this, a slave dropped a goblet. Trimalchio eyed him, and said 'Off you go, and kill yourself for being such a fool.' The boy's lips trembled, and at once he began to beg for mercy. Trimalchio responded: 'Why address me? I'm not hounding you. I suggest that you prevail upon yourself not to be a fool.' But eventually we pleaded successfully with him, and he let the slave off. The boy celebrated his acquittal by prancing round the table ...

Trimalchio called out: 'Out with the water, down with the wine!' We hailed his witty quip, led by Agamemnon who knew how to earn a further invitation to dinner. He was now very nearly drunk. 'Will none of you ask my dear Fortunata to dance? Believe me, nobody does the cordax better.' He himself then placed his hands over his brow, and began to ape the actor Syrus, while the whole ménage sang in chorus: 'Madeia, perimadeia.' He would have advanced to the centre of the floor, if Fortunata had not whispered in his ear; I suspect that she told him that such degrading tomfoolery detracted from his high dignity. But he was the personification of vacillation supreme, for at one moment he would respectfully heed Fortunata, and at the next would revert to his natural self.

Source

Walsh, P.G. (ed.), 1996, *Petronius: The Satyricon*, Oxford, Clarendon Press: 40–41

Notes

1　Tacitus' Petronius died in early AD 66; Lucan committed suicide in AD 65. Petronius seems to know and satirise Lucan's unfinished epic.

2　On the date of the composition see Rose, 1971; for a more sceptical view see Smith, 1975. On economic and social factors see D'Arms, 1981; for literary connections see Sullivan, 1985.

3　For a discussion of Trimalchio as an example of a social type or category of this period, see Veyne, 1961.

4　See also Pliny, *HN*, 36.195 and Dio Cassius, *Roman History*, 57.21.7. From Dio we learn that the Emperor was Tiberius.

5　There are various emendations: 'patronarum unus' (Goes, 1965) and 'patronus meus' (ed. Patav, 1975) are the simplest.

6　Triple confusion by Trimalchio: in Greek mythology Niobe, wife of Amphion, a traditional King of Thebes, had nothing to do with the Trojan war and the wooden horse; nor had Daedalus the Athenian architect and craftsman who built or designed the labyrinth at Cnossos in Crete. He did, however, make a wooden cow for Pasiphaë (wife of King Minos for whom that labyrinth was built) who loved a fine white bull and hid inside the cow so as to be covered by it. She gave birth to the monstrous Minotaur for which the labyrinth at Cnossos was built (Warmington, 1969: 106–7).

7　These were gladiators and therefore vulgar. The first name appears on a first-century lamp found in Puteoli, the second on several commemorative cups speculatively dated to the Neronian period (see Walsh, 1996: 173).

References

Arrowsmith, 1966
Bourdieu, 1984
Coffey, 1989
D'Arms, 1981
Horsfall, 1989
Rose, 1971

Slater, 1990
Smith, 1975
Sullivan, 1985
Tanner, 1995
Veyne, 1961
Ville, 1964
Walsh, 1996
Warmington, 1969

31

The collection of Asinius Pollio

The collection of Asinius Pollio[1] stands between the private and the public domain and as such presents one strand of the 'intellectual humanist' approach to Greek art: interest in and respect of Greek art, put into the service of the Roman art. Unlike other collections discussed by Pliny (except perhaps of the *Horti Servilliani*), this one is treated by the writer as a unity and as evidence of Pollio's interest both in art and in the public benefit.

Previously, Pliny has also mentioned as belonging to the same collection four sculptures by Praxiteles, *Caryatids, Maenads, Sileni*, and *Thyiads* (36.23–4), a *Venus* by Kephisodotus (36.24) and a *Canephoros* (basket-bearer) by Scopas (36.25).[2] There was also there a large assemblage of portrait busts (probably following the tradition of its models, the libraries of Pergamum and Alexandria), among which it was the portrait of M. Terentius Varro (7.115; 35.9–10).

The collection was held in the edifice that Asinius Pollio had built after his triumph against the Parthians in 39 BC. He was the first Roman to establish a library and most probably it was joined to this edifice. The building was part of the complex called *Atrium Libertatis* which, according to Livy (34.33.5), was restored and enlarged in 194 BC. Augustus had given Pollio permission to restore the old edifice in commemoration of his victory and thus to honour his own memory. Consequently, Pliny uses the appellation *monumenta Asini Pollionis*. Subsequently, it gave way to the Trajan Forum (Richardson, 1992: 41; Isager, 1991: 164–5; Pellegrini, 1867; André, Bloch and Rouveret, 1981: 145ff).

The selection and setting of the works of art have been subject to rigorous discussion. Becatti (1956: 208) images an antithetical grouping of the statues of the collection: Jupiter against Jupiter *Hospitalis*, Thespiads against Appiads, Centaurs against Sileni, Oceanus against Dionysus, and Venus surrounded by Cupids. The *Punishment of Dirke* was perhaps, according to that arrangement, placed in the centre to enable viewing from all angles. Gros (1976: 164) argues that Pliny's account of the setting of the works of art very much resembles that of somebody who walks in front of the objects, and describes them as one succeeds the other. Besides their setting, the choice of the works themselves present great interest. The 'old masters', Praxiteles, Kephisodotus and Scopas, are present, but the emphasis seems to be on a more recent generation of artists, those of the first century BC (Becatti, 1956: 207–8). This led to the conclusion that what differentiates the collection of Asinius Pollio is the fact that unlike other military leaders, instead of plundering works of art for his *monumenta*, he had chosen to commission them from Greek artists active in Rome during this period. His intention, therefore, was to create an architectonic and artistic whole and to exhibit it in a specially constructed 'museum'. Furthermore, his taste is considered to be in absolute accordance with Augustus' political aims, which discouraged private collections in order to benefit the public ones, as well as with plundering as a practice (see also Becatti, 1956: 270ff; Isager, 1991: 167).

PLINY, *HISTORIA NATURALIS*, 36.4.33–37.

Asinius Pollio, being an ardent enthusiast, was accordingly anxious for his collection to attract sightseers. In it are Centarus Carrying Nymphs by Arcesilas, the Muses of Helicon by Cleomenes, the Oceanus and Jupiter by Heniochus, the Nymphs of the Appian Water by Stephanus, the double bursts of Hermes and Eros by Tauriscus (not the well-known worker in metal and ivory, but a native of Tralles), the Jupiter Patron of Strangers by Papylus, the pupil of Praxiteles, and a composition by Apollonius and Tauriscus which was brought from Rhodes, namely Zethus and Amphion, and then Dirce and the bull with its rope, all carved from the same block of stone. These two artists caused a dispute as to their parentage, declaring that their putative father was Menecrates and their real father Artemidorus. In the same galleries there is a Father Liber by Eutychides which is warmly praised, and close by the Portico of Octavia an Apollo by Philiscus of Rhodes standing in the temple of Apollo, and furthermore a Latona, a Diana, the Nine Muses, and another Apollo, which is naked. The Apollo With His Lyre in the same temple was made by Timarchides, and in the temple of Juno that stands within the Portico of Octavia the images of the goddess herself was made by Dionysius, although there is another by Polycles, while the Venus in the same place was executed by Philiscus and the other statues by Praxiteles. Polycles and Dionysius, who were the sons of Timarchides, were responsible also for the Jupiter in the adjacent temple, while in the same place the Pan and Olympus Wrestling, which is the second most famous grappling group in the world, was the work of Heliodorus, the Venus Bathing of Daedalsas, and the Venus Standing of Polycharmus. It is clear from the honour accorded to it that a work much esteemed was that of Lysias which Augustus of Revered Memory dedicated in honour of his father Octavius in a niche embellished with columns upon the arch on the Palatine. This work consists of a team of four horses with a chariot and Apollo with Diana all carved from one block of marble. In the Gardens of Servilius I find that works much admired are the Apollo by the eminent engraver Calamis, the Boxers by Dercylides, and the historian Callisthenes by Amphistratus. Beyond these men, there are not a great many more that are famous. The reputation of some, distinguished though their work may be, has been obscured by the number of artists engaged with them on a single task, because no individual monopolizes the credit nor again can several of them be named on equal terms. This is the case with the Laocoon in the palace of the emperor Titus, a work superior to any painting and any bronze. Laocoon, his children and the wonderful clasping coils of the snakes were carved from a single block in accordance with an agreed plan by those eminent craftsmen Hagesander, Polydorus and Athenodorus, all of Rhodes.

Source

Eichholz, D.E. 1971, *Pliny Natural History*, Vol. 10, Loeb Classical Library, London and Cambridge, Mass., Heinemann and Harvard University Press: 27–31

Notes

1   For his biography see André, 1949.
2   In the same paragraph are also mentioned two pendants of Vesta by Scopas, which was in the *Horti Serviliani*; scholars do not agree on what exactly these were.

References

André, 1949
André, Bloch and Rouveret, 1981
Becatti, 1956
Gros, 1976
Isager, 1991
Pellegrini, 1867
Richardson, 1992

32

A letter from Cicero to one of his purchasing agents

Cicero, the republic's most famous and competent orator, was also an avid collector of works of Greek art; through his correspondence with friends and agents the most direct evidence about the Roman art market and the tastes of the collectors come forward. It is also a unique first-hand testimony, the only direct communication of a Roman collector with his agents and suppliers available down to our days, and as such has often been regarded as representative of the era as a whole, and thus used as a textual support for many discussions of archaeological data.[1] These are real letters, not written in order to be published, and show the unofficial side of Cicero, who reveals and shares his thoughts, doubts, fears, concerns and wishes. The style in which they are written confirms their genuine character, and reflects the everyday language of Rome. The letter that follows belongs to the first set of letters of the four that have been transmitted to us: it consists of sixteen books of *Epistulae ad Familiares*, letters to friends and relatives, which date from 62 to 43 BC (Conte, 1994: 202–3).

The letter to M. Fabius Gallus dates to 46 BC and is one of the most revealing items of evidence regarding the orators' personal collection and the rationale that led to its formation. Gallus, like T. Pomponius Atticus, had undertaken the assignment of finding and purchasing statues for Cicero, and it is to this project that the orator refers in his letter. Cicero endowed his commissioners with complete confidence, justified in the case of Atticus, not quite so in the case of Gallus. This, along with the brevity of his references to the subject (sometimes just a short phrase), and the lack of details regarding his commissions (such as style, date, workmanship, beauty, originality, artist and so on) have been interpreted as personal indifference and/or lack of aesthetic judgement (Vermeule, 1977).

The truth, though, is far from this. This letter outlines the principles defining the formation of a collection by a Roman noble, who had an interest in assembling works of art and artefacts, but who claimed superiority to those enslaved Romans, who were emotionally dependent on such works. Cicero draws his collecting profile in opposition to that of the 'connoisseur' who is uncritically enslaved by material culture and prepared to go to

114

extreme lengths in order to acquire the objects of his desire. He, on the other hand, is prepared to acquire only what fits into the main notions of Roman aesthetics, namely suitability (*decor*) and utility (*utilitas*).

Decor, clearly, is the first notion that this 'intellectual' collector takes into account. It is the aesthetic equivalent of the ethical term of *decorum* (Pollitt, 1974). It can be broadly defined as 'suitability of style to place and purpose, or to tradition' (Rawson, 1985: 187). Cicero himself defines the notion in the *Orator* (21.69–23.74): 'propriety is what is fitting and agreeable to an occasion or person', and he develops it in his ethical system presented in *De Officiis* (1.93–8).

We thus come to the second value, *utilitas*. The works of art Cicero assembled were more than appropriate for their setting. They also served the purpose of creating and promoting an identity for their owner, of enhancing his image. Cicero spoke of the utility of art in order to manifest the relation between beauty and function. It is, again, a notion originating in Greek ethical philosophical thought.

CICERO, *EPISTULAE AD FAMILIARES*, TO M. FADIUS[2] GALLUS ROME, 46 (?) BC[3]

I had only just arrived from Arpinum when a letter from you was delivered to me; and by the same hand I received one from Avianius,[4] containing this very handsome offer, that when he came he would enter my debt to him on whatever day I pleased. Pray put yourself in my place. Is it consistent with either your sense of honour or mine, first to haggle about the day, and then to ask for more than a year's credit? But everything would have been easy, my dear Gallus, had you bought only what I wanted, and that only up to the price I had in my mind. But for all that, the actual purchases mentioned in your letter I shall ratify, and they will gratify me too; for I quite understand that you showed not only your anxiety to please, but your affection also, in buying up, because you considered them worthy of me, things which gave pleasure to yourself, who, as I have always thought, show most refined taste wherever critical skill is needed.

Still I should like Damassipus[5] to stick to his intention; for out of all your purchases there is absolutely not one that I should really prize. You however, in ignorance of my regular practice, took over your four or five statues at a price beyond what I set on the whole collection of statues in the world. You compare your Bacchantes with Metellus's[6] Muses. Where is the analogy? In the first place, I should never have thought those

Muses themselves worth all that money, and all the Muses would have agreed. Still it would have been suitable for a library, and would harmonize with my literary pursuits. But as for Bacchantes, which is there room for them at my house? Ah but, you will say, they are beautiful little figures. I know them perfectly well, and have often seen them. Had I fancied them, I should have specifically commissioned you to buy statues that were known to me. For I often buy the sort of figures that would adorn a place in my palaestra, and make it look like the gymnasia. But a statue of Mars! What do I, the advocate of peace want with that? I am glad there was not one of Saturn for I should suspect these two statues of having brought debt upon me. I should rather there had been some sort of a statue of Mercury.[7] I might have had better luck perhaps in my transaction with Avianius.

As for the table-support you had intended for yourself, if you like it, you must keep it; if however you have changed your mind, you may be sure that I shall keep it. For the sum you have expected, I declare I would much rather have bought a lodging house at Tarracina,[8] so as not to be an everlasting burden upon my host. On the whole I take it that the fault lies with my freedman, whom I had definitely commissioned to make certain purchases, and also with Junius, whom I think you know, Avianius' friend.

I have built some new reading-rooms in a little colonnade at my Tusculan villa, and I should like to decorate them with pictures; as a matter of fact, if anything of that sort gives me any pleasure at all, it is painting.

Anyhow, if I am to take over your purchases, I wish you would notify me where they are, when they are to be sent for, and in what kind of conveyance; for if Damassipus has not the courage of his opinions, I have got to find some *soi-disant* Damassipus, even if I lose by it.

Source

Williams, Glyn W. 1952, 1953, 1972, 1979, Vol. 1, Vol. 2, Vol. 3, Vol. 4, *Cicero: The Letters to his Friends*, Loeb Classical Library, London, Heinemann: 67–71

Notes

1 Together with the text of Petronius on Trimalchio; see, for example, Leach, 1988; Wallace-Hadrill, 1994.
2 Usually, but wrongly, called Fadius; he was a friend of Cicero's, author, Epicurean and connoisseur of art.

3 The date of the letter is unknown and has been an issue of dispute: in the Loeb edition the letter is dated in 61 BC, whereas Shackleton Bailey (1978) dates it in December 46 BC.

4 He is the sculptor C. Avianius Evander.

5 Damassipus was probably an art dealer, specialised in buying and selling statues for gardens.

6 Probably Metellus Scipio.

7 In astrology, Saturn and Mars bring bad luck, whereas Mercury brings gain.

8 Cicero had recently visited his Campanian villas and will have stayed at Tarracina en route; perhaps Gallus was his host.

References

Conte, 1994
Lafon, 1981
Pollitt, 1974
Rawson, 1985
Vermeule, 1977

33

Letters from Cicero on his collection

Cicero was particularly interested in acquiring objects suitable for the decoration of his private villa at Tusculum. For this reason he had commissioned his childhood friend Atticus to buy for him all objects that he considered suitable for decorating his private space.

The list of the statues that Atticus had bought for Cicero are quite indicative of his views on what consists an appropriate collection for a man of his social position and intellectual claims. Atticus sends a Hermathena (double bust of Minerva and Hermes, made of Pentelic marble with bronze heads). The object meets Cicero's most unreserved approval and satisfaction both for himself and his academy. Atticus and Cicero knew that the Athenian Academy had a sanctuary of Minerva in it, one of the tutelary deities of the place. This, along with the philosophical connotations of Minerva as goddess of wisdom, is seen to fit well into Cicero's views about what is appropriate as a personal symbol and as a piece in a gymnasium. Similarly, the promise of Atticus to send him a Heracles herm[1] is accepted with enthusiasm. In his letter to Brutus (24), we also learn about a statue of Plato that Cicero possessed, although it is unclear whether this was part of his Tusculan collection, or was kept at another of his villas (see also Valenti, 1936: 265).[2]

The attempt to create evocative spaces in a villa is quite typical, as excavated material and literary evidence came to show. Atticus, for instance, shared his friend's collecting paradigm and had created in his house an Amaltheium. Cicero asks Atticus for a description of the place, as well as for poems and tales about Amaltheia, in order to decide whether it would have been 'appropriate' for his public persona to create one at his villa at Arpinum, something which he actually does, as we find out in other letters of the series. Varro, earlier had created a *musaeum* in his villa (Varro, *RR*, 3.5.9). The finds from the villa of the Papyri form another example of a decorative arrangement by the owner (Calpurnius Piso) to reveal the Epicurean ideals (Sauron, 1980). Sperlonga is also an example of the transformation of a grotto into a landscape of heroic mythology (Marvin, 1989: 33). In the Palatine there was a *Hermaeum* where Emperor Claudius sought refuge (Suetonius, *Claudius*, 10). Finally, the villa of Hadrian at Tivoli, in the second century AD, also used sculpture in architectural settings to elicit a special world for the visitor. These decorative programmes are centred around the parts of the Roman house that would be accessible to the public, and thus allow for the public image to be created (Lafon, 1981: 157–8).

CICERO, *LETTERS TO ATTICUS*

November 68 BC
I am glad you are pleased with your purchase in Epirus. Yes, do please look after my commissions and anything else that may strike you as suitable to my place in Tusculum, so far as you can without putting yourself into too much trouble. It is the only place where I rest from troubles and toils.

November 68 BC
That is about all I have to tell you. If you succeed in finding any *objets d'art* suitable for a public hall, which would do for you know where, I hope you won't let them slip. I am delighted with my place at Tusculum, so much so that I feel content with myself when, and only when, I get there. Let me know in full detail about everything you are doing and intending to do.

February 67 BC
All is in order at your mother's and I am not forgetting her. I have arranged to pay L. Cincius HS 20,400 on the Ides of February. I should be grateful if you would see that I get the articles which you say you have bought and have ready for me as soon as possible. And please give some thought to how you are to procure a library for me as you have promised. All my hopes of enjoying myself as I want to do when I get some leisure depend upon your kindness.

February 67 BC
I have paid L. Cincius the HS 20,400 for the Megarian statues in accordance to your earlier letter. I am already quite enchanted with your Pentelic herms with the bronze heads, about which you write to me, so please send them and the statues and any other things you think would do credit to the place in question and to my enthusiasm and to your good taste, as many and as soon as possible, especially any you think suitable to a lecture hall [*gymnasi xystique*] and collonade. I am so carried away by my enthusiasm for this sort of thing and it's your duty to help me – and other people's perhaps to scold me. If a ship of Lentulus' is not available, put them aboard any you think fit.

March or April 67 BC

I am eagerly expecting the Megarian statues and the herms you wrote to me about. Anything you may have of the same sort which you think suitable for the Academy, don't hesitate to send it and trust my purse. This is how my fancy takes me. Things that are especially suitable for a lecture hall [*gymnasium*] are what I want. Lentulus promises his ships. Please attend to this carefully.

May 67 BC

Yes. I should be grateful if you could ship when you most conveniently can my statues and Heracles herms and anything else you may discover that would be convenable you know where, especially things you think suitable to a palaestra and lecture hall [*gymnasium*]. In fact I am sitting there now as I write, so that the place itself is a reminder. Further please get me some bas-reliefs which I can lay in the stucco of the small entrance hall and two figured puteals. Mind you don't engage your library to anyone, no matter how ardent a wooer you may find. I am putting all my little gleanings aside to pay for this stand-by for my old age.

August 67 BC

Please send the things you have got for my Academy as soon as possible. The very thought of the place, let alone the actual use of it, gives me enormous pleasure. Mind you don't hand over your books to anybody. Keep them for me, as you say you will. I am consumed with enthusiasm for them, as with disgust for all things else. It's unbelievable in so short a time how much worse you will find them than you left them.

End of 67 BC

The statues you acquired for me have been disembarked at Caieta. I have not seen them, not having had an opportunity of leaving Rome. I have sent a man to pay the freight. I am most grateful to you for taking so much trouble and getting them cheaply.

First half 66 BC

I am very grateful for what you say about the Hermathena. It's an appropriate ornament for my Academy, since Hermes is the common emblem of all such places and Minerva special to that one. So please beautify it with other pieces, as you promise, as many as possible. I have not yet seen the statues you sent me earlier. They are in my house at Formiae, which I am now preparing to visit. I shall take them all up to Tusculum, and decorate Caieta if and when I begin to have a surplus. Hold on to your books and don't despair of my being able to make them mine. If I manage that, I am richer than Crassus and can afford to despise any man's manors and meadows.

Shortly before 17 July 65 BC

I am quite delighted with your Hermathena. It's so judiciously placed that the whole hall [*gymnasium*] is like an offering at its feet. Many thanks.

June 61 BC

Please write me a description of your Amaltheum, its adornment and situation; and send me any poems and tales you have about Amalthea. I should like to make one too in my place at Arpinum. I will send you some of my writings; but there is nothing finished.

Cumae, Apr. 22, 55 BC

And I would rather be in that niche of yours under Aristotle's statue than in their curule chair, and take a walk with you at home than have the company which I see will be with me on my path.

Arpinum, July 3, 44 BC

I will send you my book *On Glory* soon. I will hammer out something in the style of Heracleides to be stored up in your treasure-house. I remember about Plancus. Attica has a good reason for grumbling. I am much obliged to you for telling me about the garlands for Bacchus and the statues. Please don't omit any detail of the same importance, or even the smallest importance in the future.

Source

Schackleton Bailey, D.R. 1965, *Cicero's Letters to Atticus*, Vol. 1, Cambridge: 109, 111, 113, 115, 117, 121, 123–4, 129

Notes

1   'Herm' is the archaeological term used for this particular type of quadrangular shaft surmounted by a sculptured head (Pollitt 1974: 76, nt. 138).
2   In the *Orator* 110, there is a reference to a bronze statue of Demosthenes held in a Tusculan villa, most probably that of Cicero's brother Quintus. Also in a letter to Atticus (4.10), Cicero expresses the wish to have been able to be in his friend's house, which is denoted with the phrase 'in that niche of yours under Aristotle's statue', an indication of space decorated with a work of art appropriate for both men. It is interesting that the whole house is connoted by that little corner.

References

Lafon, 1981
Marvin, 1989
Neudecker, 1988
Sauron, 1980
Valenti, 1936

34

The Emperor Augustus as collector

Gaius Octavius Augustus (63 BC–AD 14) became the first Emperor of Rome, who brought the city and the empire from the chaos of civil war to a system of ordered government (Shotter 1991: 1). He developed an interest in public and private collecting alike, and his activities and choices were determined by political reasons along with personal interests.

Augustus returned many of the 'spoils of war' to their provenance (Pliny, *HN*, 34, 58), while he let it be known that Greek art should henceforth be considered public property and should be used in the service of the state (Pollitt, 1978: 65). Finally, he became the primary patron of the arts; this pre-eminence was due to his *auctoritas*: a central concept to the Augustan Principate, synonymous with influence and prestige, which embraced the idea of acquiring these through a combination of heredity, personality and achievement. Importantly, it implies the ability to patronize on a large scale (Shotter, 1991: 90) and an essential element of Augustus' *auctoritas* was control of patronage (Morford, 1986: 2007–8).

Apart from political reasons, Augustus' relationship with Hellenism was rather ambiguous; although he had to discourage the accumulation and admiration of Greek works of art by the Roman patricians, personally he was not indifferent to them. He had received a classical education from the rhetorician Apollonius of Pergamum (Suetonius, Augustus, 89), and he identified himself with Apollo and Alexander. By the Augustan Age, a study of all things Greek was an essential feature of the classical heritage of which Rome was a part (Shotter, 1991: 66). Augustus' interest in public collections was further expressed by his dedications of Greek works of art to public buildings and temples.

In his private domain, however, Augustus seems to have practised what he forbade to others. His political enemies accused him of being an avid collector of Corinthian bronzes before he came into power. Augustus' interest in rarities is recorded in other sources, as well as in the paragraph that follows. Pliny refers to the *mirabilia* that Augustus had devoted to sanctuaries, for example, four elephants from obsidian (35.196).

In short, Augustus, having limited the collection of Greek works of art to the public domain for political reasons, developed an interest in nature and the creation of knowledge. Being the creator of the phenomenon of the empire, Augustus developed an encyclopaedic curiosity and sought to create around him a 'microcosm'. He wanted to 'conquer' the natural world and become *invare mortalem*, useful to human beings. Thus, Augustus became the *Princeps* of the cabinets of curiosities which would become influential during the Renaissance (Serbat, 1986: 2094).

SUETONIUS,[1] *AUGUSTUS*, LXXII. 3

He disliked large and sumptuous country palaces, actually razing to the ground one which his granddaughter Julia built on a lavish scale. His own villas, which were modest enough, he decorated not so much with handsome statues and pictures as with terraces, groves, and objects noteworthy for their antiquity and rarity; for example, at Caprae the monstrous bones of huge sea monsters and wild beasts, called the 'bones of the giants', and the weapons of the heroes.

Source

Rolfe, J.C. 1951, 1979, *Suetonius, The Twelve Caesars*, Loeb Classical Library, London and Cambridge, Mass.: Heinemann and Harvard University Press: 237

Note

1   Gaius Suetonius Tranquillus (AD 75–160), most probably in Rome. He wrote in Greek and Latin, in the fields of biography, antiquities, natural history and grammar. *The Twelve Caesars* was published in AD 120.

References

Morford, 1986
Pollitt, 1978
Serbat, 1986
Shotter, 1991
Strong, 1976

35

Verres: the archetype
of the passionate collector

Having won the reputation of an honest and scrupulous governor
during his quaestorship in Sicily in 75 BC, Cicero was asked by the
Sicilians to prosecute their case against Verres, the governor of
their province for the years 73 to 71 BC.[1] The representatives of
important cities of the island (except of Messina and Syracuse)
demanded Verres' punishment for the systematic and rapacious
looting of their province. Cicero managed to overcome the problems Verres' supporters, the old Roman nobility, brought in his
way and to collect the necessary evidence in a short enough time
that allowed for the trial to take place before the change of the
year, a fact which would have had an immediate impact on the
verdict, since the political conditions of the following year were
far more favourable to Verres (Q. Hortensius Hortalus, his defence
orator, would become a consul in 69 BC). In order to speed up the
process, Cicero chose to deal with the political background of the
trial rather than the facts of the case in his opening speech, and to
proceed immediately in calling up the witnesses and letting them
present the evidence. Overwhelmed by it, Verres fled into exile
before the second part of the trial, and was sentenced by default.[2]
Subsequently, Cicero published the second part of the prosecution
speech, *Actio Secunda in Verrem*, in order to demonstrate the
oratorical abilities which he had not been able to show in the first
part and to justify Verres' conviction.[3]

The portrait which is created is that of a passionate collector,
who did not hesitate for any reason to enrich his collection of fine
art objects and luxury goods. Thefts from private individuals,
from sacred sanctuaries and temples, as well as from public places
in the province, were most common for Verres, who did not respect friends or enemies, gods or humans. Cicero summarises
Verres' activities with this phrase: 'reveal you not merely his
greed, but the insanity, the madness, that sets him apart from all
other men' (*'rem eius modi ut amentiam singularem et furorem
iam, non cupiditatem eius perspicere possitis'*) (2.4.38).

The paragraph that follows lists some of Verres' thefts from
individuals. Among the people who had suffered from Verres was
Diodorus from Melita, whom the governor attempted to deprive
of his embossed silverware, of the Thericlian type, made by

Mentor. Verres conceived a passionate desire for the objects, without actually having seen them. When he sent to ask for them, Diodorus left the island and chose to stay in exile rather than lose his exquisite plate. Verres considered himself 'robbed' of the objects he did not succeed in acquiring, and felt an irrational rage about the loss. Cicero compares his feelings with that of Eriphyle, the mythic queen who became responsible for her husband's death because of her greed for an object. Verres was even worse, according to Cicero, since his passion was aroused merely by hearing about the objects' beauty; he did not need to see them (2.4.39).

CICERO, *VERRINE ORATIONS*, 2.4.37–9

XVII. From Marcus Coelius, an excellent young Roman knight at Lilybaeum, you carried off all you cared to take. Without scruple, you carried off all the furniture of the active, accomplished and exceptionally popular Gaius Cacurius. From Quintus Lutatius Diodorus, who through the kind offices of Quintus Catulus was made a Roman citizen by Lucius Sulla, you carried off a large and handsome table of citrus-wood, to the certain knowledge of everyone in Lilybaeum. I will not charge you with your treatment of a very proper victim of your villainy, Apollonius the son of Nico, of Drepanum now called Aulus Clodius, whom you despoiled and pillaged of all his admirable silver plate. Let that pass: for this man does not think himself wronged inasmuch as you rescued the fellow when he was already lost and the halter closing round his neck in that affair where you went shares with him in the patrimony of which he robbed his wards at Drepanum. Any theft of yours from him gives me actual pleasure; I hold that you have never done a more honest action than this. But it was certainly not a proper thing to carry off that statue of Apollo from Lyso, the leading citizen of Lilybaeum, in whose house you were a guest. You will tell me you bought it. I know you did – for ten pounds. 'Yes, I think so.' I know you did, I tell you. 'I will produce the record.' Still, it was not a proper transaction. And as for Heius, the boy whose guardian is Gaius Marcellus, and from whom you took a huge sum of money will you claim to have bought from him his chased goblets at Lilybaeum, or will you confess to having taken them?

But why, in dealing with this part of the man's offences, do I thus assemble his more commonplace outrages, which would seem to amount to nothing more than theft by himself and loss for his victims? Let me now tell you of an affair that will reveal to you not merely his greed, but the insanity, the madness, that sets him apart from all other men.

XVIII. There is a man of Melita named Diodorus, whose evidence you have already heard. For many years he has been living at Lilybaeum; he comes of a good family at Melita, and his high character has brought him distinction and popularity in his adopted home. It was reported to Verres about him that he owned some really good chased silver, and in particular, some cups of the kind called Thericliam, highly finished specimens of the art of Mentor. On hearing this, Verres conceived so passionate a desire not only to examine them but to carry them off that he summoned Diodorus and asked for them. Diodorus, having no objection to keeping them, replied that he had not them with him at Lilybaeum; that he had left them with a relative of his at Melita. Verres forthwith sent special messengers to Melita, and wrote to certain people there, telling them to search for these vessels; he also asked Diodorus to write to this relative of his. Never did time pass so slowly as while he was waiting to set eyes on that silver. Diodorus, being a good careful fellow who was anxious to keep what was his, wrote to his relative bidding him tell Verres' men, when they arrived, that within the last few days he had sent the silver off to Lilybaeum. Meanwhile he himself left the country: temporary exile seemed better than staying to witness the loss of his exquisite silver plate. When Verres heard this, he was so thoroughly upset that everyone felt sure he had taken complete leave of his senses. Because he could not himself rob Diodorus of his silver, he talked of himself as 'robbed of those lovely vessels', threatened the absent Diodorus, uttered open cries of rage, and now and then even shed tears. The legend tells us that when Eriphyle saw the necklace – made, I suppose, of gold and jewels – its loveliness so excited the grasping woman that she betrayed her husband to his death. The greed of Verres was like hers; but his was of an ever fiercer and wilder type, since her desire was for a thing she had seen, while his passions were aroused not only by his eyesight but by his hearing also.

Source

Greenwood, H.G. 1948, 1953, *Cicero: The Verrine Orations*, Loeb Classical Library (in two volumes); 1: *Against Caecilius – Against Verres*, books 1 and 2, 2: books 3, 4, and 5: 325–9

Notes

1   C. Verres was born at the end of the second century BC (121/2, or 151, or 115 BC, according to different scholars), when luxury had already invaded

Rome and established a new way of life. He was the son of a senator, and he was soon involved in the overcrowded and highly competitive world of Roman politics himself, finally becoming propraetor in Sicily in 73–70 BC. Verres also succeeded in gaining the friendship of a number of leading nobles. Foremost among them were the celebrated orator Q. Hortensius and the three brothers of the powerful Metellan clan, Quintus, Marcus and Lucius. Furthermore, Verres accumulated sufficient wealth to allow full exploitation of his expertise in political bribery and machination. Cicero implied more than once that his friends' support was sustained by bribes. Such collaboration with the powerful was typical of Verres' political life, and his opportunism, combined with effective use of his wealth and brought him a place of considerable prominence and influence in Roman politics.

2   There is a debate about the actual delivery of a defence speech by Hortensius, with some scholars denying it in view of information presented by other writers and Cicero himself, whereas some others believe that Hortensius did defend his client, although not successfully. It is generally agreed, though, that it is a great misfortune that we have intact only one side of the story. For a detailed review of both sides, and support of the latter, see Alexander, 1976.

3   For a detailed account of Cicero's profits from publishing the second speech see Peterson, 1920: 142, and May, 1988.

References

Alexander, 1976
Bieber, 1977
May, 1988
Peterson, 1920

36

Perceptions of collecting psychology, as seen by Pliny

The discussion of Corinthian bronze in Book 34 of *Historia Naturalis* (*Natural History*) is very illuminating as far as Pliny's and his contemporaries' ideas on value and collecting are concerned. Corinthian bronze offers the best opportunity to tackle these issues. Pliny records that Corinthian bronze was appreciated more than silver (34.1), and he criticises the fact that artistry has come in his era to hold a secondary role compared to material. The story of the creation of this special alloy of bronze during the capture of Corinth is presented in 34.6–8. Then, the 'wonderful mania' for possessing this metal is highlighted, and for its illustration Verres and Mark Antony are employed. The former, whose name was enough to denote passion for objects (see Cicero, *Verrine Orations*), is paired with the latter in order, firstly, for Pliny to make a political statement (Mark Antony is one of the men that Pliny constantly refers to as an example of degeneracy), and secondly, to underline the dangers involved in the passion for artefacts: it could lead to proscriptions, death, eternal disgrace.

It is in relation to Corinthian bronze that Pliny takes the opportunity to distinguish between real connoisseurship and pretension. He explains that the latter is employed by those who wish to differentiate themselves from the uneducated mass, without having any real insight into the matter. To prove his point, he unveils the 'truth' about Corinthian bronze.[1] He argues that Corinth was conquered when metalworking had already ceased to be so prominent a craft, and when famous workers in this medium had long perished. Still, the pseudo-connoisseurs appreciated the 'artistry of their Corinthian bronzes'. Pliny corrects this fallacy on the grounds that genuine Corinthian vessels were the ones that the false connoisseurs did not respect much, and converted into dishes, lamps or wash basins (34.11–12).[2]

PLINY, *HISTORIA NATURALIS*, 34.3.6–8

Of the bronze which was renowned in early days, the Corinthian is the most highly praised. This is a compound that was produced by accident, when Corinth was burned at the time of its capture; and there has been a

129

wonderful mania among many people for possessing this metal – in fact it is recorded that Verres, whose conviction Marcus Cicero had procured was, together with Cicero, proscribed by Antony for no other reason than because he had refused to give up to Antony some pieces of Corinthian ware; and to me the majority of these collectors seem only to make a pretence of being connoisseurs, so as to separate themselves from the multitude, rather than to have any exceptionally refined insight in this matter; and this I will briefly show. Corinth was taken in the third year of the 158th Olympiad, which was the 608th year of our city, when for ages there had no longer been any famous artists in metalwork; yet these persons designate all their work as Corinthian bronzes. In order therefore to refute them we will state the periods to which these artists belong; of course it will be easy to turn the Olympiads into the years since the foundation of our city by referring to the two corresponding dates given above. The only genuine Corinthian vessels are then those which your connoisseurs sometimes convert into dishes for food and sometimes into lamps or even washing basins, without nice regard for decency (or for the neatness of workmanship). There are three kinds of this sort of bronze: a white variety, coming very near to silver in brilliance in which the alloy of silver predominates; a second kind, in which the yellow quality of gold predominates and a third kind in which all the metals were blended in equal proportions. Besides these there is another mixture the formula for which cannot be given, although it is man's handiwork; but the bronze valued in portrait statues and others for its peculiar colour, approaching the appearance of liver and consequently called by a Greek name 'hepatizon' meaning 'liverish' is a blend produced by luck; it is far behind the Corinthian blend, yet a long way in front of the bronze of Aegina and that of Delos which long held the first rank.

Source

Rackham, H. 1952, *Pliny, Natural History*, Vol. 9, Loeb Classical Library, London and Cambridge, Mass., Heinemann and Harvard University Press: 131–3

Notes

1 For Corinthian bronze, see Emanuele, 1989.
2 For a discussion of this see Gros, 1976 and Rouveret, 1989: 454; Rouveret, 1989 also connects this with the notion of '*cessavit ... revixit ars*' (34.52), see esp. pp. 454ff.

References

Emanuele, 1989
Gros, 1976
Rouveret, 1989

37

Collecting values and vices as seen by Martial

The fourth book of Martial's *Epigrams* was published in Rome in AD 89. It presents a greater variety of themes than the previous ones, and there is a strong sense of a greater political and historical awareness. The percentage of satiric epigrams is lower (less than a third of the book), and Martial mentions new private patrons (Sullivan, 1991: 33–4).

Epigram 4.39 refers to Charinus, an ardent collector of antique works of art. Undoubtedly, the name is fictitious and Charinus probably a stereotype. The emphasis of the epigram is not on collecting *per se*; Charinus is 'attacked' mainly on the grounds of his private life. He has collected *all* silver plate, he *alone* possesses antique works of art by Myron, Praxiteles, Scopas, Phidias and Mentor. He *owns genuine* works of Grattius, gold-inlaid dishes and *ancestral* tables. Martial is feigning surprise, that a rich connoisseur of wrought *objets d'art* and tableware has no *argentum purum* (pure silver) in his collection. Sullivan (1991: 246–7) argues that this point has direct sexual connotations. The epigram projects the picture of a passionate relationship between the collector and his objects. The use of the words 'all', 'alone' (repeated four times), 'lack', 'collected' and 'owns' are used by Martial consciously to make a point about both Charinus and his collecting activities. They sketch the picture of a man who strives towards his completion and his purification through collecting a 'complete' as well as 'unique' set of the much-admired tokens of the antique, with all their connotations. Very much in the spirit of the theory of contemporary collecting research, Martial suggests that collecting is for Charinus a mechanism of compensation for his lost purity, along with a powerful symbol of his personal inadequacies. The objects selected and collected participate, in other words, in a process of narcissistic projection on behalf of Charinus: he extends himself to the very limits of his collection and he collects his ideal self which, as Martial ruthlessly unveils, far exceeds the actual personal quality of the collector.

Book 10 is one of the best of Martial's books, but it presents a number of problems. Posterity has the second edition, published in mid-98, when the poet was preparing to return to Spain. The earlier edition had been put out in December 95, but Martial informs his audience (10.2.3) that many of the poems of the first edition had been revised, and more importantly, that over half of them were new (Sullivan, 1991: 40).

Epigram 10.80 is a short presentation of one more of the characters of Martial's fictitious portrait gallery: it refers to another collector, Eros. He weeps and groans whenever he spots objects he desires, objects finer than usual than he cannot acquire. He wishes he could carry home the whole Saepta Julia. Eros is another stereotype, who would normally attract people's laughter, argues Martial. But he is not just that: as a personage, he is a caricature of a large number of Romans who, although laughing on the surface, in their hearts share the feelings of Eros. Martial is shocked and embarrassed to recognise that. The description of the collector makes a couple of interesting points. The name 'Eros' itself, chosen for the collector, refers to the point made by other writers as well as Martial himself about sexual undertones. The personality of the collector unfolds within the boundaries of sexual inadequacy or fetishism. The insatiable desire for objects finds an equivalent in the insatiable desire for sexual activity, and the connoisseur is also a person whose life is immoral and whose desire is impure. Furthermore, Martial criticises not collecting as such, but avarice in terms of the acquisition of material culture.

MARTIAL, *EPIGRAMS*, 4.39

You have collected every kind of silver plate, and you alone possess Myron's antique works of art, you alone the handiwork of Praxiteles and of Scopas, you alone the chased product of Phidias' graving chisel, you alone the results of Mentor's toil. Nor do you lack genuine works of Grattius, or dishes overlaid with Gallician gold, or pieces in relief from ancestral tables.[1] Nevertheless, I wonder why, amid all your silver plate, you, Charinus, have nothing chaste.

MARTIAL, *EPIGRAMS*, 10.80

Eros weeps whenever he inspects cups of spotted murrine,[2] or slaves, or a citrus-wood table finer than usual and heaves groans from the bottom of his chest because he – wretched man[3] – cannot buy up the whole Saepta and carry it home. How many act like Eros! But with dry eyes the greater part laugh at his tears – and have them in their hearts.

Source

Ker, Walter, C.A. 1919, (two volumes): Vol. 1 and Vol. 2, *Martial Epigrams*, Loeb Classical Library, London and Cambridge, Mass., Heinemann and Harvard University Press: 257, 217

Notes

1   We have in this poem a complete list of all the values attributed by collectors to their objects. A collector aims to acquire 'all' the objects of his collecting interest, what is called in modern collecting research 'to fill a complete set'; he also aims to be the 'only' possessor of a particular category of artefacts, in other words to gain 'uniqueness' through material culture; he is also interested in acquiring 'genuine' works in an attempt to be original and reach 'authenticity', since it is the 'real' thing that attracts interest and has the power to transmit its qualities to the owner; he aims at the acquisition of ancestral possessions, which have a special meaning and value for collectors, since they allow for interrelations to be achieved between the original owner of the work and the collector, and also to found the collector deeply in a social and historical background.
2   Transparency or paleness was a defect.
3   An interesting perception of collectors by their contemporaries.

References

Sullivan, 1991

38

The passion for murrhine crystalware, recorded by Pliny

During the discussion about murrhine cups, Pliny refers to a collection of murrhine artefacts that Nero had taken away from the children of a collector after his death, and exhibited for a short time in a private theatre. Pliny was very surprised to see the fragments of a broken cup included in the exhibition, since it was decided that the fragments of that cup would have the same treatment as the body of Alexander the Great. The equation between the body of the king, and the fragments of the object is indicative of the fetishisation of the artefact (and of Alexander).

In the following paragraph another similar incident is recorded. It is the well-known one of Petronius smashing his cup in order to prevent it decorating Nero's table after his death. Petronius thought of the object as a symbol of himself, standing for his perishable body, and therefore he wished to destroy it, exactly like himself (he committed suicide), rather than surrender it to his enemies (Bounia, 1998: Chapter 8). A similar pattern of thought is detached in Nero's behaviour, when he decided to punish his contemporaries, and take vengeance for his death by making it impossible for another man to drink from his vessels; thus he broke his crystal cups in a final outburst of rage.

In relation to issues of value, we may also refer to the anecdotes mentioned by Pliny. They are all meant to criticise collectors, as people whose sound judgement has been destroyed through their irrational dependence on objects. As one of the stories goes, an ex-praetor gnawed the rim of his already extremely expensive cup, only to see its value enhanced by those who favoured prestigious associations and passionate relationships with objects. A similar process of enhanced value due to interaction with an object is recorded in 34.63–4. Nero had asked for a statue by Lysippus to be gilded; but that diminished its artistic value, so it was decided to remove the gilding, which unfortunately left traces on the statue. Remarkably, this incident increased its monetary worth.

PLINY, *HISTORIA NATURALIS*, 37.7.18–20

That same victory first brought myrrhine ware to Rome. Pompey was the first to dedicate fluorspar bowls and cups from his triumph to Capitoline Jupiter. Vessels of fluorspar immediately passed into everyday use, and even display stands and tables were eagerly sought. This kind of extravagance increases daily. An ex-consul drank from a fluorspar cup for which he had paid 70,000 sesterces, although it held only 3 pints. He was so enamoured of it that he used to chew the rim. Yet this damage increased its value, and no item of fluorspar today bears a higher price-tag on it.

The amount of money he dissipated in acquiring his other pieces can be gauged from their large number; there were so many that when they were confiscated from that man's children by Nero and put on show, they filled the private theatre in Nero's gardens across the Tiber! This structure was large enough even for Nero to sing in before an audience while he was rehearsing for Pompey's Theatre.

When the ex-consul Titus Petronius was at the point of death, he broke a fluorspar ladle for which he had paid 300,000 sesterces, thus depriving the emperor's dining-room table of this legacy. Nero, however, as was fitting for an emperor, outdid everyone else by paying a million sesterces for a single bowl. That a commander-in-chief and Father of his Country paid so much to drink is a matter worthy of record.

Source

Healy, J.F., 1991, *Natural History – A Selection*, Pliny the Elder, translated with an introduction, Harmondsworth, Penguin Books: 366–7

References

Bounia, 1998

39

The Roman art market

The art market in Rome was a thriving business, supported by Roman collectors who were willing to pay enormous amounts to acquire the objects of their desire. These reached their final destination, the stands of the auctioneers in the portico of Saepta Julia in Rome, as Martial informs us (2.14; 9.59), through the mediation of agents who arranged for locating, transporting and selling them. The most common way of transferring the artefacts would be by sea. Cicero mentions Lentulus as the person who would undertake the transportation.

Direct testimony about these transportations and the routes of the art trade are available from the archaeological remains. Shipwrecks on the seabed of the Mediterranean have been very valuable in determining these routes, as well as aspects of the Roman taste. Among the most well-known wrecks that provide information on the art trade are those of Madhia, that dates from approximately 86 BC, and Antikythera (c. 80–70 BC), the first testifying to a trade from Athens, the second to one from Delos.[1] Examples of similar cases are the Riace warriors, found in Sicily (1972), and the discovery at Piraeus in 1959 of a quantity of works, possibly part of the booty of Sylla ready to be transferred to Italy. The intermediaries in this art trade, however, were not only friends. They were also specially employed agents, like the ones Verres had hired, or the more decent Damassipus whom both Cicero and Horace mention (Horace, *Satires*, 2.3.18). The trade also supported a range of other professionals, among whom were conservators, like C. Avianus Evander mentioned by Cicero (*ad Famil.* 12.2;13.23), and fakers, like those named by Martial (4.88; 8.34).

The prices of works of art that writers record for us also indicate not only their importance, but also the folly of collectors (this is the context where these are usually presented), as well as the prosperity of the market. Cicero often refers to prices, either to suggest that the ones Verres paid to his victims as compensation were ridiculous, in which case he expects the judges to understand and appreciate this as an argument, or in order to express his desire for his own objects, in which case he urges Atticus to acquire them without sparing any money.

CICERO, *VERRINE ORATIONS*, 2.4.12–14

Let us see, then, how large the sum was that could make a man who had so much money as Heius, and who cared for it so little, no longer behave like an honourable and conscientious gentleman: You instructed him, it appears, personally to record in his accounts the sale to Verres of these statues, the work of Praxiteles, Myron, and Polyclitus, for a total sum of sixty-five pounds:[2] and he did so. – Read us out the entry in the accounts. The clerk reads it: It is amusing to hear that the high reputation of the artists whom those Greeks extol to the skies has crashed so completely in the judgement of Verres. A Cupid by Praxiteles for £16! This surely explains the saying 'Better buy than beg.' VII. 'Well', someone may say, 'but do you yourself set any very high value upon such things?' I reply that, from my own point of view, and for my own purposes, I do not. But what you, I think, have to consider is what such things are worth in the opinion of those who do care for them; what they are as a rule sold for; what these particular things could have been sold for, if they had been sold openly and freely; and finally, what Verres himself thought them worth. Would he have exposed himself to popular scandal and violent censure for the sake of the Cupid, if he had really valued it at no more than £16? Well, gentlemen, you are all aware what the value placed upon things really is. Have we not seen bronzes of quite moderate size fetch £400 at a sale? Could I not name persons who have paid as much as that for them, or even more? The fact is that the value of these things corresponds to the demand for them; you can hardly limit the price of them, unless you can limit the desires of men.

Source

Greenwood, H.G., 1948 (in two volumes); 1: *Against Caecilius – Against Verres*, books 1 and 2, 2: books 3, 4, and 5, 1953, *Cicero: The Verrine Orations*, Loeb Classical Library, London and Cambridge, Mass., Heinemann and Harvard University Press: 295–7

Notes

1   For the Madhia wreck see, for instance, Fuchs, 1963; Hellenkemper Sallies, 1994; on the Antikythera wreck, see Weinberg et al., 1965; Bol, 1972.
2   The prices that Cicero mentions in the *Verrines* in the Loeb tradition have been transferred to pounds (naturally, prices of 1953).

References

Bol, 1972
Coarelli, 1983
Fuchs, 1963
Weinberg, Grace, Edwards, Robinson, Throckmorton and Ralph, 1965
Hellenkemper Sallies, 1994

40

Public displays of works of art, recounted by Pliny

The dichotomy between public and private often appears in discussions of collecting and collections.

Pliny recounts assemblages of works of art and natural curiosities, deposited by celebrated personalities of the Roman world in public buildings, mainly but not exclusively temples. The definition of the work of art itself is quite broad, since it includes sculpture in bronze or marble and paintings, and also products of fine craftsmanship, like bowls and cups – what we would call decorative arts. The collections described by Pliny are part of his 'art history' discussion and his presentation of famous artists and personalities of the Greek and Roman worlds.

Pliny's discussion of Greek art is dominated by concepts as *honos* (honour) and *auctoritas* (influence), although we normally find these concepts in the sphere of politics and not of the arts (Isager, 1991: 158). The selection of those words signals that Pliny considered the given work of art from the point of view of the political usefulness it might have had for the person who had brought it to Rome. This also indicates that the political propaganda had been an important aspect of public, and private, collections and determined their nature.

As far as the setting of works of art within these public buildings is concerned, before the second century BC, works of art were put into temples and other buildings without much thought given to their arrangement. But when the importance of this dedication developed, the architecture was adapted to receive them (Strong, 1975). Worth mentioning are C. Vermeule's studies on the subject (1967; 1968; 1977).

In both public and private settings, works of art soon became the essential furnishing of architectural monuments and in some cases dominated their settings. Their importance was so great, that they also influenced the development of art and architecture. By the first century BC no major building would be planned without suitable works of art to furnish it (Strong, 1976).

PLINY, *HISTORIA NATURALIS*, 36.4.38–43

Similarly, the imperial mansions on the Palatine were filled with excellent statues made by pairs of artists, Craterus and Pythodorus, Polydeuces and Hermolaus, another Pythodorus and Artemon, and individually by Aphrodisius of Tralles. The Pantheon of Agrippa[1] was embellished by Diogenes of Athens; and among the supporting members of this temple there are Caryatids that are almost in a class of their own, and the same is true of the figures on the angles of the pediment, which are, however, not so well known because of their lofty position. A work that is without honour and stands in no temple is the Hercules before which the Carthaginians were wont to perform human sacrifices every year. This stands at ground level in front of the entrance to the Portico of the Nations. Formerly too there were statues of the Muses of Helicon by the temple of Prosperity, and a Roman knight, Junius Pisciculus, fell in love with one of them, according to Varro, who incidentally was an admirer of Pasiteles, a sculptor who was also the author of a treatise in five volumes on the World's Famous Masterpieces. He was a native of Magna Graecia and received Roman citizenship along with the communities of that region. The ivory Jupiter in the temple of Metellus at the approaches to the Campus Martius is his work. Once, he was at the docks, where there were wild beasts from Africa, and was making a relief of a lion, peering as he did so into the cage at his model, when it so happened that a leopard broke out of another cage and caused serious danger to this most conscientious of artists. He is said to have executed a number of works, but their titles are not recorded. Arcesilaus too is highly praised by Varro, who states that he once possessed a work of his, namely Winged Cupids Playing with a Lioness, of whom some were holding it with cords, some were making it drink from a horn, and some were putting slippers on its feet, all the figures having been carved from one block. Varro relates also that it was Coponius who was responsible for the fourteen figures of the Nations that stand around Pompey's theatre.[2] I find that Canachus, who was much admired as a maker of bronzes, also executed figures in marble. Nor should we forget Sauras and Batrachus, who build the temples that are enclosed by the Porticoes of Octavia. They were mere natives of Sparta. And yet, some people actually suppose that they were very rich and erected the temples at their own expense because they hoped to be honoured by an inscription; and the story is that, although this was refused, they attained their object in another way. At any rate, on the moulded bases of the columns there are still in existence carvings of a lizard and a frog in token of their names.

Source

Eichholz, D.E., 1971, *Pliny Natural History*, Vol. 10 (libri 36–37), Loeb Classical Library, London and Cambridge, Mass., Heinemann and Harvard University Press: 31–5

Notes

1   The Pantheon of Agrippa was erected as part of a complex consisting of the Baths, the Temple of Neptune and Saepta Julia. The exact relationship between them is not clear, since their functions seem to have been very different, but they were all major monuments. An inscription on the façade dates the Pantheon to 27 BC, but Cassius Dio (53.27.2) implies that it was finished in 25 BC and was called 'Pantheon' because of the number of statues it contained. (See the discussion in Richardson, 1992: 283–6, also Bibliography). It is considered an example of the 'new' architecture, taking into account the 'museographic' significance of the temples (Gros, 1976: 160ff).
2   The Porticus Pompeii, dedicated in 52 BC, contained a collection of paintings by Polygnotus (35.59), Pausias (*Sacrifice of an Ox*, 35. 126), Nikias (*Alexander*, 35.132) and Antiphilos (*Cadmos and Europe*, 35. 114), as well as fourteen figures by Coponius representing the Fourteen Nations (36.41).

References

Gros, 1976
Richardson, 1992
Strong, 1975
Strong, 1976
Vermeule, 1967
Vermeule, 1968
Vermeule, 1977

41

A private picture gallery, described by Philostratus

Following the tradition of the Greek sanctuaries, where the rooms for the display of picture-panels had been an almost standard feature (for example, the Propylaea on the Athenian Acropolis, the Stoa Poikile in the Athenian Agora, the Lesche of the Cnidians in Delphi), private art collections were formed in Rome. Testimonies about picture galleries in private or public settings are available from many sources (for example see Ebert, 1950 with references; Leach, 1982b, 1988). They were held in public or private spaces, and their presence was taken for granted. They formed a characteristic element in the luxurious mansions of the period, and were a manifestation of the aesthetic tendencies of the age – collection and appreciation. (*Pinacothecae* are described from the time of Lucullus (Varro, *RR* 1.2. 10) and Varro (*RR* 1. 59.2).) The elder Pliny (*HN*, 35.4; 148) was not very favourable towards those who collected *pinakes*, although it was a widespread practice in his era. Imperial *pinacothecae* are also mentioned in an inscription dated in AD 153 (*CIL* VI. 10234 = Dessau *ILS*, 7213, line 2ff).

Philostratus' *Imagines* ascribe to the tradition of the textual collections, that is, collections of ideas, *objets d'art*, information on various topics, that the ancient writers were keen on collecting and saving for the future. Whether *Imagines* refers to an actual collection, as Lehmann (1941) suggested, or a imaginary one (see Bryson, 1994), it is true that it relies on notions and practices well known to the Romans. It is an extensive account of what a Roman picture gallery, a Roman catalogue of pictures and the Roman viewing of pictures may have been like. Philostratus claims that his verbal descriptions of sixty-odd panels are rendered after original paintings (*pinakes*) housed in a single collection in Neapolis (Naples) (Bryson, 1994: 255).

The treatise, of which the paragraph that follows is part, was written by the Elder Philostratus from Lemnos, member of a prominent family of men of letters. There are two works with the same title, written the first by the Elder Philostratus, who was contemporary of Septimius Severus, the second by his grandson, the Younger Philostratus, who was active in c. AD 300. (Pollitt, 1983: 219).

The *Imagines* of the Elder Philostratus enjoyed an enormous appreciation during subsequent periods (witnessed, for example,

by the translations that Isabella d'Este commissioned), since besides being a unique testimony about the context, setting and
appreciation of pictures collections in antiquity it contains the
promise that all ancient textual collections have shared, that is, the
promise of resurrection: the entire gallery described in the pages
of Philostratus, along with the context of their arrangement and
reception became part of the museological tradition of the Renaissance onwards (Bryson, 1994: 255–6).

PHILOSTRATUS, *IMAGINES*, 1. 4 (295.15–35 – 296.1–4)

Now the story of the men who have won mastery in the science of
painting, and of the states and kings that have been passionately devoted
to it, has been told by other writers, notably by Aristodemus of Caria,
whom I visited for four years in order to study painting; and he painted in
the technique of Eumelus, but with much more charm. The present discussion, however, is not to deal with painters nor yet with their lives;
rather we propose to describe examples of paintings in the form of
addresses which we have composed for the young, that by this means
they may learn to interpret paintings and to appreciate what is esteemed
in them.

The occasion of these discourses of mine was as follows: It was the
time of the public game at Naples, a city in Italy settled by men of the
Greek race and people of culture, and therefore Greek in their enthusiasm
for discussion. And as I did not wish to deliver my addresses in public,
and young men kept coming to the house of my host and importuning
me. I was lodging outside the walls in a suburb facing the sea, where
there was a portico built on four, I think, or possibly five terraces, open to
the west wind and looking out on the Tyrrhenian sea. It was resplendent
with all the marbles favoured by luxury, but it was particularly splendid
by reason of the panel-paintings set in the walls, paintings which I thought
had been collected with real judgment, for they exhibited the skill of very
many painters. The idea had already occurred to me that I ought to speak
in praise of the paintings, when the son of my host, quite a young boy,
only ten years old but already an ardent listener and eager to learn, kept
watching me as I went from one to another and asking me to interpret
them. So in order that he might not think me ill-bred, 'Very well', I said,
'we will make them the subject of a discourse as soon as the young men
come.' And when they came, I said, 'Let me put the boy in front and
address to him my effort at interpretation; but do you follow, not only
listening but also asking questions if anything I say is not clear.'

Source

Fairbanks, A. 1931, *Philostratus, Imagines – Callistratus. Descriptions*, Loeb Classical Library, London and New York, Heinemann and G.P. Putnam's Sons: 5–7

References

Bryson, 1994
Ebert, 1950
Lehmann-Hartleben, 1941
Pollitt, 1983
Leach, 1982
Leach, 1988

42

Temporary exhibitions in the city of Rome

The triumphs of Roman generals became the first temporary exhibitions organised in Rome, and the middle stage from the processual displays of earlier antiquity to the permanent public collections and the temporary exhibitions organised to celebrate an office, or to display a collection (see *HN*, Chapter 40 in this volume).

The passage that follows describes a triumphal procession held in AD 75. It is part of the *Jewish War*, a seven-book historical treatise covering the period from Antiochus Epiphanes' conquest of Jerusalem in 170 BC to the tragedy of Masada in AD 74, which was written by Flavius Josephus, a priest from Jerusalem (c. AD 38–100). He enjoyed the patronage of Vespasian and wrote several works of history that deal with the history, topography, and social, political and economic life of Judaea (Jerusalem and Palestine). The works were originally written in his native Aramaic and were later translated in Greek with the help of assistants in Rome. The *Jewish War* was probably translated toward the end of Vespasian's reign, between AD 75 and 79 (Cornfeld, 1982: 6).

FLAVIUS JOSEPHUS, *JEWISH WAR*, VII. 132–62

It is impossible adequately to describe the multitude of those spectacles, and their magnificence under every conceivable aspect, whether in works of art or diversity of riches or natural rarities; for almost all the objects which men who have ever been blessed by fortune have acquired by one – the wonderful and precious productions of various nations – by their collective exhibition on that day displayed the majesty of the Roman empire. Silver and gold and ivory in masses, wrought into all manner of forms, might be seen, not as if carried in procession, but flowing, so to speak, like a river; here were tapestries borne along, some of the rarest purple, others embroidered by Babylonian art with perfect portraiture; transparent gems, some set in golden crowns, some in other fashions, swept by in such profusion as to correct our erroneous supposition that any of them was rare. Then, too, there were carried images of their gods, of marvellous size and no mean craftsmanship, and of these not one but was of some rich material. Beasts of many species were led along all caparisoned with appropriate trappings. The

146

numerous attendants conducting each group of animals were decked in garments of true purple dye, interwoven with gold; while those selected to take parts in the pageant itself had about them choice ornaments of amazing richness. Moreover, even among the mob or captives, none was to be seen unadorned, the variety and beauty of their dresses concealing from view any unsightliness arising from body disfigurement.

But nothing in the procession excited so much astonishment as the structure of the moving stages; indeed, their massiveness afforded ground for alarm and misgivings as to their stability, many of them being three or four stories high, while the magnificence of the fabric was a source at once of delight and amazement. For many were enveloped in tapestries interwoven with gold, and all had a framework of gold and wrought ivory. The war was shown by numerous representations, in separate sections, affording a very vivid picture of its episodes. Here was to be seen a prosperous country devastated, there whole battalions of the enemy slaughtered; here a party in flight, there others led into captivity; walls of surpassing compass demolished by engines, strong fortresses overpowered, cities with well-mannered defences completely mastered and an army pouring within the ramparts, an area all deluged with blood, the hands of those incapable of resistance raised in supplication, temples set on fire, houses pulled down over their owners' heads, and, after general desolation and woe, rivers flowing, not over a cultivated land, nor supplying drink to man and beast, but across a country still on every side in flames. For to such suffering were the Jews destined when they plunged into the war; and the art and magnificent workmanship of these structures now portrayed the incidents to those who had not witnessed them, as though they were happening before their eyes. On each of the stages was stationed the general of one of the captured cities in the attitude in which he was taken. A number of ships also followed.

The spoils in general were borne in promiscuous heaps; but conspicuous above all stood out those captured in the temple at Jerusalem. These consisted of a golden table, many talents in weight, and a lampstand, likewise made of gold, but constructed on a different pattern from those which we use in ordinary life. Affixed to a pedestal was a central shaft, from which there extended slender branches, arranged trident-fashion, a wrought lamp being attached to the extremity of each branch; of these there were seven, indicating the honour paid to that number among the Jews. After these, the last of all the spoils, was carried a copy of the Jewish Law. Then followed a large party carrying images of victory, all made of ivory and gold. Behind them drove Vespasian, followed by Titus; while Domitian rode beside them, in magnificent apparel and mounted on a steed that was itself a sight ...

The triumphal ceremonies being concluded and the empire of the Romans established on the firmest foundation, Vespasian decided to erect a temple of Peace. This was very speedily completed and in a style surpassing all human conception. For, besides having prodigious resources of wealth on which to draw he also embellished it with ancient master-pieces of painting and sculpture; indeed, into that shrine were accumu-lated and stored all objects for the sight of which men had once wandered over the whole world, eager to see them severally while they lay in various countries. Here, too, he laid up the vessels of gold from the temples of the Jews, on which he prided himself; but their Law and the purple hangings of the sanctuary he ordered to be deposited and kept in the palace.

Source

Thackeray, H. St. J., 1956, *Josephus, The Jewish War*, Vol. 2, Loeb Classical Library, London and Cambridge Mass., Heinemann and Harvard University Press: 544–47

References

Cornfeld, 1982

43

Pliny and natural history collecting: a source of inspiration for Renaissance collectors

Many paragraphs in different parts of Pliny's *Natural History* read like the standard list of wonders in any respectable museum. For example, in paragraphs 32.144–5 marine animals are listed.

Renaissance museums owe to the past more than their name. There is a profound association between ancient models and subsequent practices; this contributed to the philosophical programmes that underlay their collecting practices. Museums of natural history are usually associated with the reformulation of the history of nature in the eighteenth and nineteenth centuries (Linnaeus and Darwin); but although undoubtedly this is true, so it is the fact that they originated within a predominately Aristotelian and Plinian framework. Naturalists of the Renaissance had the natural philosophers of antiquity as guidance during their researches. Aristotle, for instance, offered philosophical purpose for the collecting of nature, or the method by which one can arrive at a proper name for a previously unidentified phenomenon (Findlen, 1994: 57). Pliny's contribution is even more profound, however.

His encyclopaedic spirit, his classification principle, his aim to assemble the world, his notions of commemoration, memory and so on, have influenced (and in many senses continue to do so) the collecting process from the Renaissance onwards.

The encyclopaedic notion is responsible for a wide range of influences. It inspired naturalists to extend their curiosity to the farthest ends of the known world, and catalogue its wonders. The format of *Natural History* reminded collectors that all details of nature deserve to be assembled. It offered the compilation of a comprehensive encyclopaedia as a model for imitation, and the pursuit of knowledge as the ultimate desire of man (Findlen, 1994: 63–4). Aldrovaldi or Gesner, for instance, perceived the encyclopedia of nature as dependent on the encyclopaedia of knowledge. For example, they hoarded bibliographies, as if the assemblage of the books' titles alone could symbolically convey the possession of the contents (Findlen, 1994: 59–60). Consumed by their pursuit of knowledge, they committed themselves to a life organised around collecting, and the organisation of the objects and information they possessed.

The conscious imitation of Pliny is evidenced in the direct references to him that we find in Renaissance writings. Federico

Borromeo wrote at the beginning of his *Musaeum* (1625): 'To begin this work, I think first of Pliny, above all others, not for the desire that I have to emulate him, which would be excessively foolish and audacious, but, in spite of myself, for the excellence of his example'.[1] Elsewhere Aldrovaldi, referring to the lessons naturalists could receive from *Natural History*, asserts: 'There is nothing under the sun that cannot be reduced to one of the three genus, that is, inanimate things and fossils, extracted from the bowels of the earth, plants, or animals. Even artificial things may be included in one of these three genus according to the materials [of their composition].'[2]

Having the expansive and wide character of *Natural History* in mind, Renaissance collectors of nature included in their *Wunderkammern* works of art, antiquities and scientific instruments, too. Mercati, for instance, included descriptions of some of the Belvedere statues as examples of marble in his *Metallotheca* (Findlen, 1994: 61–3). In Italy, in particular, by the end of the sixteenth century works of art and naturalia, that is, artistically arranged natural specimens, were introduced into collections (Schulz, 1990: 4).

PLINY, *HISTORIA NATURALIS*, XXXII.53. 144–5

To begin with large beasts, there are 'sea-trees', blower-whales, other whales, saw-fish, Tritons, Nereids, walruses (?) so called 'men of the sea', and others having the shape of fishes, dolphins, and seals well known to Homer, tortoises on the other hand well known to luxury, beavers to medical people (of the class of beavers we have never found record, speaking as we are of marine animals, that otters anywhere frequent the sea); also sharks, 'drinones', horned rays (?), sword-fish, saw-fish; hippopotamuses and crocodiles common to land, sea, and river; and, common to river and sea only, tunnies, other tunnies, 'siluri', 'coracini', and perches.

Source

Jones, W.H.S., 1963, *Pliny Natural History*, Vol. VIII, (libri XXVIII–XXXII), Loeb Classical Library, London and Cambridge, Mass., Heinemann and Harvard University Press: 553

Notes

1 Translated by Luigi Grasselli, in *Il Museo del Cardinale Federico Borromeo*, Milan 1909, p. 44.
2 Quoted in Findlen, 1994: 62; from *BAV*, Vat. Lat. 6192, Vol. 2, f. 656v.

References

Findlen, 1994
Schulz, 1990

44

'Textual collections' and Pliny's influence on later collectors

In the Plinian discourse and hierarchy of values, the recording of artefacts corresponds to the assemblage of a 'textual collection' and is opposed to 'sacrilegious acts of luxury', that is 'actual collection', in the sense that by being a collection in paper it respects nature and safeguards it for the future, without destroying it as the formation of private collections of artefacts does. On the one hand, the notion of public as opposed to private is of prevailing importance. Textual collections undoubtedly serve a public role, since they allow more individuals to access them, while they also permit the appropriate conditions of thorough enjoyment of them to be reached.

Pliny has a long tradition of textual collections to follow. It is the tradition created by the antiquarians which was taken over by Pliny's ideal *vir bonus*, M. Terentius Varro, who had assembled along with an actual collection (33.155; 36.41), a textual one of portraits. Other antiquarians, like Atticus, were also devoted to such projects. Even artists like Pasiteles (first century) had assembled in five volumes the '*opera nobilia in toto orbe*', all the noble works of art in the city – and Pliny uses him as a source in Books 34 to 36 (Rouveret, 1989: 459). Just the title of Pasiteles' work is indicative: it is an appreciation of all the works of art produced until then, in a wide geographical and chronological spectrum, expressed in an assemblage, and a reclassification of a sort that reminds one of an imaginary museum. Rouveret (1989: 460) attributes to Pliny a similar wish achieved in the 'art history' chapters, especially in Book 36, where Pliny most explicitly adopts a wider stance and views the world with the eyes of a critic (as Rouveret argues). I would suggest that this is undoubtedly true in *HN*, but the scope is much wider than has been indicated, so that it includes the whole of *HN* and not just the art history chapters. Pliny aimed to assemble, to hoard, a *musée imaginaire* – that is, the universe. The sanctity of the subject reifies the outcome as well. Words, images, and texts are incorporated into a universal encyclopaedia of knowledge.

PLINY, *HISTORIA NATURALIS*, 36.24.101

But this is indeed the moment for us to pass on to the wonders of our own city, to review the resources derived from the experiences of 800 years, and to show that here too in our buildings we have vanquished the world; and the frequency of this occurrence will be proved to match within a little the number of marvels that we shall describe. If we imagine the whole agglomeration of our buildings massed together and placed on one great heap, we shall see such grandeur towering above us as to make us think that some other world were being described, all concentrated in one single place.[1]

Source

Eichholz, D.E., 1971, *Pliny Natural History*, Vol. X (Books 36–37), Loeb Classical Library, London and Cambridge, Mass., Heinemann and Harvard University Press: 79–81

Notes

1   For Rome as the 'archetypal museum', see Elsner, 1994b; Déotte, 1995; Bounia, 1998a: 21.

References

Bounia, 1998
Déotte, 1995
Elsner, 1994
Findlen, 1994
Rouveret, 1989

45

Pausanias and cultural tourism

In the later second century AD, Pausanias, a man likely born in
Lydia, travelled to mainland Greece and recorded his experience
in a kind of early guidebook to Greece. Although Pausanias had
his predecessors (for example Scylax wrote a guidebook in c. 350
BC, and Heracleides of Crete offered a description of the appearance and customs of Greek cities in the second or first century
BC), his is the only one that survives intact and has influenced
subsequent generations to any great extent.

Pausanias was an antiquarian: he was interested in the works
of man and not in nature; in rituals and legends, but not in geography, economics or anthropology. His aim was to preserve a memory
of the past through the recording of its relics and the stories that
went with them (Eisner, 1993: 30–3). Pausanias was concerned
with contexts – the sites' history, their historical topography – as
well as with objects (Arafat, 1992).

Pausanias' *Description of Greece* could be quoted in full as
an example of the Roman interest in cultural tourism and pilgrimage, and as a source of information on their interests and
concerns (for example Elsner, 1994, 1997). Nevertheless, here
we include only two brief passages in order to illustrate the
interest of the ancient world in sites or things that are 'worth
seeing'. Although this epithet is not used frequently enough to
qualify as a criterion for the study of Pausanias' selectivity
(Arafat, 1992: 389), it is indicative of the notion of travelling in
order to visit things or sites that are worth a visit. The first refers
to the theatre at Epidaurus, a monument that has a central place
in the modern touristic guides to Greece, and forms part of the
cultural tourist's itinerary. The second refers to the temple of
Hera at Plataia (Boetia), a monument that today is at the margin
of touristic interest.

PAUSANIAS, *DESCRIPTION OF GREECE*, 2.27.5

The Epidaurians have a THEATRE in their sanctuary that seems to me
particularly worth a visit. The Roman theatres have gone far beyond all
the others in the whole world: the theatre of Megalopolis in Arkadia is
unique for magnitude; but who can begin to rival Polykleitos for the

beauty and composition of his architecture? It was Polykleitos who built the theatre and the round building.

PAUSANIAS, *DESCRIPTION OF GREECE*, 4.2.7

In the city itself as you advance from the altar and statue erected to Zeus of Freedom you come to the shrine of the divine heroine Plataia: I have already spoken about her, dealt with her legend, and offered a conjecture. They have a TEMPLE OF HERA at Plataia, worth seeing for its size and fine statues. Inside is Rea bringing Kronos the rock wrapped in swaddling clothes as if it were the child she bore; then there is Perfect Hera, an upright statue of great size. They are both in Pentelic stone, by Praxiteles.

Source

Levi, P., 1971, Pausanias, *Guide to Greece, Central Greece*, Vol. 1, Harmondsworth, Penguin Books: 195, 313–14

References

Arafat, 1992
Eisner, 1993
Elsner, 1994a
Elsner, 1997

46

'Curator' as a technical term, as Suetonius records

During the Republic the contents of temples and public buildings were under the responsibility of the *censors* and *aediles*. The *censors* were responsible for the cataloguing and distribution of the *res sacrae* ('sacred things'); they also had to prepare lists of the contents of the buildings. The *aediles*, on the other hand, had the general supervision of the buildings, which means that they were responsible for the maintenance of the buildings and the supervision of the custodians, the *aeditui*. They also had responsibility for dedications in public places.

As soon as Augustus gained control, and because of his interest in public collections, the authority of temples and public collections passed to two '*curatores aedium sacrarum et operum locorumque publicorum*' (RE, 1901, s.v. *curator*); the third of those 'curatorial boards' was established between 11 BC and AD 14, and the *curatores* undertook the role of both the *censors* and the *aediles*. There is not enough information about the exact duties of curatores (most of the existing information comes from inscriptions), but they operated under tight imperial control; one of them must have been responsible for the public buildings and the other for the sacred shrines. The large imperial collections must have been separately administered. It is interesting to notice that the term '*curatores*' has survived up to our times. 'Curators' of contemporary museums are distant in time, but vocationally close descendants of those '*curatores*' (Strong, 1975: 250–55; Chevallier, 1991; Beaujeu, 1982).

In the passage that follows, the 'curator' of the public works is accused of not being particularly trustworthy and of having misused his office for stealing works of art and precious offerings.

SUETONIUS, *THE LIVES OF THE CAESARS*, VITELLIUS, 5[1]

V. Having in this way through the favour of three emperors been honoured not only with political positions but with distinguished priesthoods as well, he afterwards governed Africa as proconsul and served as curator of public works (*curamque operum publicorum*), but with varying purpose and reputation. In his province he showed exceptional integrity for two successive years, for he served as deputy to his brother, who succeeded him; but in his city offices he was said to have stolen some of the offerings and ornaments from the temples and changed others, substituting tin and brass for gold and silver.

Source

Rolfe, J.C., 1914, in 2 volumes, *The Lives of the Caesars*, Vol. 2, Loeb Classical Library, London and New York, Heinemann and MacMillan: 255

Notes

1   Vitellius was one of the three emperors of the chaotic (for Roman politics) year of AD 69. The other two were Galba and Otho.

References

Beaujeu, 1982
Chevallier, 1991
Strong, 1975

47

Women collectors: extravagance, folly and fetishism, as Martial shows

Roman authors present women's relation to material culture as structured around the traditional female stereotypes. According to these, women can be associated with the domestic environment, the female domain and the adornments of the house, or religious practices and the objects that are used for these.

The second stereotype that associates women with material culture, is the one that refers to objects of personal adornment. Material acquisitions of this category, mainly jewellery, offer the model of the woman as a frivolous, vain, time-wasting person, unconcerned with the civil life, who instead presents a danger to society, since personal adornment of this sort aims at men's seduction, and the making of biased decisions.

The use of both these stereotypes implies an unnatural and irrational relation to material culture, and thus aims to alert the male readers of the dangers involved in such behaviour. Women are expected to be more passionate and irrational when it comes to acquiring personal property, and therefore, passionate collecting can be related to behaviour appropriate for women.

It follows that, just as the wrong sort of attention to his appearance is considered to undermine man's status as a male and exposes him to the charges of effeminacy (Wyke, 1994), so does interest in 'things female'. In this sense, collections that belong to the household, silverware, statuettes, furniture, and so on, along with objects that traditionally belong to the adornment of women, such as jewellery and rings, are meant to imply a man's unorthodox behaviour, that exceeds what is appropriately male, and thus puts at risk his male identity. Interest in them can therefore be considered a sign of effeminacy, and hence degeneracy.

Martial's eighth book appeared in December 94 AD, and is explicitly dedicated to Domitian (Sullivan, 1991: 40). Like his other books, this one consists of epigrams that share the professed aims of the satire. In other words, without aiming to address or denigrate specific persons, his aim was to castigate vice, ridicule wickedness and inanity, to satirise the social vices of Rome – extravagance, social climbing, legacy-hunting, pretentiousness, greed, stupidity and other human frailties – but also to entertain.

Epigram VIII.81 refers to a woman collector, Gellia, and her passionate relationship to her pearls. She appreciates them more than anything, and they are above any sacred or familial relationship in her hierarchy. Thus Martial wishes for Annaeus Serenus to have been employed; we do not know who this man was, whether a thief, as Shackleton-Bailey (1993) suggests, or some notorious wearer of pearls (Ker, 1919). In any case, Martial's wish is for him to remove Gellia's pearls so that 'she would not live an hour' away from her ridiculous – according to Martial – passion.

The same misogynistic attitude is exemplified in other epigrams as well, see for instance epigrams 7.13 and 1.102. Martial's argument is that women cannot possess precious objects, since they lack the essential property in order to appreciate them, namely rationality.

MARTIAL, *EPIGRAMS*, VIII. 81

Gellia does not swear by the mystic rites of Dindymene, nor by the bull of Nile's heifer,[1] nor in fine by any god or goddesses, but by her pearls. These she embraces, these she covers with kisses, these she calls her brothers, these she calls her sisters, these she loves more passionately than her two children.[2] If the poor thing were by some mischance to lose them, she says she would not live an hour. Ah, Papirianus, how well the hand of Annaeus Serenus might now be employed![3]

Source

Shackleton Bailey, D.R., 1993, *Martial Epigrams*, Cambridge, Mass., Harvard University Press, Vol. 2, Loeb Classical Library: 231

Notes

1 Apis, the sacred Egyptian bull, representing Osiris, the husband of Isis, who was represented as a heifer: cf. ii.xiv.8.
2 The passionate element in the relationship with material culture is often emphasised in the writing of ancient authors. The vocabulary is that of an erotic relationship, and it is exactly this point that the writers aim to reveal. Passionate relationships with material possessions, fetishistic relationships, aim only to provoke the disapproval of the audience, and reveal a personality that is far from sane and respectable.
3 An obscure allusion. Perhaps Serenus was notoriously a wearer of pearls.

Some commentators take him for a noted thief. But Martial would then hardly have mentioned his name.

References

Coffey, 1989
Howell, 1980
Ker, 1919
Sullivan, 1991

Part IV
Early Medieval Voices

48

The author of *The Ruin* describes life and wealth

Among the donations Leofric, Bishop of Exeter, made to his cathedral library about AD 1060 was a book of Anglo-Saxon poems, described as '*i mycel englisc boc*', 'the big English book'. This is the Exeter Book, most important of the four surviving books on Old English poetry: it is still in the Cathedral Library at Exeter. One of the poems written in the book is that known as *The Ruin*, perhaps originally composed around AD 700. The poem describes a ruined stone-built Roman settlement, almost certainly Bath, given the mention of hot springs.

The poet imagines life in the Roman buildings to have been like life in contemporary and recent royal halls (either in fact or in imagination). It is clear that gazing on wrought gemstones and on hoarded gold is among the highest of earthly pleasures.

EXTRACT FROM *THE RUIN*

Bright were the buildings, halls where springs ran,
high, horngabled, much throng-noise;
these many meadhalls men filled
with loud cheerfulness: Wierd[1] changed that.

Came days of pestilence, on all sides men fell dead,
death fetched off the flower of the people;
where they stood to fight, waste places
and on the acropolis, ruins.
         Hosts who would build again
shrank to the earth. Therefore are these courts dreary
and that red arch twisteth tiles,
wyryeth from roof-ridge, reacheth groundwards …
Broken blocks …

         There once many a man
mood-glad, gold-bright, of gleams garnished,
flushed with wine-pride, flashing war-gear,

gazed on wrought gemstones, on gold, on silver,
on wealth held and hoarded, on light-filled amber,
on this bright burg of broad dominion.

Stood stone houses; wide streams welled
hot from source, and a wall all caught
in its bright bosom, that the baths were
hot at hall's hearth; that was fitting ...

Thence hot streams, loosed, ran over hoar stone
unto the ring-tank ...
... It is a kingly thing
... city ...

Source

Alexander, M., 1966, *The Earliest English Poems*, London, Penguin Books: 29–31

Notes

1   'Wierd' is 'Fate'. The word survives in modern English as 'weird', that is, strange and fateful.

References

Chadwick and Chadwick, 1932–40
Ker, 1957

49

Notions about treasure in *Beowulf*

Three key passages from *Beowulf* are given here, describing the gifts given to Beowulf by Hrothgar after he had mortally wounded the monster Grendel, Beowulf's fight with the dragon and capture of its treasure hoard, and Beowulf's burial. *Beowulf* was composed in England, probably in the eighth century AD, but, like all such early Germanic verse, draws on much earlier stories and themes. The royal hall of Hrothgar, King of the Danes, has been troubled by the monster Grendel. The young Beowulf sails from Sweden to Denmark, waits for Grendel and mortally wounds him by tearing off his arm, and Hrothgar rewards Beowulf with rich gifts. Much later, Beowulf has been King of the Geats (in southern Sweden) for many years when a dragon whose ancient treasure has been looted, ravages the country. Beowulf and his younger kinsman Wiglaf fight and kill the dragon and gain his treasure hoard, but Beowulf is mortally wounded and dies in Wiglaf's arms. The Geats build a funeral pyre for Beowulf's body and build a mound over the remains in which the dragon's treasure is also placed.

The motif of the treasure hidden in darkness and guarded by an other-worldly being, together with that of the power of individual objects, runs through early Germanic literature. Similarly, the idea of the treasure buried in the death mound recurs, and its actual, as opposed to literary, expression appears in the rich burial at Sutton Hoo, which was deposited around AD 600. Treasure hoards are accumulated and dispersed through the twin activities of warfare and plunder, and gift giving which rewards followers, binds their loyalty, and increases a king's war-band.

BEOWULF IS REWARDED FOR KILLING GRENDEL

The goblet was brought to him [Beowulf][1] with a friendly invitation to drink, and he was made a generous present of golden metal-work – two armlets, rings, a shirt of mail, and the finest golden collar in the world. They say that nowhere, in any treasury, has there been a richer jewel since Hama carried off to his glittering stronghold the Brosings' necklet[2] together with its precious setting. [Hama fled from Eormenric's hot pursuit and died.] The great Hygelac of the house of Swerting, later took this collar with him on his final expedition, when he had to make a last stand to defend his treasury and booty. He met with his end because he went recklessly in search of trouble, and began a feud with the Frisians. So the great prince, after carrying the treasure and jewels overseas, died shield in hand. Hygelac's body, his armour and the golden collar as well, fell into the hands of the Franks. For when the slaughter was over lesser men looted the dead Geats whose bodies covered the battlefield.

THE DRAGON'S TREASURE

The great kingdom of the Geats came into the hands of Beowulf. He ruled it well for half a century. But when he was an aged and veteran king, a certain Dragon began to exert its power in the darkness of night. In its upland lair it kept guard over a treasure in a huge funeral barrow, under which ran a secret passage. Some man wandering near that pagan hoard found his way in and stole a great jewelled cup. The Dragon, tricked by a thief's cunning while it slept, made its loss known; and the neighbourhood soon discovered how enraged it was.

The man who so provoked the Worm did not violate its treasure wilfully or on purpose, but through sheer necessity. He was a slave belonging to somebody or other, and was running away from a beating. This guilty fellow, being in need of shelter, had forced his way in. Stark terror took hold of the intruder the moment he entered, but nevertheless the fugitive, when the sudden peril came upon him, escaped from the Worm and took to his heels with a jewelled cup.

Many such ancient treasures lay in the tumulus, where in times gone by an unknown man had carefully hidden the immense ancestral wealth of some great race. All had long been dead; and the chieftain who survived them, disconsolate at the loss of his kinsmen, supposed that, like them, he would possess their slowly gathered wealth for a short time only. Ready to hand upon a cliff near the sea stood a newly completed barrow, which had been fortified to make it impregnable. Into this the guardian of the hoard had carried rings and beaten gold, the richest part of the treasure. He said:

'Earth, hold what men could not, the wealth of princes. For heroes won it from you long ago. The holocaust of battle has claimed every mortal soul of my race who shared the delights of the banqueting hall. I have none to wield the sword, none to polish the jewelled cup. Gone are the brave. The tough helmet, overlaid with gold, must be stripped of its golden plates. They sleep who should burnish the casques. Armour that stood up to the battering of swords in conflict, among the thunder of the shields, moulders away like the soldier. Nor shall the corselet travel hither and yon on the back of a hero by the side of fighting-men. There is no sweet sound from the harp, no delight of music, no good hawk swooping through the hall, no swift horse stamping in the castle yard. Death has swept away nearly everything that lives.'

In this fashion the one survivor sadly lamented, wandering mournfully about night and day, till death touched his heart.

The treasure in the open barrow was found by the primeval enemy that haunts the dusk; the scaly malicious Worm which seeks out funeral mounds and flies burning through the night, wrapped about with flame, to the terror of the country folk. Its habit is to seek out treasure hidden in the earth and mount guard over the pagan gold, but, though ancient in years, it will profit nothing thereby.

BEOWULF IS BURIED

Then, Wiglaf[3] gave orders to the soldiers, householders, and chieftains, to fetch timber for the hero's pyre.

'Now let black flames shoot up and fire swallow this prince of fighting-men, who so often faced a rain of steel, when sped by bowstrings a gale of arrows hurtled over sheltering shields, and the feather-flighted shaft did its work, driving home the barb.'

Wiglaf next summoned seven of the king's best men from the host, and with them entered the unfriendly vault. The leading man carried a burning torch in his hand. When the troops saw the bulk of the treasure lying mouldering and unguarded in the vault, no lots needed to be drawn as to who should loot the hoard; no one had the least scruple over pillaging the valuables as quickly as possible. They heaved the Worm over the cliff as well, and let the waves bear away and the sea cover the guardian of the treasure. A quite incalculable amount of twisted gold was loaded upon a wagon;[4] and the old king was carried up to Hronesness.

The people of the Geats prepared for Beowulf, as he had asked of them, a splendid pyre hung about with helmets, shields, and shining corselets. Then, mourning, the soldiers laid their loved and illustrious prince in the midst. Upon the hill the men-at-arms lit a gigantic funeral fire. Black wood-smoke whirled over the conflagration; the roar of flames mixed with the noise of weeping, until the furious draught subsided and the white-hot body crumbled to pieces. Sadly they complained of their grief and of the death of their king. A Geat woman with braided hair keened a dirge in Beowulf's memory, repeating again and again that she feared bad times were on the way, with bloodshed, terror, captivity, and shame.[5] Heaven swallowed up the smoke.

Upon the headland the Geats erected a broad, high tumulus, plainly visible to distant seaman. In ten days they completed the building of the hero's beacon. Round his ashes they built the finest vault that their most skillful men could devise. Within the barrow they placed collars, brooches, and all the trappings which they had plundered from the treasure-hoard. They buried the gold and left the princely treasure to the keeping of earth, where it yet remains, as useless to men as it was before.

Then twelve chieftains, all sons of princes, rode round the barrow lamenting their loss, speaking of their king, reciting an elegy, and acclaiming the hero. They praised his manhood and extolled his heroic deeds. It is right that men should pay homage to their king with words, and cherish him in their hearts, when he has taken leave of the body. So the Geats who had shared his hall mourned the death of their lord, and said that of all kings he was the gentlest and most gracious of men, the kindest of his people and the most desirous of renown.

Source

Wright, D., 1994, *Beowulf*, London, Penguin Books: 55, 79–80, 100–101

Notes

1   A few pages before this excerpt, a poet has composed a new poem in honour of Beowulf in which his exploit with Grendel is compared with the story of Sigemund, the father of Sigurd, here said to be the hero of the dragon slaying and treasure gaining story.
2   In Old Norse legend, a tribe called the Brisings, who may be meant here, made a magic necklace for the goddess Freyja. Eormenric was king of the Ostrogoths. Hygelac was Beowulf's uncle and King of the Geats.
3   Wiglaf is the son of Weohstan, kinsman of Beowulf, said elsewhere in the poem to be a Swedish prince.
4   The poem means that Wiglaf and the men entered the barrow which had been the lair of the dragon until it was killed by Beowulf; they threw the dragon's body over the cliff and took away the treasure it had guarded.
5   The identity of this Geat woman has been much – but not very profitably – debated.

References

Carver, 1998
Hines, 1989
Newton, 1993

50

The story of the Volsung Treasure

The history of the great Volsung Treasure and of the fates of those involved with it is the Germanic equivalent of the Greek story of the Trojan War and, as the accounts of the Trojan War look back to the local Bronze Age (however difficult it may be to establish the detail of how they do so), so the Germanic story looks back to the Age of Migration, roughly 350–600 AD, when Germanic-speaking groups were moving across the Rhine and settling within the old Roman empire (a process equally open to various interpretations). During this time, practices with a long history in northern Europe, notably rich burials of which that at Sutton Hoo, Suffolk, is the best known, reappear, and they are part of the psychological world of the stories represented here.

The stories belong to two main traditions, that of the North in Scandinavia and Iceland, and that of southern Germany. Although the course of the main story is similar, the casts of characters have different names. The northern hero is Sigurd, the leading female Brynhild, her rival Gudrun who marries first Sigurd and then Atli the Hun (historically Attila), and Atli's enemies are Gunnar and Hogni, Gudrun's brothers. In brief, Sigurd wins a great treasure called Andvari's Hoard by killing the dragon Fafnir who guards it, but the gold is accursed. Sigurd marries Gudrun but a quarrel between her and Brynhild leads to Sigurd's death through the plotting of Gunnar and Hogni, and so the working-out of the curse. Atli, jealous of Gunnar and Hogni who now possess the gold, summons them to his court; they go, though full of foreboding, and are captured in the ensuing fight. Gunnar taunts Atli into cutting out his brother's heart, and then dies himself rather than reveal to Atli the hiding-place of the gold, now sunk in the Rhine; Gunnar dies in a snake-pit, playing his harp until the adder poison reaches his heart.

The story seems to have been told originally in a loosely linked group of lays. Versions of these are incorporated in the poetic collection known as the *Elder Edda* which may have taken shape in tenth- to twelfth-century Iceland, where the only manuscript of the collection reappeared in the seventeenth century. The *Elder Edda* contains the lay known as the *Lay of Atli*, which tells a version of the story. Sometime around 1250 an unknown author in Iceland wrote the *Volsunga Saga*, a prose version of the Eddic lays which connects them into a single story and adds material from sources now lost to us.

The pieces from the Volsunga Saga are here taken from the version made by William Morris. In 1868 Morris became acquainted with the Icelander Eirikr Magnusson and with him studied the language and travelled in Iceland: the two collaborated on *Volsunga Saga* which appeared in 1870. For Morris, it was an immensely significant aspect of the renewal of medieval ideals, to which he devoted his life.

FROM THE *VOLSUNGA SAGA* BY WILLIAM MORRIS

Now yet again spake Regin to Sigurd, and said –

'Not enough is thy wealth, and I grieve right sore that thou must needs run here and there like a churl's son; but I can tell thee where there is much wealth for the winning, and great name and honour to be won in the getting of it.'

Sigurd asked where that might be, and who had watch and ward over it.

Regin answered, 'Fafnir is his name, and but a little way hence he lies, on the waste of Gnita-heath; and when thou comest there thou mayst well say that thou hast never seen more gold heaped together in one place, and that none might desire more treasure, though he were the most ancient and famed of all kings.'

'Young am I,' says Sigurd, 'yet know I the fashion of this worm,[1] and how that none durst go against him, so huge and evil is he.'

Regin said, 'Nay it is not so, the fashion and the growth of him is even as of other lingworms, and an over great tale men make of it; and even so would thy forefathers have deemed; but thou, though thou be of the kin of the Volsungs, shalt scarce have the heart and mind of those, who are told of as the first in all deeds of fame.'

Sigurd said, 'Yea, belike I have little of their hardihood and prowess, but thou has naught to do, to lay a coward's name upon me, when I am scarce out of my childish years. Why dost thou egg me on hereto so busily?'

Regin said, 'Therein lies a tale which I must needs tell thee.'

'Let me hear the same,' said Sigurd ...

[The story follows:]

'Loki took a stone and cast it at Otter, so that he gat his death thereby; the gods were well content with their prey, and fell to flaying off the otter's skin; and in the evening they came to Hreidmar's house, and showed him what they had taken: thereon he laid hands on them, and doomed them to such ransom, as that they should fill the otter skin with gold, and cover it without with red gold; so they sent Loki to gather gold together for them; he came to Ran, and got her net, and went therewith to Andvari's force,[2] and cast the net before the pike, and the pike ran into the net and was taken. Then said Loki –

> "What fish of all fishes,
> Swims strong in the flood,
> But hath learnt little wit to beware?
> Thine head must thou buy,
> From abiding in hell,
> And find me the wan waters flame."

'He answered –

> "Andvari folk call me,
> Call Odin my father,
> Over many a force have I fared;
> For a Norn of ill-luck,
> This life on me lay
> Through wet ways ever to wade."

… So Loki beheld the gold of Andvari, and when he had given up the gold, he had but one ring left, and that also Loki took from him; then the dwarf went into a hollow of the rocks, and cried out, that the gold-ring, yea and all the gold withal, should be the bane of every man who should own it thereafter.

'Now the gods rode with the treasure to Hreidmar, and ful-filled the otter skin, and set it on its feet, and they must cover it over utterly with gold: but when this was done then Hreidmar came forth, and beheld yet one of the muzzle hairs, and bade them cover that withal; then Odin drew the ring, Andvari's loom, from his hand, and covered up the hair therewith; then said Loki –

> "Gold enow, gold enow,
> A great weregild, thou hast,
> That my head in good hap I may hold;
> But thou and thy son
> Are naught fated to thrive,
> The bane shall it be of you both."

'Thereafter', says Regin, 'Fafnir slew his father and murdered him, nor got I aught of the treasure, and so evil he grew, that he fell to lying abroad, and begrudged any share in the wealth to any man, and so became the worst of all worms, and ever now lies brooding upon that treasure: but for me, I went to the king and became his master-smith; and thus is the tale told of how I lost the heritage of my father, and the weregild for my brother.'

So spake Regin; but since that time gold is called Ottergild, and for no other cause that this.

But Sigurd answered, 'Much hast thou lost, and exceeding evil have thy kinsmen been! But now, make a sword by thy craft, such a sword as that none can be made like unto it; so that I may do great deeds therewith, if my heart avail thereto, and thou wouldst have me slay this mighty dragon.'

Regin says, 'Trust me well herein; and with that same sword shalt thou slay Fafnir.' ...

Now falls Atli to thinking of where may be gotten that plenteous gold which Sigurd had owned, but King Gunnar and his brethen were lords thereof now.

Atli was a great king and mighty, wise, and a lord of many men; and now he falls to counsel with his folk as to the ways of them. He wotted well that Gunnar and his brethren had more wealth than any others might have; and so he falls to the rede of sending men to them, and bidding them to a great feast, and honouring them in diverse wise, and the chief of those messengers was high Vingi.

Now the queen wots of their conspiring, and misdoubts her that this would means some beguiling of her brethren; so she cut runes, and took a gold ring, and knit therein a wolf's hair, and gave it into the hands of the king's messengers.

Thereafter they go their ways according to the king's bidding; and or ever they came aland Vingi[3] beheld the runes, and turned them about in such a wise as if Gudrun prayed her brethren in her runes to go meet King Atli.

Thereafter they came to the hall of King Gunnar, and had good welcome at his hands, and great fires were made for them, and in great joyance they drank of the best of drink.

Then spake Vingi, 'King Atli sends me hither, and is fain that ye go to his house and home in all glory, and take of him exceeding honours, helms and shields, swords and byrnies, gold and goodly raiment, horses, hosts of war, and great and wide lands, for, saith he, he is fainest of all things to bestow his realm and lordship upon you.' Then Gunnar turned his head aside, and spoke to Hogni – 'In what wise shall we take this bidding? Might and wealth he bids us take; but no kings know I who have so much gold as we have, whereas we have all the hoard which lay once on Gnita-heath; and great are our chambers, and full of gold, and weapons for smiting, and all kinds of raiment of war, and well I wot that amidst all men my horse is the best, and my sword the sharpest, and my gold the most glorious.'

Hogni answers, 'A marvel is it to me of his bidding, for seldom hath he done in such a wise, and ill-counselled will it be to wend to him.' ...

Then spake King Atli with Gunnar the king, and bade him tell out concerning the gold, and where it was, if he would have his life.

But he answered, 'Nay, first will I behold the bloody heart of Hogni, my brother.'

So now they caught hold of the thrall again, and cut the heart from out of him, and bore it unto King Gunnar, but he said –

'The faint heart of Hjalli may ye here behold, little like the proud heart of Hogni, for as much as it trembleth now, more by the half it trembled whenas it lay in the breast of him.'

So now they fell on Hogni even as Atli urged them, and cut the heart from out of him, but such was the might of his manhood, that he laughed while he abode that torment, and all wondered at his worth, and in perpetual memory is it held sithence.

Then they showed it to Gunnar, and he said –

'The mighty heart of Hogni, little like the faint heart of Hjalli, for little as it trembleth now, less it trembled whenas in his breast it lay! But now, O Atli, even as we die so shalt thou die; and lo, I alone wot where the gold is, nor shall Hogni be to tell thereof now; to and fro played the matter in my mind whiles we both lived, but now have I myself determined for myself, and the Rhine river shall rule over the gold, rather than that the Huns shall bear it on the hands of them.'

Then said King Atli,' Have away the bondsman,' and so they did.

But Gudrun called to her men, and came to Atli, and said –

'May it fare ill with thee now and from henceforth, even as thou hast ill held to thy word with me!'

So Gunnar was cast into a worm-close, and many worms abode him there, and his hands were fast bound; but Gudrun sent him a harp, and in such wise did he set forth his craft, that wisely he smote the harp, smiting it with his toes, and so excellently well he played, that few deemed that they heard such playing, even when the hand had done it. And with such might and power he played, that all the worms fell asleep in the end, save one adder only, great and evil of aspect, that crept unto him and thrust its sting into him until it smote his heart; and in such wise with great hardihood he ended his life days.

Source

Morris, W. (trans.), 1963, *Volsunga Saga: the Story of the Volsungs and Niblungs*, New York, Collier Books: 126–219

Notes

1 'Worm' is a version of the Old Norse 'orm' meaning snake, serpent or dragon.
2 Loki is the Norse trickster god, Ran is a sea-goddess, Fafnir and Otter are Regin's brothers, and Andvari is a dwarf. Fafnir's evil deeds turn him into a worm.
3 In the saga, Ginki (or Vinki) rules south of the Rhine. He is the father of Gunnar, Hogni and Guttorm, and daughter Gudrun. His wife is Grimhild.

References

Ker, 1957
Todd, 1992
Vestergaard, 1987

51

The magical power of the cursed sword Tyrfing

This piece comes from the same Northern world as *Beowulf* and the *Volsunga Saga*, and is involved in the mass of confused tradition surrounding Attila the Hun and his campaigns against the Germanic kingdoms in the early fifth century AD. The poem known as *The Waking of Angantyr*, from which these excerpts are taken, was incorporated in the *Saga of King Heidrek the Wise* composed in Iceland probably in the twelfth century. The date of the poem is uncertain.

Two men called Angantyr seem to have been confused. The earlier seems to have been a king of the Goths at the time before Attila's campaigns when the Goths had reached and settled in the Carpathian mountains near the Danube. The later (how much later is unclear) was a berserk fighter killed in a famous fight on the island of Samsey (now called Samsø, between Jutland and Zealand), and there buried with others in a great burial mound in a cemetery of similar barrows.

In the poem Angantyr's sword is Tyrfing, forged by dwarfs, desirable for its power and beauty but carrying a curse which means that it brings ruin to its possessors. The sword's name has attracted much commentary, and it may reflect the name *Tervingi* used by Roman writers for the Visigoths, one of the two branches into which the Goths were divided, east and west of the Dnieper.

The poem is important for its emotional intensity. The grim dead lie lifeless but sometimes wakeful in their burial mounds while the barrow fires burn round them. Both Angantyr and Hervor his daughter desire Tyrfing, although both know that it is cursed.

ANGANTYR'S SWORD

Then she spoke:

Wake, Angantýr,
wakes you Hervör,
Sváfa's offspring,
your only daughter;

175

the keen-edged blade
from the barrow give me,
the sword dwarf-smithied
for Sigrlami ...

Then Angantýr answered her:

Why do you hail me,
Hervör, daughter?
To your doom you are faring
filled with evil!
Mad you are now,
your mind darkened,
when with wits wandering
you wake the dead.

No father or kinsman
in cairn laid me;
they kept Tyrfing,
the two survivors –
one alone did
wield it after.

Hervör answered:
You give me a lie!
May the god let you
rest whole in your howe
if you're holding not
Tyrfing with you;
unwilling you are
to give the heirloom
to your only child.

Then the barrow opened, and it was as if the whole mound were in flame.
Angantýr spoke again:

Hell's gate is lifted
howes are opening
the isle's border
ablaze before you;
grim outside now
to gaze around you –
to you ships, if you can,

quick now, maiden!

She answered:

> No blaze can you light,
> burning in darkness,
> that your funeral fires
> should with fear daunt me;
> unmoved shall remain
> the maiden's spirit,
> though she gaze on a ghost
> in the grave-door standing.

Then Angantýr said:

> I tell you, Hervör –
> hear my words out! –
> what shall come to pass,
> prince's daughter:
> trust what I tell you,
> Tyrfing, daughter,
> shall be ruin and end
> of all your family.

> You shall bear offspring
> who in after days
> shall wield Tyrfing
> and trust in his strength;
> by the name Heidrek
> known to his people,
> born the strongest
> beneath the sun's curtain.[1]

Then Hervör said:

> I will guard it
> and grasp it in hand,
> the keen-edged sword,
> can I but obtain it;
> no fear have I
> of the fire burning;
> the flame grows less
> as I look towards it.

Angantýr answered:

> Fool you are, Hervör,
> in your heart's daring,
> with eyes open
> to enter the fire!
> The blade from the barrow
> I will bring, rather;
> O young maiden
> I may not refuse you.

Hervör answered:

> Son of warriors,
> you do well in this,
> the blade to me
> from the barrow yielding;
> king, to keep it
> I count it dearer
> than were all Norway
> beneath my hand.

Angantýr spoke:

> You see it not –
> you're in speech accursed,
> woman of evil! –
> why you're rejoicing;
> trust what I tell you,
> Tyrfing, daughter,
> shall be ruin and end,
> of all your family.

Hervör spoke:

> I will go my way
> to the wave-horses,[2]
> chieftain's daughter
> cheerful-hearted;
> I care not at all
> O kings' companion,
> how my sons shall
> strive hereafter.

Angantýr spoke:

> You shall keep Tyrfing
> with contentment long;
> the bane of Hjálmar
> in hiding keep;
> touch not the edges –
> in each is poison;
> worse than deadly,
> doom-bringer to men.

And now Hervör said:

> May you all lie unharmed
> in the howe resting –
> to hasten hence
> my heart urges;
> I seem to myself
> to be set between worlds,
> when all about me
> burnt the cairn-fires.

Source

Tolkien, C., 1960, *The Saga of King Heidrek the Wise*, Nelson and Sons, London: 14–19

Notes

1 'Sun's curtain' means that which frames the sun, that is, the sky.
2 'Wave-horse' is a ship, which rides the waves.

References

Todd, 1992
Wulfram, 1988

52

Wealth in early Welsh imagination and society

An interest in wealth and its accumulation, parallel to that in the Germanic-speaking world, appears equally in the Britonic (roughly early Welsh) literature, first written down in the eight, ninth or tenth centuries AD. This literature gathers in traditions current in a wide arc of western Britain, from southern Scotland, through Cumbria and Wales, to Cornwall and the south-west. Its themes are, like the Germanic literature, heroic, but it shows a strong, perhaps a stronger or at any rate a differently toned, interest in the Other World.

The details, or even the broad outlines, of the process have been much disputed for many years, but there is general agreement that, somehow, this early Welsh literature is bound up with the development of the Arthurian Cycle. A great mass of Arthurian literary material was produced in medieval Europe from about 1100 AD, has been produced ever since and continues to be so today. Throughout this long period, it has continued to show interest in the symbolic quality of special objects and groups of objects, in heroic conduct, and in the interface between this world and the Other World; and these themes are the major part of its appeal.

The piece chosen here comes from *The Dream of Macsen Wledig* which is itself one of the romances grouped together as *The Mabinogion*. It is not specifically an Arthurian story, as others in *The Mabinogion* are, but it involves characters like Mascen Wledig, and Cynan and Gadeon, the sons of Eudaf, who were players in the early development of the Arthurian stories. More importantly, the land which Macsen visits in his dream is both an idealised version of Britain where, in the story, Macsen eventually finds his bride, and a typical expression of an other-world castle of the kind that appears often later in the medieval stories with Arthurian connections.

The composition date of *The Mabinogion* as we have it (the name probably means 'the stories of young men') may be the twelfth century AD, but the stories it contains draw on a range of material, earlier but difficult to date. Many motifs are not specifically 'Welsh' but belong to the general stock of folk tale.

180

FROM *THE DREAM OF MACSEN WLEDIG*

And amidst the fleet he [i.e. Macsen Wledig][1] saw a ship; and bigger was that by far and fairer than all the others. And what he might see of the ship above water, one plank he saw of gold, and the next of silver. He saw a bridge of walrus-ivory from the ship to the land, and he thought how he came along the bridge on to the ship. A sail was hoisted on the ship, and away she went over sea and ocean. He saw how he came to an island, the fairest in the whole world, and after he had traversed the island from sea to answering sea, even to the uttermost bound of the island, he could see valleys and steeps and towering rocks, and a harsh rugged terrain whose like he had never seen. And from there he saw in the sea, facing that rugged land, an island. And between him and that island he saw a country whose plain was the length of its sea, its mountain the length of its woodland. And from that mountain he saw a river flow through the land, making towards the sea. And at the river mouth he could see a great castle, the fairest that mortal had ever seen, and the gate of the castle he saw open, and he came to the castle. Inside the castle he saw a fair hall. The roof of the hall he thought to be all of gold; the side of the hall he thought to be of glittering stones, each as costly as its neighbour; the hall doors he thought to be all gold. Golden couches he saw in the hall, and tables of silver. And on the couch facing him he could see two auburn-haired youths playing at gwyddbwyll.[2] A silver board he saw for the gwyddbwyll, and golden pieces thereon. The garments of the youths[3] were of pure black brocaded silk, and frontlets of red gold holding their hair in place, and sparkling jewels of great price therein, rubies and gems alternately therein, and imperial stones. Buskins of new cordwain were on their feet, and bars of red gold to fasten them.

And at the foot of the hall-pillar he saw a hoary-headed man seated in a chair of ivory, with the images of two eagles in red gold thereon. Armlets of gold were upon his arms, and many gold rings on his hands; and a golden torque about his neck; and a golden frontlet holding his hair in place; and his presence august. A board of gold and gwyddbwyll was before him, and in his hand a rod of gold, and hard files. And he was carving men for gwyddbwyll.

And he saw a maiden[4] sitting before him in a chair of red gold. No more than it would be easy to look on the sun when it is brightest, no easier would it be than that to look on her by reason of her excelling beauty. Vests of white silk were upon the maiden, with claps of red gold at the breast; and a surcoat of gold brocaded silk upon her, and a mantle like to it, and brooch of red gold holding it about her; and a frontlet of red gold on her head, with rubies and gems on the frontlet, and pearls alternatively, and imperial stones; and a girdle of red gold around her; and the fairest sight to see of mortal kind.

And the maiden arose to meet him from the chair of gold, and he threw his arms around the maiden's neck; and they both sat down in the chair of gold. And the chair was not straiter for them both than for the maiden alone.

And when he had his arms around the maiden's neck, and his cheek against her cheek, what with the dogs straining at their leashes, and the shoulders of the shields coming against each other, and the spear shafts striking together, and the neighing and the stamping of the horses, the emperor awoke. And when he awoke neither life nor existence nor being was left him, for the maiden he had seen in his sleep.

Source

Jones, G. and Jones, M., 1963 (ed. and trans.), *The Mabinogion*, London, Dent: 80–81

Notes

1 Macsen Wledig, which translates roughly as Prince (or Ruler) Magnus, was an historical character, the Spanish-born Magnus Maximus who rose to high military command in the late Roman army in Britain. In 383 he was proclaimed emperor and invaded Gaul, but in 388, after a defeat in north Italy at the hands of the reigning Emperor Theodosius, he was executed.
2 'Gwyddbwyll' is a board game of the 'hunt' type (rather than, like chess, of the 'battle' type). A king piece, at the centre of the board, tries to break through to the safe edge, while a 'hunting party' tries to pen and capture him.
3 Later, the young men turn out to be Cynan and Gadeon, and the older man their father, Eudaf son of Caradawg. All these figures have complicated roles in the broad mass of British and Arthurian literature.
4 The maiden turns out to be Elen, or Helen, probably originally a separate character in Welsh mythology, who seems to have been specially associated with Roman roads. She became early confused with St Helena, the mother of the Emperor Constantine the Great, who was believed to have discovered the True Cross in Jerusalem.

References

Bromwich, 1978
Gantz, 1976
Loomis, 1959

53

The statues on show in the late Roman and Byzantine city of Constantinople

When Constantine the Great created his new capital on the Bosphorus, he moved to it a large range of statues from the neighbouring parts of the empire; many of these were famous pieces by well-known earlier sculptors and from important sites. Successive emperors continued Constantine's policy. The number of statues was originally considerable – several hundred – and although many were destroyed between 400 and 1200, an impressive collection remained in 1204.

Throughout the medieval period, Constantinople was seen as a fabulous place by those living in the west, with its splendid churches, palaces and gardens, its relic collection, and its public places of which these statues were a part. Knowledge of them encouraged a continuing interest in classical matters and collections.

In addition to the open-air public statuary, Constantinople also had private or quasi-private collections. One of the most important of these seems to have belonged to Lausus, an imperial chamberlain, who probably died sometime after 436. Lausus apparently had an impressive palace near the Hippodrome where was assembled a major collection of pagan statues. Two chroniclers, Georgius Cedrenus writing about 1080 and Joannes Zonaras writing about 1130, give some details of what Lausus' collection held; there are some difficulties with their accounts but they do draw on earlier material.

Lausus was known as a devout Christian, which makes his collection of pagan art the more interesting. The statues seem to have been arranged deliberately in the long hall of the palace, with the great statue of Zeus fitting into an apse at the far end and dominating the scene. The youthful figures of Eros and Kairos (Chance) may have been either side, with the goddess figures along one wall and the animal figures on the opposite one. All this was probably meant to have an allegorical significance showing the triumph of Virtue over Eros and Chance. The statues seem to have been lost in a disastrous fire in AD 475.

ANTIQUE STATUARY AND THE BYZANTINE BEHOLDER

The deliberate assembling of ancient statues in Constantinople constitutes something of a paradox. We must not forget that paganism was very
much of a live issue, not only in the fourth century, but until about the
year 600. Statues of pagan divinities were, of course, an essential part in
the celebration of pagan rites. The lives of the saints are full of reference
to the destruction of pagan statues...

Granted this attitude, how are we to explain the fact that the first
Christian Emperor[1] used statues of pagan divinities to decorate Constantinople? How was it also that these statues remained for the most part
unmolested for so many centuries?

It would be a mistake, I think, to suggest – as some modern scholars
have done – that these statues were used simply for decoration. The
answer is rather to be sought in the ambiguity of the religious policy
pursued by Constantine's government. Nor must we hold Constantine
himself responsible: the task of decorating the capital must have been
entrusted to subordinate officials – the *curatores* – who were probably
pagan, and they simply did the kind of job that was expected at the
time...

In addition to the Delphic tripods,[2] Constantine also erected in the
Hippodrome the statues of the Dioscuri, whose temple had stood on that
spot. On the agora of ancient Byzantium he went so far as to build a
temple to the Fortuna of Rome, and to restore another one, dedicated to
Cybele, the Mother of the Gods. The statue of Cybele was of venerable
antiquity: allegedly it had been made by Jason's companions. In the
Senate House Constantine erected statues of the Muses, taken from Mount
Helicon, and in front of it he set up on stone pedestals the statues of Zeus
of Dodona and Athene of Lindos.[3] The Muses perished in the great
conflagration of 404, caused by the followers of St. John Chrysostom,
but the gods were unexpectedly preserved: a pagan miracle that gave
comfort to the 'more cultivated' ... persons dwelling in the city, as
Zosimus tells us.[4] Then, most important, there was a great bronze statue
representing Apollo/Helios which Constantine set up in 328 as his own
effigy on top of the porphyry column of the Forum; it wore a radiate
crown, held a spear in its right hand and a globe in its left. Tradition
affirmed that it had been brought from Phrygia.[5]

A great collection of statues were also assembled in the baths of
Zeuxippus: these are known to us through a tedious poem by the Egyptian Christodorus, which forms Book II of the Palatine Anthology. In all,
eighty statues are described, all of them antique, and most, if not all, of
bronze. The greater number represented mythological heroes, but there
were also nine statues of gods, many of poets, orators, philosophers,

historians, and statesmen. Very few were of Roman origin: a Julius Caesar, a Pompey, an Apuleius, a Virgil, as well as a group of the pugilists Dares and Entellus borrowed from Book V of the Aeneid. The baths of Zeuxippus were burnt down in 532 and the statues must have perished at the same time. When, in 1928, part of the baths was excavated, two inscribed statue bases were found. They bore the names of Hecuba and Aeschines, both mentioned by Christodorus.

GEORGIUS CEDRENUS

Note that in the quarter of Lausus ... there used to be various buildings and certain hostels at the place where [the cistern of] Philoxenus provided its water, whence its name. There stood there also a statue of Lindian Athena, four cubits high, of emerald stone, the work of the sculptors Scylis and Dipoenus, which once upon a time Sesostris,[6] tyrant of Egypt, sent as a gift to Cleobulus, tyrant of Lindus. Likewise the Cnidian Aphrodite of white stone, naked, shielding with her hands only her pudenda, a work of Praxiteles of Cnidus.[7] Also the Samian Hera, a work of Lysippus and the Chian Bupalus; a winged Eros holding a bow, brought from Myndus,[8] the ivory Zeus by Phidias, whom Pericles dedicated at the temple of the Olympians;[9] the statue representing Chronos, a work of Lysippus, bald at the back and having hair in front; unicorns, tigresses, vultures, giraffes, an ox-elephant [buffalo?], Centaurs and Pans...

When he [Basiliscus] had been proclaimed there occured a conflagration in the City which destroyed its most flourishing part. For it started in the middle of the Chalkoprateia [Copper Market] and consumed both porticoes and everything adjacent to them and the so-called Basilica, wherein was contained a library that had 120,000 books. Among these books was a dragon's gut 120 ft. long upon which Homer's poems, namely the Iliad and the Odyssey, were written in gold letters together with the story [or the pictures ...] of the heroes' deeds. [The fire] also destroyed the porticoes on either side of the street Mese and the excellent offerings ... of Lausus: for many ancient statues were set up there, namely the famous one of the Aphrodite of Cnidus, that of the Samian Hera, that of Lindian Athena made of a different material which Amasis, King of Egypt, had sent to the wise Cleobulus, and countless others. The fire extended as far as the Forum of the great Constantine, as it is called.

Sources

Mango, C., 1963, 'Antique Statuary and the Byzantine Beholder', *Dumbarton Oaks Papers*, 17: 253–7

Bekker, I. (ed.), 1838, *Georgius Cedrenus*, Vol. 1, Bonn: 564, 616

Notes

1 The Emperor Constantine (288–337) was the first emperor to support Christianity. In 312, before a crucial battle outside Rome, he was reported as seeing in the sky a vision of the Cross and the words 'In this conquer'. After the victory he issued the Edict of Milan (313) which made Christianity a legal religion. He was baptised on his deathbed.
2 The Delphic tripods had belonged to the prophetic shrine at Delphi.
3 All these figures are of important mythological or legendary figures, somewhat at variance with the Christian city.
4 The statues brought in by Theodosius II included the four bronze horses from Chios, which he put in the Hippodrome; they are now on the façade of St Marks, Venice, having been taken there in the aftermath of the Fourth Crusade in 1204, when Western crusaders captured the city.
5 This Zeus was one of the most famous statues in the ancient world.
6 The pharaoh was Amasis (569–525 BC) not Sesostris. The second excerpt is correct.
7 Praxiteles was an Athenian not a Cnidian.
8 The Samian Hera was by Bupalus, while Lysippus made the Eros stringing his bow.
9 Pericles did not dedicate the Olympian Zeus. The Zeus was nearly 12.5m high, and showed the god seated. It stood originally in the temple of Zeus at Olympia.

References

Mango, Vickers and Francis, 1992

54

A late Roman treasure hoard buried near Thetford, Suffolk

The Thetford treasure was a rich example of an important group of over sixty hoards made up of gold objects, silver objects, silver plate and gold and/or silver coins which were buried, presumably deliberately, in late Roman Britain (and also in the north-western part of the Continent). There are also a number of known hoard finds comprising pewterware, which may be cheaper equivalents of the treasures. One of the most famous treasure hoards has been found fairly recently at Water Newton.

The character of these hoards, and the reasons for their burial, have been much debated. Some seem to be personal or family wealth hidden for security; some may be offerings at sacred sites; some seem to be the sacred vessels from temples, and others apparently have Christian connotations, whether personal or related to church organisation. It is, of course, possible that many have a mixed character and combine many of these motifs.

THE THETFORD TREASURE

In 1979, at Gallows Hill, Thetford, a rich hoard of late Roman gold jewellery and silver utensils was found. The conclusions of the scholars who subsequently published the Thetford Treasure have far-reaching ramifications for the identification of Christian objects in the Roman world. Hence it is essential that these conclusions be closely examined in the light of the available evidence. A reappraisal of the Treasure will, it is believed, reveal a Christian component in this predominantly pagan hoard.

The Treasure comprises eighty-one items: twenty-two gold finger rings, twenty-one other items of gold jewellery, one unmounted gem (these contained in a shale box with lid), plus thirty-three silver spoons and three silver strainers. Of the spoons, thirty-two were engraved with a mixture of pagan and what could in another context be considered Christian symbols or inscriptions. The pagan element related to the ancient Latin god Faunus, either by that name or given a Celtic epithet, such as *Dei Fau(ni) Medugeni:* of the god Faunus Medugenus ('the Mead Begotten'); the jewellery appears to have iconographical links with this deity.

The cult was of a Bacchic type popular in the fourth century, especially as a counter-influence to Christianity.

Summarizing their research, Johns and Potter see the spoons as part of the ritual plate of a sanctuary for the worship of Faunus. They regard the jewellery as a jeweller-merchant's stock and offer three possible solutions: that it comprised regalia specially commissioned for the cult; that the jeweller-merchant, a devotee of Faunus, incorporated some of his religious beliefs into his creations and kept his wealth in a (presumed) sanctuary or temple; or that, ignoring all iconographical references, the jewellery was but the stock of a jeweller-merchant located in a wealthy part of Roman Britain, a stock stolen and hidden with silver looted from the sanctuary.

In view of what may be shown to be a definite Christian element in the hoard, another hypothesis is now proposed: that the whole was a cult treasure, kept for safety at a temple or in the hands of someone associated with the cult. The jewellery was a votive offering to Faunus, either specially commissioned by the various members of the sect for this purpose or, in one or two cases, the devotee's personal property. The spoons and strainers were in some instances owned and previously used by members, the others made and intended for use in a ritual honouring Faunus. To explain the Christian element, it is suggested that the owners of the spoons with fish-and-plant,[1] *uti felix* and *viv bone vivas*,[2] plus Agrestius, Auspicius, Ingenuus, Persevera, Primigenia, Silviola and perhaps Restituts,[3] were lapsed Christians. The accession of Julian (A.D. 360–63) and the return to paganism must have been a stimulus for nominal or half-hearted Christians to revert to the pagan cults; and the policy of religious toleration of the Christian Valentinian I (364–75) would have secured at least security for such cults well into the second half of the fourth century, perhaps until the decree of Theodosius in 391, which closed all temples and banned pagan cults.

Source

Watts, D., 1988, 'The Thetford Treasure: A Reappraisal', *Antiquaries Journal* 68: 55

Notes

1   Spoon 67 (according to the numbers given by Johns and Potter for the whole find) bears a fish and plant motif, interpreted here as Christian symbols.

2   *Uti felix* ('Be happy') and *viv bone vivas* ('good life to you'), both inscribed
     on spoons, are regarded as Christian in character.
3   All these names are inscribed on the bowls of the spoons in the treasure.

References

Bland and Johns, 1993
Johns and Potter, 1983
Painter, 1977
Poulton and Scott, 1985
Milton, 1994
Johns, 1994

55

Wilfred of Northumbria and his relic-collecting activities in Rome

In the Catholic church particular attention has always been focused upon the relics of saints, considered primarily as actual body parts of the person concerned, or secondarily of objects like clothes or earth which had had intimate contact with the saint, either alive or dead. The central belief was that the saint, through the merits of his or her life (or death in the case of martyrs) had achieved an especially close relationship to God. As a result there flowed to the saint the particular powers of sainthood: the ability to heal sickness, to prophesy and to work wonders within the natural world. The saint could intercede with God on behalf of supplicants, and use his powers accordingly.

The relationship between saint and worshipper did not cease at death. Saints were conceived as dwelling both with God in heaven, and in the tomb in their churches. As a result, churches with famous saints became important places of pilgrimage, and their resting places rich in gold-work, enamel and gems. The treasures which accumulated in such churches combine characteristics of surplus community wealth, deposition in a sacred place, and a created relationship with the mighty dead.

The Life of Wilfred was written around 720 by the priest Stephanus, who knew Wilfred, seems to have gone to Rome with him, and returned with him to Ripon. Stephanus succeeded in producing a genuine biography of his hero, rather than a piece of stock hagiography. Wilfred was born in 634, in Northumbria, and entered the monastery at Lindisfarne as a boy. He became Bishop of Ripon soon after 664, but much of his life was spent in quarrels with fellow bishops and successive kings of Northumbria. This involved periods of exile, some of which he spent in Rome, like the two described in the pieces included here, and during these times he made substantial collections of saintly relics and church furnishings which went to endow the Northumbrian churches.

OUR BISHOP RETURNS

Wilfrid's long stay in Rome[1] was brought to an end by the injunction of the pope and synod to return home, taking with him the orders of the

190

Holy See which he was to show to Archbishop Theodore[2] and King Ecgfrith.[3] Our holy bishop carried out these commands with unwavering loyalty as he had promised, but before setting out he spent several days going round the shrines of the saints making his devotions. He managed to obtain, much to the comfort of the churches of Britain, a large supply of relics, each of which he labelled with a description of the object itself and the name of the saint. In his usual way he acquired numerous other articles to decorate the house of God, but it would be tedious to give a list of them all here. Finally he and his company set out for home in great joy with the blessing of pope and synod and with the help of God...

WILFRID IS ORDERED TO RETURN HOME AND BRINGS BACK THE HOLY RELICS

After several months of almost daily examination and close questioning, Wilfrid emerged completely exonerated. His case was won. His one wish now was to remain permanently in the Holy City and there end his days, crucifying himself to the world (as St Paul said) in his old age; but he had promised humble obedience to the pope and synod and they both ordered him to leave for home. Now that his long period of affliction had been brought to an end by complete acquittal from every charge both particular and general, they bade him return to present the findings in writing to the kings and archbishops, to soothe his subjects' grief and give his friends cause for rejoicing. Our holy bishop knew how to obey. He went round the shrines of the saints with his companions making a collection of relics, each labelled with the saint's name, and he bought purple cloth and silk vestments to decorate his churches. Then, with the blessing of the saints upon him, he made his way homewards by paths rough and smooth, over mountain and plain, till after a long journey he reached the Kingdom of Gaul.

Source

Eddius Stephanus, *Life of Wilfred*, in Webb, J. (ed.), 1970, *Lives of the Saints*, London, Penguin Books: 165–92

Notes

1 Wilfred appealed to Rome twice, and went in person to the Pope on each occasion, first in 677–80, and secondly in 702–704. These two texts refer to the two visits.
2 Theodore was Archbishop of Canterbury. He was born in Tarsus, and in 667 was living in Rome with a reputation as a scholar and philosopher. In 668 he was consecrated Archbishop by the Pope: an unexpected appointment but a very successful one. After an uneasy relation over the organisation of the church in Northumbria, Theodore and Wilfred were reconciled in 686. Theodore died in 690.
3 Ecgfrith was King of Northumbria; he quarrelled with Wilfred, and ultimately expelled him from the kingdom. He died in 685.

References

Brown, 1982
Obelkavich, 1979

56

Relic collections listed in
The Resting Places of the Saints

The document known as *The Resting Places of the Saints*, completed around 1031, gives a kind of 'Cook's Guide' to the whereabouts of famous saintly relics in England at that time. Many of the saints concerned had rested in the same churches for a considerable period by 1031, a few perhaps from as early as the sixth century AD, and others from the seventh century. Lists like this were a common feature of Western Christendom and may have been intended to direct pilgrims, although this list is not directly arranged for this purpose.

This is the only guide of its kind known to have survived, although it is unlikely to have been unique. The formula used takes the form of 'Holy X rests at Y', but often, especially in the first half, there is a further reference to a topographical feature, often a river. The list throughout contains details of a large number of saints who spent their working lives in England, but the first half has a Northumbrian orientation, while the second half concentrates upon Wessex and southern England generally, and there is an especial emphasis on Winchester.

It is clear that this kind of hagiographical list was a popular form among the Anglo-Saxons. Part of the reason for this may have been its relationship to Roman models, and its harmony with the Roman cult of relics, for of all the peoples of Western Christendom, the Anglo-Saxons, who owed their conversion to a papal initiative, were particularly reverential towards Rome.

THE SAINTS WHO REST AT CANTERBURY AND WINCHESTER

29. Truly the most blessed apostle of the English Augustus[1] and many more of his successors rest in the monastery of the Apostles Peter and Paul outside the city of Durovernum which is called Canterbury;[2] and holy Dunstan and many others [rest] in that same city in the monastery of the St Saviour.
30. And Holy Paulinus[3] [rests] in the place which is called Rochester.
31. Truly blessed Birinus and holy Heada and holy Swithin and holy

Justus the Martyr and many others [rest] with them in the monastery which is called the Old Minister at the city of Winchester.[4]
32.   And holy Judoc and Grimbald [rest] in the monastery which is called the Newminster.
33.   Holy Aedburh [rests] in the monastery which is called the Nunsminster in that same city.[5]

Source

Liebermann, F., 1889, *Die Heiligen Englands*, Hannover: 9–19

Notes

1   Section 29 of *The Resting Places* describes the saints' relics considered to be within the monastery of St Peter and St Paul outside Canterbury, and those in the cathedral church of Christ Church (monastery of St Saviour). Augustine had started his conversion of the English at Canterbury in 597. Dunstan was Archbishop of Canterbury in the tenth century.
2   This was the Roman name of the city; Canterbury is the English name.
3   Paulinus was Bishop of Rochester. He had come to England with the mission of 601 (linked with Augustine's of 597) and was originally Bishop of York, but the political climate in Northumbria forced him to flee, and he was made Bishop of Rochester in 632 (section 30).
4   Section 31 lists the relics held in the Old Minster at Winchester. Birinus, Haeddae and Swithin were all West Saxon bishops of Winchester.
5   The Newminster and the Nunsminster were both separate institutions in the city of Winchester (sections 32 and 33).

References

Rollason, 1989
Ridyard, 1988
Conner, 1993
Rollason, 1978

57

The Exeter Cathedral relic collection

The manuscripts from the Cathedral Church, Exeter, contain a list of relics headed by the claim 'these are the names of the holy relics which are held in the monastery of St Mary and St Peter the Apostle at Exeter, the greater part of which the most glorious and victorious King Athelstan gave'. Athelstan (king from 925 to 939) was King Alfred's grandson, and consolidated the defences of southern England following Alfred's victories against the Danes. Athelstan was supremely a man in tune with his times, and his relic-collecting activities reflect this.

Athelstan's later reputation was that of a great benefactor to the south-western churches, including St Buryan in Cornwall, Exeter and Hartland in Devon, and Milton Abbas in Dorset. Athelstan did indeed have a number of contacts in Brittany, probably with the bishopric of Dol, and this may have been the source of some of the relics in this Exeter list.

Lists of relics like this were usually made in all the major churches. Two lists survive from Exeter, apart from this one, which seems to belong to the eleventh century. A similar list, but not identical, appears at the beginning of manuscript presented to Exeter by Leofric (Warren, 1883: 1xi), and another forms part of the cathedral archive (Chapter MS 2861). This is probably late twelfth century, since it includes relics of Thomas Becket. The presence of most of the relics themselves in the church is, of course, much earlier, although exactly how much earlier is difficult to say.

ITEMS CHOSEN FROM THE LIST TO GIVE AN APPRECIATION OF THE VARIED CHARACTER OF THE MATERIAL

Of the tomb of the Lord[1]
Of the Jordan where the Lord was baptised
Of the garments of Holy Mary the Mother of the Lord
Of the body of St John the Baptist
Of the relics of the Holy Innocents
Of the Mount of Olives from which the Lord ascended into Heaven
Of the beard of St Peter the Apostle

Of the blood of St Stephen the Protomartyr, and of his relics
The relics of St Sebastian, Martyr
Of the relics of the Holy Martyrs who were martyred in Jerusalem
Of the relics of St Martin, Confessor
Of the relics of St Pancras, Martyr[2]
Of the relics of St Winwaloe[3]
Of the relics of St Winard
Of the body of St Withenoc
Of the relics of St Tudwal
Of St Cecilia[4]
Of St Agatha, Virgin

Apart from these, there are many other holy relics the names of which we cannot find written down, and are ignorant of whom they might be.

Source

Warren, F., 1883 (ed.), *The Leofric Missal*, Oxford, Clarendon Press: 354

Notes

1 This entry, and the next nine, refer generally to events connected with the Gospel stories and the Holy Land. The routes by which they reached Exeter are now likely to be difficult or impossible to trace.
2 Both Martin and Pancras were very well-known saints whose supposed relics were widely dispersed.
3 Winwaloe, and probably Winard, Withenoc and Tudwal have Breton, and also some Cornish, connections. They may have derived from Athelstan's activities, but there are a large number of other trans-Channel connections which could account for the Exeter traditions.
4 The female saints are listed separately at the end, and in rather perfunctory terms. Cecilia and Agatha were both saints well known in Western Christendom.

References

Ward, 1982
Geary, 1979
Rollason, 1989
Connor, 1993

58

The pilgrim traffic which went to view the relics gathered in Constantinople

Rome was a famous storehouse of relics, but so was Constantinople. Its churches and palaces, with their gold furnishings, rich decoration and relics, exercised an immensely powerful attraction upon the Western world. Pilgrims continued to reach Constantinople from the West throughout the early medieval centuries, but major contact was made with the First Crusade, which reached Constantinople soon after 1096, and with many succeeding crusading ventures. Eventually the Fourth Crusade of 1204 took and sacked the city, and finally Constantinople fell to the Turks in 1453; as a result much ecclesiastical and other material arrived in the West.

HOLY RELICS IN CONSTANTINOPLE

Throughout the eleventh century till its last two decades, an unending stream of travellers poured eastward, sometimes travelling in parties numbering thousands, men and women of every age and every class, ready, in that leisurely age, to spend a year or more on the voyage. They would pause at Constantinople to admire the huge city, ten times greater than any city that they knew in the West, and to pay reverence to the relics that it housed. They could see there the Crown of Thorns, the Seamless Garment and all the major relics of the Passion. There was the cloth from Edessa on which Christ had imprinted His face, and Saint Luke's own portrait of the Virgin; the hair of John the Baptist and the mantle of Elijah; the bodies of innumerable saints, prophets and martyrs; an endless store of the holiest things in Christendom.[1] Thence they went on to Palestine, to Nazareth and Mount Tabor, to the Jordan and to Bethlehem, and to all the shrines of Jerusalem. They gazed at them all and prayed at them all; then they made the long voyage homeward, returning edified and purified, to be greeted by their countrymen as the pilgrims of Christ who had made the most sacred of journeys.

Source

Runciman, S., 1951, *A History of the Crusades*, Vol. 1, *The First Crusade*, Cambridge University Press: 272–3

Notes

1   These are all major relics of the Passion, as Runciman says, and other supreme relics connected with Christ himself and his immediate followers.

References

Ward, 1982
Obelkevich, 1979

59

Carolingian art in the Abbey of St Denis, Paris

Among the gifts sent by the eastern Emperor Michael the Stammerer to the Holy Roman Emperor Louis the Debonnaire in AD 827 was a Greek manuscript of the works of the writer known as Dionysius the Areopagite. By 838 this manuscript had been deposited in the Benedictine Abbey of St Denis on the outskirts of Paris. St Denis was the patron saint of the Carolingian family, and Dionysius, the Greek version of the name 'Denis', was believed to be the same man as the French dedication.

The work was not translated until 858, by an Irish scholar, John the Scot. The work included the tract called the 'Celestial Hierarchy' which is a discussion of angelic lore and encouraged the artists at St Denis to include more, and more elaborate, scenes including angels in their work. St Denis was the most important royal abbey in northern France and during the later ninth century became an extremely important artistic centre for the production of gold-work, ivory carving, manuscript illumination and rock crystal carving. The theology of Dionysius and the artistic production within the abbey are closely interwoven, and the assemblage of treasure at St Denis was very important for the future of artistic appreciation and collecting.

TREASURES OF ST DENIS

We may ask ourselves the question: In what place could the artists of the eclectic school of Corbie get hold of and copy manuscripts of all the previous schools of Carolingian illumination? Where could they see and work with some of the very manuscripts we have seen them copying? Nowhere, it seems to me, save in the library of Charles the Bald,[1] in the Abbey of St. Denis ...

Now if we consider the second of our categories of material, the group of works in gold *repoussé*, other reasons for thinking St. Denis the place of origin for all these objects become apparent. In the first place we know that the abbey was famous for its goldsmithery under the abbot Louis, the predecessor of Charles the Bald. Lupus of Gerrières, in one of his letters to Louis, announces that he is sending up two of his monks to be trained with the workers of gold and silver in St. Denis who are famous far and wide as the most skilful. The group of objects we are considering[2] consists of (1) the gold cover of the Ashburnham Gospels; (2) the gold cover of the Gospels of St. Emmeran, in the State Library at Munich; (3) the portable altar of Arnulf in the Schatzkammer in Munich, and (4) the old high altar of the abbey of St. Denis itself, which though destroyed in the French revolution is luckily preserved in style and design by an old Franco-Flemish painting, in the Collection of Mrs. Stuart MacKenzie, London. The first three have always been regarded as belonging to the same workshop if not made by the same hand. The second, the book cover in Munich is the binding for the gospels of St. Emmeran which we have discussed above. The manuscript was illuminated in St. Denis and the history of its travels is known from the time that Odo took it from the treasury of St. Denis and presented it to Arnulf. At that time it possessed its gold cover and there is no reason to suppose that the beaten gold plates which compose this cover were made anywhere else, particularly if the figure style of the gold work and the illuminations be compared. The high altar of St. Denis would probably have been made in the abbey itself. The gold plates with figures in relief given by Charles the Bald were used as an antependium. Suger, the great minister of Louis VII, completed the altar and placed a commemorative inscription on it ...

All the evidence for a definite provenance for this group of metal work points overwhelmingly to St. Denis.

The ivories which Adolph Goldschmidt has placed in his Luithard group, including the ivory crucifixion at Munich which I have discussed above, are intimately associated with the so-called Corbie school of manuscripts, in several cases being the actual or former covers thereof. Goldschmidt has intimated that the center of that school cannot be Corbie – 'Corbie wie Janitschek vermutete, ist es voraussichtlich nicht'. As we have seen, it is probably St. Denis, and all the Luithard group of ivories were sculptured there or under the influence of the abbey...

The fourth category for our consideration, that of carved rock crystal, nets us very little for proving the St. Denis origin of our school. The gems are rather the reflection of painting, and the iconographic point I mentioned above is the only significant feature. The other carved crystals show the general iconography of the late Metz school of ivories which I consider late St. Denis.

The Art of the Abbey of St. Denis in Carolingian times may be divided into three periods. We begin with the period of the domination of the Franco-Saxon style, which lasted till about 867. In that year Charles the Bald became secular abbot of St. Denis and must have put his great library at the disposal of the St. Denis monks. From 867 till 877, the year of Charles's death, the abbey was the most fecund center of art in Europe, producing the group of manuscripts usually called the School of Corbie, the group of ivories which Goldschmidt calls the Luithard group, and the great works in the precious metals together with carved crystal gems. The period of decline was long and important because of the influence the abbey exerted in England, Belgium and Germany.

Source

Friend, A., 1923, 'Carolingian Art in the Abbey of St Denis', *Art Studies* 1: 72–5

Notes

1   Charles the Bald, grandson of Charlemagne, ruler of the Carolingian empire and Holy Roman Emperor (died 877).
2   All of this list are pieces of gold-work created, as here argued, in St Denis around 860.

References

Beckwith, 1964

Part V
Voices from the Twelfth to the Fifteenth Centuries

60

Abbot Suger considers the art treasures of the Abbey Church of St Denis, Paris

Suger seems to have come from an unimportant family, perhaps in the Paris region, and to have entered the Abbey of St Denis as a boy, in around 1091. He was educated at various monastic schools, and in 1106 was appointed Secretary to the Abbot of St Denis. He had experience of diplomatic and administrative work in Rome in the years around 1120, and in 1122 was appointed Abbot of St Denis. He was one of the Regents of the Kingdom while Louis VII was absent on the Second Crusade (1147–49) and died in 1151.

The Dionysius the Areopagite mentioned as a convert of St Paul's was identified in France with the St Denis who was held to be the Apostle of the Gauls, and whose relics lay in the abbey church dedicated to him. Moreover, the same Dionysius/Denis was also identified with a theological writer now known to have been a Syrian (name unknown) writing about AD 500 in Greek. A Greek manuscript of his writings had been deposited in St Denis by Emperor Louis the Pius, and had been translated by an Irishman, John the Scot, a guest of the Emperor Charles the Bald, in the tenth century. It was this work which had a profound effect upon Suger, and upon his work at St Denis.

The Syrian writer (known as Dionysius the Pseudo-Areopagite) had fused Christianity and the Neoplatonic thinking of writers like Plotinus and Proclus to create a doctrine in which the universe is created and animated by the Divine One and where, therefore, there is a hierarchy between God and the humblest material created thing, which partakes of the essence of God and can show forth his glory. This is the theme of the Syrian's most important work *De Celesti Hierarchia* (*Concerning the Celestial Hierarchy*). These ideas can lead to a notion that all material things can rightly be used to praise and worship God, and consequently lead to the creation of a Christian aesthetic in which objects of art and fine craftsmanship are intrinsically good, and proper within a church.

Such ideas were fundamentally in tune with Suger's character, and enabled him to bring together the royal history of his church, its supposed founding saint and his relics, the supposed writings of that saint, and the opportunities on offer in the mid-eleventh century, to create an abbey church of unparalleled magnificence. The church was rebuilt in what we call Gothic style, with its lightness and grace, and was the very first of the major churches to be so redesigned. Inside, the building was enriched with every piece of artwork which Suger could collect.

The reorganisation of the church included cast bronze gilded doors, coloured glass windows, a golden altar frontal studded with gems placed in front of the body of St Denis, a great gold cross with gemstones and golden panels to clad the main altar of St Denis. Some of the pieces were already ancient, and had been in the church for generations, like the Cross of St Eloy, the standing ornament known as the Crest, the pulpit with its ivory panels and the throne of King Dagobert. With all this went altar vessels, chalices and a stone (porphyry) vase of classical workmanship which was converted into an eagle shape. As a result of Suger's aesthetic, and through his building and his deliberate collecting activities, St Denis was converted into a new kind of experience of lightness and richness which was to have enormous influence.

OF THE GOLDEN ALTAR FRONTAL IN THE UPPER CHOIR

Into this panel, which stands in front of his most sacred body,[1] we have put, according to our estimate, about forty-two marks of gold; [further] a multifarious wealth of precious gems, hyacinths, rubies, sapphires, emeralds and topazes, and also an array of different large pearls – [a wealth] as great as we had never anticipated to find. You could see how kings, princes, and many outstanding men, following our example, took the rings off the fingers of their hands and ordered, out of love for the Holy Martyrs, that the gold, stones, and precious pearls of the rings be put into that panel. Similarly archbishops and bishops deposited there the very rings of their investiture as though in a place of safety, and offered them devoutly to God and His Saints. And such a crowd of dealers in precious gems flocked in on us from diverse dominions and regions that we did not wish to buy any more than they hastened to sell, with everyone contributing donations. And the verses on this panel are these:

Great Denis, open the door of Paradise
And protect Suger through thy pious guardianship.
Mayest thou, who hast built a new dwelling for thyself through us,
Cause us to be received in the dwelling of Heaven,
And to be seated at the heavenly table instead of at the present one.
That which is signified pleases more than that which signifies.

Since it seemed proper to place the most sacred bodies of our Patron Saints in the upper vault as nobly as we could, and since one of the side-tablets of their most sacred sarcophagus had been torn off on some unknown occasion, we put back fifteen marks of gold and took pains to have gilded its rear side and its superstructure throughout, both below and above, with about forty ounces. Further we caused the actual receptacles of the holy bodies to be enclosed with gilded panels of cast copper and with polished stones ...

Therefore, we searched around everywhere by ourselves and by our agents for an abundance of precious pearls and gems, preparing as precious a supply of gold and gems for so important an embellishment as we could find, and convoked the most experienced artists from diverse parts. They would with diligent and patient labor glorify the venerable cross on its reverse side by the admirable beauty of those gems...

One merry but notable miracle which the Lord granted us in this connection we do not wish to pass over in silence. For when I was in difficulty for want of gems and could not sufficiently provide myself with more (for their scarcity makes them very expensive): then, lo and behold [monks] from three abbeys of two Orders – that is, from Citeaux and another abbey of the same Order, and from Fontevrault – entered our little chamber adjacent to the church and offered us for sale an abundance of gems such as we had not hoped to find in ten years, hyacinths, sapphires, rubies, emeralds, topazes. Their owners had obtained them from Count Thibaut for alms; and he in turn had received them, through the hands of his brother Stephen, King of England, from the treasures of his uncle, the late King Henry,[2] who had amassed them throughout his life in wonderful vessels. We, however, freed from the worry of searching for gems, thanked God and gave four hundred pounds for the lot through they were worth much more...

Often we contemplate, out of sheer affection for the church our mother, these different ornaments both new and old; and when we behold how that wonderful cross of St. Eloy – together with the smaller ones – and that incomparable ornament commonly called 'the Crest' are placed upon the golden altar, then I say, sighing deeply in my heart: *Every precious stone was thy covering, the sardius, the topaz, and the jasper, the chrysolite, and the onyx, and the beryl, the sapphire, and the carbuncle, and the emerald.* To those who know the properties of precious stones it becomes evident, to their utter astonishment, that none is absent from the number of these (with the only exception of the carbuncle), but that they abound most copiously. Thus, when – out of my delight in the beauty of the house of God – the loveliness of the many-colored gems has called me away from external cares, and worthy meditation has induced me to reflect, transferring that which is material to that which is immaterial, on the diversity of the sacred virtues, then it seems to me that I see myself dwelling, as it were, in some strange region of the universe which neither exists entirely in the slime of the earth nor entirely in the purity of Heaven; and that, by the grace of God, I can be transported from this inferior to that higher world in an analogical manner...

We also caused the ancient pulpit, which – admirable for the most delicate and nowadays irreplaceable sculpture of its ivory tablets – surpassed human evaluation also by the depiction of antique subjects, to be repaired after we had reassembled those tablets which were moldering all too long in, and even under, the repository of the money chests; on the right side we restored to their places the animals of copper lest so much and admirable material perish, and had [the whole] set up so that the reading of Holy Gospels might be performed in a more elevated place. In the beginning of our abbacy we had already put out of the way a certain obstruction which cut as a dark wall through the central nave of the church, lest the beauty of the church's magnitude be obscured by such barriers.

Further, we saw to it, both on account of its so exalted function and of the value of the work itself, that the famous throne of the glorious King Dagobert,[3] worn with age and dilapidated, was restored. On it, as ancient tradition relates, the kings of the Franks, after having taken the reins of government, used to sit in order to receive, for the first time, the homage of their nobles ...

Also, with the devotion due to the blessed Denis, we acquired vessels of gold as well as of precious stones for the service of the Table of God, in addition to those which the kings of the Franks and those devoted to the church had donated for this service. Specifically we caused to be made a big golden chalice of 140 ounces of gold adorned with precious gems, viz., hyacinths and topazes, as a substitute for another one which had been lost as a pawn in the time of our predecessor.

We also offered to the blessed Denis, together with some flowers from the crown of the Empress, another most precious vessel of prase [a green quartz], carved into the form of a boat, which King Louis, son of Philip, had left in pawn for nearly ten years; we had purchased it with the King's permission for sixty marks of silver when it had been offered to us for inspection. It is an established fact that this vessel, admirable for the quality of the precious stone as well as for the latter's unimpaired quantity, is adorned with 'verroterie cloisonnée' work by St. Eloy which is held to be the most precious in the judgment of all goldsmiths.

Still another vase, looking like a pint bottle of beryl or crystal, which the Queen of Aquitaine[4] had presented to our Lord King Louis as a newly wed bride on their first voyage, and the King to the Divine Table for libation. We have recorded the sequence of these gifts on the vase itself, after it had been adorned with gems and gold, in some little verses:

As a bride, Eleanor gave this vase to King Louis,
Mitadolus to her grandfather, the King to me, and
   Suger to the Saints.

We also procured for the services at the aforesaid altar a precious chalice
made out of one solid sardonyx, which [word] derives from 'Sardius' and
'Onyx'; in which one [stone] the sard's red hue, by varying its property,
so keenly vies with the blackness of the onyx that one property seems to
be bent on trespassing upon the other.

Further we added another vase shaped like a ewer, very similar to the
former in material but not in form, whose little verses are these:

Since we must offer libations to God with gems and gold,
   I, Suger, offer this vase to the Lord.

We also gladly added to the other vessels for the same office an excellent
gallon vase, which Count Thibaut of Blois had conveyed to us in the
same case in which the King of Sicily had sent it to him.

Also we deposited in the same place the little crystal vases which we
had assigned to the daily service in our [private] chapel.

And further we adapted for the service of the altar, with the aid of
gold and silver material, a porphyry vase, made admirable by the hand of
the sculptor and polisher, after it had lain idly in a chest for many years,
converting it from a flagon into the shape of an eagle; and we had the
following verses inscribed on this vase:

This stone deserves to be enclosed in gems and gold.
It was marble, but in these [settings] it is more precious than
marble.

Source

Panofsky-Soergel, G., 1979, *Abbot Suger on the Abbey Church of St Denis and
   its Art Treasures*, second edition, Princeton University Press: 55, 57–9, 63–5,
   73, 77–9

Notes

1   'his most sacred body' refers to the relics of St Denis.
2   Henry I of England (1099–1135) and his nephew King Stephen of England
    (1135–54).

3   Dagobert I was king of all the Merovingian Frankish lands from 632 to 639, and when he died he was buried at St Denis. His court was at Paris, where his treasurer was the goldsmith St Eloi.

4   Eleanor, Duchess (rather than Queen) of Aquitaine in her own right, through inheritance. She married first Louis VII of France and then Henry II of England in 1151.

References

Panofsky-Soergel, 1979

61

Bishop Henry of Winchester brings ancient statues from Rome to Winchester

John of Salisbury finished his *Historia Pontificalis* in 1164 or soon after. John studied in Paris, and then spent most of his life as a clerk, what we might think of as a civil servant, at the papal court in Rome, and the archbishop's court at Canterbury. His *History* covers his own lifetime, and he was an eyewitness of many of the events he discusses. The political background to the piece given here is the reign of King Stephen. The English bishops, at the command of the King, had failed to attend the church council of Rheims and were consequently suspended by the Pope. All but Henry, Bishop of Winchester, were received back on the authority of the Archbishop of Canterbury, but Henry was treated differently.

Henry of Blois, Bishop of Winchester, was King Stephen's brother. He lived in princely style, building palaces within his diocese. He had had hopes of being appointed Archbishop of Canterbury, and when he was disappointed, was created Papal Legate, which made him the most senior churchman in England. But he also desired to raise Winchester to the level of an archbishopric for the west of England, although these efforts were unsuccessful.

His commission as legate lapsed on the death of Pope Innocent II in September 1143, and he travelled to Rome before Christmas 1143 in the hope of persuading the new Pope, Celestine II, to renew the position. Political events in Rome made his efforts unsuccessful, but Henry was apparently released from his suspension.

In 1151 Henry visited Rome again in an effort to persuade the Pope to elevate his see of Winchester to an archbishopric. The Pope was deaf to his demands, and did not treat his request seriously. John tells us that in his disappointment he took to buying ancient statues at Rome and sending them back to Winchester. John describes a grammarian as mocking Henry, and this no doubt describes his own feelings towards these activities: presumably collecting antique statues was regarded as eccentric and perhaps foolish.

Henry of Blois was in most ways very much a man of his times – born into the feudal ruling class, a prince of the church, an ambitious politician. He was devoted to the great reformed abbey of Cluny in France, where he regularly spent periods of retreat. His collecting activities are an important witness to the developing interest in the classical past which runs through the twelfth century; but John's distaste is also significant.

JOHN OF SALISBURY, *HISTORIA PONTIFICALIS*

Theobald Archbishop of Canterbury relaxed the suspension of the bishops and abbots of England, apart from Henry of Winchester, who went to Rome and received satisfaction in his own person.[1] Indeed, the man was received with grace by Guy of Summa, Bishop of Ostia, Gregory of St Angel, and others of his friends. His purpose, as they afterwards confessed, was to ask that a pallium[2] should be given to him so that he might be made Archbishop of Wessex, or that the position of Legate of the kingdom be given to him, or at least that his church should be exempted from the jurisdiction of Canterbury. However, he was sent away without having achieved any of these. Finally, he asked that he might be personally exempt. But to all these requests the Lord Pope was deaf, because he suspected that Henry wished to throw the whole of England back into evil courses, and because the church of Canterbury was renewing its probity [and proper relationship with the Pope]...

When the Bishop finally realised that he would obtain absolution but nothing else, having received leave to depart, he bought ancient statues in Rome, which he arranged to transfer to Winchester. When a learned teacher with a long beard, together with other grave philosophers, saw him buying marvellous images in the market ... he mocked him saying

> Damassipus was insane about buying ancient statues

To this sound advice, the Bishop returned another quotation, which was deliberately meant to insult:

> May the gods and goddesses, Damassipus, give you a barber for your sound advice[3]

The Bishop gave few presents and received few,[4] and returned by sea to avoid the dangers of Tuscany, Lombardy and Burgundy, travelling across Spain to the shrine of St James,[5] from whence safe and prosperous he returned home.

Source

Poole, R., 1927, *Iannis Sareberiensis, Historia Pontificalis*, Oxford University Press: 80–82

Notes

1 The texts seems to confuse several separate episodes into one.
2 The pallium was a circular band of white material marked with six dark purple crosses which is granted by the Pope to archbishops; its symbolic significance was such that its award amounted to the creation of an archbishopric.
3 These are quotations from the Roman poet, Horace (firstly *Satires* 2, 3: 64, secondly *Satires* 2, 3: 16–17). It is interesting that the two men knew Horace well enough to engage in this kind of quotation game.
4 That is, his visit to Rome had not been a success.
5 This is the famous shrine of St James at Compostela in north-west Spain.

References

Beckwith, 1964
Frisch, 1971
Poole, 1958

62

The goldsmith at work

In medieval England generally, the term 'goldsmith' seems to have covered a wide range of expertise in metalworking techniques. The first piece shows how the goldsmith was expected to produce leaf gold and sheet silver, copper and other metals, to carry out engraving work, to repair damaged objects, and to engrave hard and softer gemstones. He was also required to understand the technical properties of iron and steel.

The earliest ordinances concerning goldsmiths in London date from 1238, and these forbid the plating of base metal with gold or silver, a regulation later relaxed in respect of church plate. The list of Exeter Cathedral treasure (see Chapter 65 in this volume) shows how common gilt vessels were in the later medieval period. The first royal charter was granted to the Goldsmiths' Company in 1327, but a statute of 1300 had already started to regulate gold working.

This regulation produced the leopard-head hallmark, stamped on each piece of silver as a guarantee of its purity by the Wardens of the Company as proof that the piece had been assayed (tested).

Independent, or semi-independent, goldsmithing centres also developed in the fourteenth century at cities like Chester, Norwich, Exeter and York, and an ordinance of 1378–79 laid down that in places like these the master of the local mint was to mark plate with the mark of the city after it had been assayed.

The second piece given here dates to 1292 and is a rare surviving example of a contract between a goldsmith and a customer. It determines how Roger of Faringdon, a London goldsmith, will make for the religious community of St John of Beverley in Yorkshire a shrine for their patron saint. The shrine must have been broadly similar to that of St Thomas at Canterbury. The desire to accumulate valuable pieces, and the prestige attached to them, supported the craftsworkers, who were maintained by surpluses yielded by the socio-economic arrangements of later medieval England.

THE WORK OF THE GOLDSMITH

The goldsmith[1] should have a furnace with a hole at the top so that the smoke can get out ... Let there be an anvil of extreme hardness on which iron and gold may be softened and take the required form. They can be stretched and pulled with the tongs and the hammer. There should be a hammer also for making gold leaf, as well as sheets of silver, tin, brass (*oricalceas*), iron, or copper. The goldsmith must have a very sharp chisel by which he can engrave in amber, diamond, or *ophelta* [?], or marble, or *jacinth*, emerald, sapphire, or pearl, and form many figures. He should have a touchstone for testing metals, and one for distinguishing steel from iron. He must also have a rabbit's-foot for smoothing, polishing, and wiping the surface of gold and silver, and the small particles of metal should be collected in a leather apron. He must have ... gold and silver wire, by which broken objects can be mended or properly constructed. The goldsmith should be skilled in engraving [?] (*in opera plumiali*) as well as in bas-relief, in casting as well as in hammering. His apprentice must have a waxed table, or one covered with clay, for portraying little flowers and drawing in various ways. He must know how to distinguish solid gold from brass and copper.

A GOLDSMITH AND HIS CUSTOMER

Roger de 'Faringdon',[2] goldsmith, servant of William de 'Farindon' [*sic*], goldsmith, covenants to make for the Chapter of St. John de Beverle[y][3] a shrine 5½ feet in length and 1½ feet in breadth, and of proportionate height, in honour of St. John the patron of the church of Beverle[y]: the shrine to be made of gold and silver provided by the Chapter and refined by the said Roger: to be adorned with columns and cunningly worked statues, in size and quantity as the Chapter may direct: and to have tabernacles and pinnacles and other ornaments of goldsmiths' work both behind and before.

Sources

Holmes, U., 1953, *Daily Living in the Twelfth Century*, London: 142
Sharpe, R., 1899, *Calendar of Letter Books ... of the City of London*, London: 180–81

Notes

1   This description was written by Alexander of Neckham (d. 1217) in about 1200. He taught for many years in Paris, and his description may be based on the Parisian smiths.

2   Faringdon was, and is, one of the Wards of the City of London; it lies to the north-west of the city.

3   St John of Beverley (d. 721) was a monk at the Northumbrian house of Whitby, and consecrated Bishop of Hexham in about 687. In 705 he was translated to York and became embroiled in Wilfred's quarrels (see Chapter 55 in this volume). Before his death, he retired to the monastery which he had founded at Beverley. His tomb became a famous shrine.

References

Frisch, 1971

63

A description of the City of Rome by Master Gregory

In 1917 M.R. James found in St Catherine's College, Cambridge, a manuscript by a Magister Gregorius, or Master Gregory, giving a description of the city of Rome. Gregory seems to have written his description around 1180 or perhaps a little later, and to have based it upon eye-witness accounts of what he himself had seen, supplemented by material from 'the cardinals and priests of the papal administration'.

Gregory's tone is secular rather than religious, and he shows a considerable interest in the relics of antiquity, both buildings and particularly, the sculptures which were still distributed around the city. It is this aspect of his work which is of particular interest here. The description shows the interest in classical pieces which was already developing in north-western Europe in the late twelfth century, and no matter how naive or unaesthetic this interest was, it forms part of the developing strain of classical humanism which had never entirely died in western Europe.

CHAPTERS 4–8

Another statue is in front of the Pope's palace, and this is the immense horse and his rider,[1] who the people of Rome say is Constantine, and the pilgrims say is Theoderic; but the cardinals and priests of the papal administration say is either Marcus or Quintus Quirinus.[2] As a result of wonderful workmanship in ancient times, this had stood upon four columns in front of the alter of Jupiter on the Capitol Hill, but the Blessed Gregory[3] separated the horse and his rider and placed the columns in the church of St John Lateran. However, the people of Rome placed the horse and rider in front of the papal palace ...

The third statue is an image of the Colossus, which all in Rome say is an effigy of the sun. The height of this statue was recorded as 26 feet. This immense statue stood in the block of buildings known as Herod's beyond the Colloseum. In his right hand he held a spear and in his left a sword ...[4]

There is another statue which, rather ridiculously, they call Priapus. It represents a boy picking a thorn out of his foot[5] ...

Among all the huge works which there once were in Rome, the greatest wonder was the group of statues which were called 'the Salvation of the City'. By magic arts were here consecrated statues of all the peoples who were subject to Roman rule, for no people or kingdom subject to Roman rule lacked their statue in this building.

CHAPTERS 12–14

Now, truly, there are only a few marble statues, because most of them were taken away or broken down by Blessed Gregory. Of these, one may be mentioned on account of its great beauty. This is an image of the Roman Venus, and is shown in that form in which, as the story tells, she appeared naked to the judgement of Paris. As the poet says, the judge acted so that Venus conquered both judge and us.

This image is made of Parian marble, and is so wonderful and completely perfect that it seems to be a living creature rather than a statue: for her nakedness is tinted like life with rosy colour. The wonderful beauty and I know not what magical persuasion drew me to the statue three times, although my hostelry was two miles distant.[6]

Not far from this are the marble horses of wonderful size and artistic composition.[7]

CHAPTERS 31–2

Close to this palace [the Colloseum] is the image of the sign given to Aeneas by the prophetic Helenus, son of Priam, showing where the city should be built, and that it would have rule over the whole earth. This statue is made by wonderful art from whitest marble ...[8]

In the portico of the winter palace of the Lord Pope is an image of that wolf which it is said suckled Remus and Romulus. This story is a fable, for Lupa was the most beautiful woman in ancient Rome. She found Remus and Romulus in the Tiber and cared for them. This same wolf was shown stalking a ram, which stood before the same palace, with water coming out of its mouth for the washing of hands. The wolf, too, once emitted a stream of water through its teats for hand washing, but now it is broken off at the foot and in a different place.[9]

Source

Rushforth, G., 1919, 'Magister Gregorius De Mirabilis Urbis Romae: a new description of Rome in the twelfth century', *Journal of Roman Studies* IX: 14–58

Notes

1   This is the equestrian statue of Marcus Aurelius now, and since 1538, at the Capitol, but in Gregory's day standing in front of the Lateran Palace.
2   The references are to the Emperor Constantine the Great (288–337), Theoderic King of the Ostrogoths (454–526), and the Emperor Marcus Aurelius (1221–80). 'Quintus Quirinus' seems to be a constructed character.
3   The pope is Gregory the Great (540–604, Pope from 590) but the story is doubtful. Gregory's writing developed the mystical teaching of Dionysius the Pseudo-Areopagite.
4   This Colossus was believed in Gregory's day to be represented by the bronze head and right arm preserved since 1471 in the Palace of the Conservatori. There is some confusion in the description with the Colossus of Rhodes, one of the Wonders of the ancient World.
5   This statue is also now in the Palace of the Conservatori, formed by Pope Sixtus IV in 1471. 'Priapus' is not recorded elsewhere as the statue's name. Priapus would be a silly name for this statue because it refers to the adult male sexual organ.
6   This Venus obviously made a profound impression upon Gregory. The perfect condition of the Venus suggests that it must have been deliberately concealed to prevent its destruction by Gregory I. Rushforth suggests it may be the Venus now in the Capitoline Museum.
7   These are the famous Dioscuri, or Horse-Tamers, of the Quirinal, which still stand approximately on their original site, as they did in Gregory's day.
8   The sign, and the statue, was of a sow with a litter of thirty piglets. The Trojan Aeneas was the legendary founder of Rome.
9   These figures stood at the entrance to the Lateran Palace. The wolf has been at the Capitol since 1471, but was at the Lateran in Gregory's day: wolf and legs are now reunited. The figures of the suckling twins now attached to the wolf, are a later (?1471) addition.

References

James, 1938

64

The will of William of Wykeham, Bishop of Winchester

William of Wykeham (1324–1404) was one of the great English churchmen of the late phase of the medieval period. He was born into a family of free peasant status but his talents enabled him to take holy orders, and his administrative abilities attracted the attention of the king, Edward III. He was overseer of royal building projects, including the new construction work at Windsor Castle (1356–61), and he served as Keeper of the Privy Seal, and Chancellor of the Kingdom from 1367.

In 1367 he succeeded his old friend and patron, John Edlington, as Bishop of Winchester, one of the wealthiest sees in Europe. Through the difficulties of Richard II's reign he was recalled to serve again as Chancellor from 1386 to 1391. He spent his final years as an elder statesman, and as an important churchman who could give time to his educational foundations.

There were two of these: New College, Oxford, founded on 26 November 1379, and Winchester College, founded 20 October 1382, the former for undergraduates, the latter for schoolboys. The intention was to train priests and theologians, of which the church was greatly in need following the warfare and plague endemic during the period, and, especially, the devastation of the Black Death which hit England in 1348. Both foundations are mentioned in the personal bequests in his will.

The mitre bequeathed to New College still survives in the college. It is of cloth-of-gold embroidered with pearls and trimmed with silver-gilt ornaments, imitation turquoises and pastes. It has a case of sheet iron covered in black leather stamped over with small fleurs-de-lis. The crozier, or pastoral staff, also survives in the college. This is an immensely imposing piece made up of three parts: the shaft, the central knob and the crozier head. The knob has an architectural form in which a central portion enriched with figures in canopied niches rises to a buttressed octagonal shaft carrying three levels of arched niches, each holding a figure of Christ, the Virgin, and saints. The crosier head is held up by a winged angel, and each side of it is decorated by enamelled plaques showing angels playing musical instruments. The whole piece, apart from the enamelled sections, is of silver-gilt. Winchester College possesses a silver-gilt spoon, known as the Founder's Spoon, which is believed to have been William's gift.

The importance of William's will is that it shows the kind of personal accumulation which a senior churchman could assemble at the end of the fourteenth century. It represents the context within which the great collections of the next century, particularly those of the early Medici, were to be made.

MOBERLY, *LIFE OF WILLIAM OF WYKEHAM*

I, William Wykeham, Bishop of Winchester, bequeath as follows:–
1. My soul to God.
2. My body to my chantry in my cathedral.[1]
3. All my debts to be paid.
4. To every poor applicant in the place when I die – 4*d*., 2*d*., or 1*d*., at my executors' discretion.
5. To every poor applicant at my funeral – 4*d*.
6. To be divided among poor prisoners in the Newgate, Marshalsea, Wolvesey, Winchester, Oxford, Berkshire, Guildford, Old and New Sarum gaols – £200.

For Cathedral Repairs:–
7. Towards the repair of the cathedral nave – £25000 marks.
8.   windows on the south side – £500 marks.

To (i) *Officials:–*
9. The king – a pair of silver-gilt ewers: remittance of a debt of £500.
10. Archbishop of Canterbury – gold ring with ruby, pair of gold beads with gold necklace, silver almsdish.
11. My successor – a pontifical and a missal, gold ring with sapphire, gilt chalice, a 'Ponsere'.
12. Bishop of London – silk bed and tapestry from Wolvesey.

(ii) *Church Establishments:–*
13. Winchester Cathedral – blue cloth vestment, twenty cloth copes, large pyx.
14. Prior of St. Swithun's – silver gilt covered jug and ewer.
15. Convent of ditto – to monks, 40*s* each, if priests, five marks; to pray for my soul.

Colleges:–
16. New College, Oxford – mitre, pastoral staff, dalmatics, and sandals.
17. Winchester College – mitre and Bible, five books.
18. Warden of New College (and successors) – 10 marks, silver-gilt covered cup and ewer...

(iii) *Convents:–*

42. St. Cross, Winchester – pair of vestments, chalice, pair of ewers.
43. St. Nicholas' Hospital, Portsmouth – pair of vestments, chalice.
44. St. Mary's Southampton – pair of vestments, chalice.
45. St. Elizabeth's College, Winchester – pair of silver basins, two silver altar flagons.
46. St. Mary Magdalen's Hospital, Winchester.
47. Sustern Spital – £2 to be divided among sisters.

(iv) *Churches:–*

48. Hambledon Church – one portifory, one chalice.
49. Eastmeon Church – one portifory, one chalice.
50. Witney, Farnham, Cheriton, Havant and Burghclere Churches – each a vestment, cope, and chalice.
51. Fawley, Crawley, Alverstoke, South Waltham, and Droxford – each a cope and chalice…

(vi) *Friends:–*

68. Chief Justices of King's Bench and Common Pleas – each a gold ring and a diamond.
69. William Hengford – a gold ring.
70. Robert Faringdon – psalter and pair of beads.
71. John Uvedale – silver jug.
72. Henry Popham – silver jug.
73. John Champflour, Nicholas Bray, Stephen Carr – each silver jug…

Source

Moberley, G., 1898, *Life of William of Wykeham*, Winchester, Warner & Son: 344–6

Notes

1 William was indeed buried in the chantry he had prepared in his cathedral church.

References

Lowth, 1759
Alexander and Binski, 1987

65

Inventory of valuable objects at Exeter Cathedral in 1327

During the later medieval centuries most great churches endeavoured to keep track of the precious objects which they had accumulated by created listed inventories. The inventory, of which part is given here, was prepared in the cathedral church of St Peter, Exeter in 1327.

The introduction to the inventory tells us that it covers books, vestments and other ornaments and goods in the cathedral church. It was made at the wish of Richard of Brailegh (or Braylegh), sub-deacon of the church, and leave to examine and list the material was given by Thomas de Hinton, treasurer of the church, whose responsibility the objects were. We are told that the list was issued on the Wednesday immediately before the Feast of the Nativity of the Blessed Virgin, (8 September) 1327, and that it was made by William Vialde, sub-treasurer of the church.

In the inventory, the books are listed first, by author and with their valuations; some 150 books are listed altogether. The chalices and silver vessels come next, and it is from this part of the list that this excerpt is taken. Over a hundred separate items are listed. The vestments follow, with over a hundred entries, many of them of sets with albs, copes, chasubles and so on. One set of red velvet chasuble, tunicle and dalmatic, for example, is said to have been given by Master William of Kilkenny. The vestments would be used during a high mass by the officiating priest, deacon and sub-deacon on days, like the feasts of martyrs, when red is the appropriate liturgical colour. Lists of cloths and pieces of furniture follow, and finally a brief list of extra objects which emerged 'after the making of the said inventory', and here one can only sympathise with William Vialde.

Exeter was not one of the wealthiest churches of the kingdom, although it had been the seat of the bishop, whose medieval diocese covered Devon and Cornwall, since 1050, and a West Saxon minster before that. Moreover, the church's governance had recently been in some confusion. James Berkley had been elected bishop on 12 December 1326, but he had died the following 24 June 1327. John de Grandisson was elected in Avignon, where the papacy was currently based, on 18 October 1327, and he arrived in Exeter in June 1328. Presumably, the desire to create the inventory was bound up with these changes.

The Bishop's registers of these years suggest that affairs at Exeter were in rather a muddle. The rebuilding of the cathedral church was less than half completed, the ecclesiastic manors had been plundered, and the cultivation of the farms had been neglected. Demands for payments were being made from the crown, the papacy and the church of Canterbury. John de Grandisson's register records requests to fellow clergy for church plate, books and vestments, suggesting various deficiencies in the stock of the cathedral. However, the inventory suggests that the possessions of the church were still relatively impressive.

FROM THE LIST BY WILLIAM VIALDE, SUB-TREASURER OF THE CHURCH

Chalices, with Other Silver Vases

Two chalices of gold, one of pure gold in weight 79s 4d, and the other 49s 6d.[1]

Twelve chalices, gilded, one of which is large and enamelled and weighs 67s 6d, one with pearls in the foot, weighing 25s 10d, and the third with an enamelled knob, weighing 27s ... the sixth has a toothed foot and a small lamb on its lid, weight 20s; the seventh with a round plain knob, weight 26s 1d; the eighth with a plain foot and a star on its lid, weight 19s 6d; the ninth with plain foot and lid, weight 21s 4d; and the tenth marked with crosses on foot and lid, weight 20s 6d ... .

One chalice of white silver, not gilded, weight 17s 6d.

Two heads of pastoral staffs [croziers] of gilded silver, of which one weighs 70s and the other 30s 6d.

One pastoral staff of ivory, bound with silver in two places.

Twelve ivory combs, of which seven are worn.

One large silver phial for oil, inscribed round the outside, without lid, weight 35s 10d.

Two phials, of gilded silver with three feet and lids, weight 18s 4.

One silver basin with three feet, gilded in places, with four images [figures], weight 39s 2d.

One silver bowl, old and broken, the gift of Theobald, Archbishop of Canterbury, of weight 17s, through the liberality of Bishop John.

Two boats[2] of silver, with two silver spoons, weight 37s 6d.

Six thuribles[3] of silver with silver chains, of which four are gilded on the exterior and weigh respectively 10 marks, 7 marks, 73s and 45s; two have the gilding damaged in places, weight 4 pounds 18s.

Two new silver candlesticks, gilded in places, the gift of Bishop Thomas, weight 5 pounds 11s 8d.

Two silver cups of which one is gilded on the outside, weight 5 pounds 6s 8d and the other of white silver gilded inside, weight 61s 8d.

One silver vessel for holy water and two silver asperges[4] gilded, the gift of Bishop Thomas, weight 5 pounds 1s, three objects of wood covered in silver and ornamented with stones.

A cross of wood ornamented with gilding and silver, with various stones and insets of carved ivory.

A small painted chest: in this are nine phials of crystal ornamented with silver holding relics and sixteen containers ornamented with silver holding relics, and one silver container with bone of Saint Brannoc, the gift of Deacon Bartholomy; and a chalice of St Dunstan with relics, and a silver hand with a joint of St Wolstan,[5] and the alabaster box of St Mary Magdalene, with a silver foot.

One large book cover of gilded silver with various stones and precious pearls, the gift of Bishop Walter Stapledon.

Source

Oliver, G., 1861, *Lives of the Bishops of Exeter*, Exeter, William Roberts: 301–19

Notes

1 Valuations are usually given, but where they are not, the piece was presumably of little value.
2 These were for carrying fresh supplies of incense: during mass they would be carried by a boat boy, who would top up the incense in the thurible at appropriate moments.
3 Thuribles are incense burners, carried and swung by a thurifer during mass.
4 These are used for scattering holy water.
5 That is a bone joint, presumably believed to be a finger joint since it was housed in a hand-shaped case.

References

Alexander and Binski, 1987

66

The author of *Pearl* shows how the aesthetic of treasure has mystical significance

The poem known as *Pearl* was composed by an unknown writer, probably somewhere in north-west England, around the 1380s. The poem achieves, in Stone's words, 'strict harmony between passionate grief, lofty moral vision, and mystical experience' (p. 137).

The poem begins with the poet in sorrow beside the grave of his dead Pearl; there he swoons and in his dream finds himself in a marvellous countryside on the banks of a stream. He sees the beautiful girl, Pearl, whom he has lost, and she rebukes his sorrow by telling him that she is now with God and immortal. She takes him to a place where he has a vision of the New Jerusalem; he sees his own Pearl among the maidens, and in a frenzy tries to join her, although the attempt brings death. God breaks the vision, and the poet resolves to submit to the will of God and prays that he in turn may deserve the blessed life in heaven.

The notion of the dream as a device for transporting narrator and reader to the other world was a normal one in medieval literature and offers great poetical potential: it permits the descriptions of the beautiful country in which the dreamer awakens, and of the New Jerusalem which he is brought to see. In this language and imaginative diction the poet draws equally on the Bible and the courtly tradition of medieval romance.

Part of this tradition was the idea that precious stones all have symbolic qualities. The 'Pearl' of the poem is both the girl and the gemstone with its symbolic identification with purity, whiteness and spiritual perfection. This derives in part from the appearance of pearls, and part from the parable of the merchant who desired a 'pearl of great price' and sold all he had to obtain it. 'Pearl' also came to mean virginity.

The extract from the poem given here shows how the qualities of pure colour and light-reflecting properties were valued in gems and objects of gold and silver. The silver, crystal and indigo are not appreciated for their monetary value, but rather for their shimmering brightness and purity, which are themselves allegories for intensity of religious feeling. These ideas should be born in mind in relation to the bald descriptions of precious objects which are preserved in church or secular inventories of treasure.

PEARL[1]

7   Adorned were all the hillsides there[2]
     With crystal cliffs, while down below
     Brilliant woodlands were everywhere.
     The boles were as blue as indigo;
     Like burnished silver the leaves swayed,
     Quivering close on the branches spread;
     They shimmered in splendour, glanced and played,
     When glinting gleams from the sky were shed.
       The gravel I ground beneath my tread
       Of precious orient pearl was formed:
       A sunbeam's light would be dull and dead
       When set by a scene so brightly adorned.

8   The adornment of those uplands fair
     Made my spirit forget to grieve
     Such freshly flavoured fruits were there
     That the good fairly made me revive.
     Birds in flocks, of flaming hues,
     Both large and small, flew in the glade;
     Melody matching their radiant mist
     No singing citherner every played.
       So sweet the harmoney their song conveyed
       As they warbled wonderfully, winging the air.
       Such marvellous music man never made
       As sight and sound's adornment there.

9   So all was adorned in a wonderful way.
     The forest where Fortune drew me forth
     Showed such splendours that none could say
     With telling by tongue their true worth.
     And still I blithely strode that strand,
     No slope so steep as to cause me stay.
     Ahead, still fairer was the forest land:
     Plant and spice and pear-tree gay.
       Hedge and border and bright mead lay
       On banks as brilliant as threads of gold,
       Between which the water cut its way –
       Lord, most truly, adornment untold!

10   The adornments of that wonderful deep
     Were banks of beryl that lambent shone;

Sweetly swirling was the water's sweep
As whisperingly it wandered on.
Dazzling stones shone in the deep
Like glint through glass, glowing and bright;
As streaming stars, when dalesmen sleep,
Flare in the welkin on winter night.
　　For every stone that met my sight
　　Was emerald, sapphire or other gem,
　　So that all the water gleamed with light
　　In the gracious adornment given by them.
　　...

14   More marvels yet daunted my mind;
　　I saw beyond that blissful stream
　　A glittering cliff of crystal kind,
　　Ablaze with many a kingly beam.
　　At its foot a girl sat, gracious sight,
　　A noble maiden most debonair
　　In garments of all glistening white,
　　And known to me well, before, elsewhere.
　　　　Like glittering gold refined with care,
　　　　So shone that glory above the shore:
　　　　Long I looked upon her there,
　　　　And gazing, knew her more and more.

15   The more I scanned her seemly face,
　　When I had found her form so fair,
　　The more I was suffused apace
　　By glorious gladness gliding there.
　　I longed to call her, but then a daze,
　　A numb surprise through my spirit spread
　　At seeing her in so strange a place:
　　My soul was struck with a sudden dread.
　　　　But then she lifted her lovely head,
　　　　With face as white as ivory pure.
　　　　It stabbed my heart, struck it with dread,
　　　　And every the longer, the more and more.

Source

Stone, B., 1964, *Medieval English Verse*, London, Penguin Books: 136–74

Notes

1 The extract is stanzas 7–10, and 14–15.
2 The poet has just fallen asleep and entered the dream country.

References

Alexander and Binski, 1987

67

The treasures of the cathedral church at Canterbury

Thomas Becket (?1118–70) was Archbishop of Canterbury from 1162, having already been appointed Chancellor by Henry II, his close friend. He resigned the chancellorship, but began to quarrel with Henry over the vexed question of the rival authority of King and Pope. In a rage, in 1170, Henry uttered the famous words 'Who will rid me of this turbulent priest?' which inspired four knights to go to Canterbury and assassinate Thomas in front of the high altar of his own cathedral.

Thomas was buried in the cathedral and miracles were soon recorded at his tomb. His relics were widely dispersed, and the tomb became one of the major focuses of pilgrimage, including, most famously, for Chaucer's storytellers in his *Canterbury Tales*. The tomb attracted gifts, the magnificence of which the two passages given here make clear.

Very little of the gold and jeweller's work that existed in later medieval England now survives. Apart from all the usual reasons for loss, the closing of the monastic houses following Henry VIII's break with Rome in 1536 involved the royal requisition of huge quantities of gold and gems. In 1538 twenty-six cartloads of gold and silver were taken from Canterbury Cathedral by Henry's commissioners, and the spoils from Thomas's shrine must have made up a good part of this load.

The first piece here comes from the description of an Italian, writing about 1480, and is plainly an eyewitness account. The shrine had been in existence for about two centuries when this description was written, but it seems to have reached this general level of magnificence quite soon after Thomas's death.

Desiderius Erasmus (?1469–1536) was one of the earliest northern humanists who became the first teacher of Greek at Cambridge, but subsequently lived much of his life on the Continent. He published a Greek edition of the New Testament and texts of the Church Fathers and also *Praise of Folly* (1509), a bitter satire on monastic and clerical corruption. He did not, however, join the Reformation movement, although Paul IV condemned his writings in 1558.

The account of the shrine, and the texture of the descriptions of goldwork and gems link with earlier medieval and later

Renaissance collections, and show how such accumulations worked on the imaginations of contemporaries.

AN EYEWITNESS ACCOUNT OF ST THOMAS'S TOMB

But the magnificence of the tomb of St. Thomas the Martyr ... is that which surpasses all belief. Notwithstanding its great size, this is entirely covered with plates of pure gold: but the gold is scarcely visible from the variety of precious stones with which it is studded, such as sapphires, diamonds, rubies, balas-rubies, and emeralds: and on every side that the eye turns, something more beautiful than the other appears. And these beauties of nature are enhanced by human skill, for the gold is carved and engraved in beautiful design, both large and small, and agates, jaspers and cornelians set in relievo, some of the cameos[1] being of such a size, that I do not dare to mention it: but everything is left far behind by a ruby, not larger than a man's thumbnail, which is set to the right of the altar. The church is rather dark, and particularly so where the shrine is placed, and when we went to see it the sun was nearly gone down, and the weather was cloudy: yet I saw that ruby as well as if I had it in my hand.

Source

Sneyd, C., 1847, *A Relation ... of that island of England about the year 1500*, Camden Society, Vol. 37: 83–4

ERASMUS DESCRIBES ST THOMAS'S TOMB

A coffin of wood [covered] a coffin of gold which, being drawn up by ropes and pullies, an invaluable treasure was discovered. Gold was the meanest thing to be seen there. All shone and glittered with the rarest and most precious jewels of an extraordinary bigness: some were larger than the egg of a goose. When this sight was shown, the prior with a white wand touched every jewel one by one, telling the name, the value, and the donor of it.[2]

Source

Erasmus, D., 1849, *Pilgrimages to Saint Mary of Walsingham and Saint Thomas of Canterbury* (trans. Nichols, J.), Canterbury: 45–56

Notes

1   It is possible that some of these carved gems were from the antique world.
2   It seems likely that this piece also describes the tomb of St Thomas, which presumably had a wooden cover over it, which would be drawn up to display the golden shrine. It is interesting that a guided tour to the shrine was available, and that local knowledge extended to a detailed catalogue of the history and provenance of each gemstone.

References

Alexander and Binsky, 1987
Frisch, 1971

68

Giovanni Dondi discusses the collecting of classical antiquities

One of the most significant testimonies to the standing of classical art towards the end of the fourteenth century comes from Giovanni Dondi dall'Orologio, a friend of Petrarch's. His strange nickname, of 'the Clock', came from a famous clock which he designed and built, and which became a showpiece at the Visconti Palace at Pavia.

Dondi was a man of wide interests, and these included classical antiquities, which he studied on a trip to Rome in 1375. His letters give a good insight into the view taken of classical art in his generation. The letter quoted here was addressed to Dondi's theologian friend Fra Guglielmo da Cremona. The text of the letter clearly shows that in Dondi's opinion, the products of classical antiquity were superior to those produced by the artists of his own day.

Alsop has an interesting interpretation of Dondi's letter (1982: 309–10). He suggests that the phrase 'avidly sought after' must mean that the classical works had attracted a number of collectors, who were also those willing to pay the large prices mentioned, as a result, presumably, of competition in the collecting field. It looks as if Italy's classical collectors were still a relatively narrow group in the 1370s, but were, nevertheless, emerging as a force in the community. As Alsop points out, this is very important. In the preceding centuries people generally expected to pay a lower price for something that was not new – and here we have old things valued in part for that reason.

There is enough evidence to give a context for Dondi's letter. We know of an Oliviero Forzetta who died in 1373, and whose will required that his art collection be sold. His collection contained classical pieces, and the proceeds were enough to endow a charity Forzetta had planned. Petrarch's friend Lombardo della Seta purchased a statue of Venus which turned up during building work in Florence, and took it back to his home in Padua. Similarly, there is also a casual note by Benvenuto da Imola, concerning another beautiful Venus statue which he saw in a house in Florence about 1390.

233

FROM A LETTER BY GIOVANNI DONDI

But who and what sort of men those Ancients were, by what customs they lived, what virtues they had, what sorts of actions gained reward, and what sorts of things were given to those who deserved well, all belong to a bygone age and cannot, like present things, be seen by our eyes or touched with our hands; they can, however, be recognized by great testimonies and reliable evidence, so that no one who looks carefully can doubt them. The best evidence consists of the writings which outstanding minds have left to the memory of posterity; their authority and majesty is so great that no one can fail to trust them. If you should ask my own opinion, their credit is so great, believe me, that I seem somehow to have seen those things that I have read. To my way of thinking, then, it is out of the question that such genuine men could have written anything except the truth, and what they had seen themselves or had accepted from those who were present, or from what they had learned from what was written by great authors – who, I am sure (especially those who were intending to write history, not poems, in which kind of writing perhaps it might be permitted to describe matters otherwise than they were), sought the truth of things above all else and eschewed every falsehood. I am sure that you have diligently read writings of this kind, or certain of the more important ones, and have in many parts of them noted customs and actions of a past Age with some admiration. If you in all fairness compare what we perceive at present with these, you will admit that justice, courage, temperance, and prudence really dwelt more profoundly in their souls, and that they who did great things by the guidance of these virtues were provided with far more worthy rewards. Moreover, proof of this is given by those objects which remain in Rome to this day as testimony to the honors that used to be conferred upon outstanding actions. For although time has consumed many of them – even many of the more magnificent – and only ruins of others appear, which present certain traces of what formerly stood, still, those things that remain, fewer and less magnificent, testify abundantly that those who decreed them must have been of great virtue, and that something great and worthy of praise must have been enacted by those for whom they were being given for their lasting honor and glory. I mean the statues which, either cast in bronze or chiseled in marble, have lasted to the present, and the many fragments of those that have been shattered lying about everywhere, the marble triumphal arches of impressive workmanship and the sculptured columns showing the histories of great deeds, and so many other things of this kind publicly built in honor of men who were distinguished, whether because they had established peace or because they had liberated the fatherland from imminent peril or had extended empire over subjected peoples, as I recall having read in some of them, not without a certain notable pleasure. And you similarly, I suspect, have noticed in passing sometimes and have stopped a little while with some amazement and perhaps have said to yourself. 'Surely these are proof of great men'. Such proof for such reasons is not forthcoming from our own time. And why, do you think, unless that there are lacking those who should act in such a way as to deserve such rewards, as well as those who would favor men acting in this way, if such there were, by whose means such rewards would be given?

Of the artistic product of ancient genius, few survive, but those that do remain anywhere are eagerly sought and seen and highly prized by those who feel strongly about such things:[1] and if you compare them with those of today, it will soon become obvious that their authors were by nature more powerful in genius and more learned in the mastery of their art. I am speaking about ancient buildings and statues and sculptures, with other things of the sort. When some artists of this time scrutinized the productions of that age carefully, they are struck with amazement. I knew a certain well-known worker in marble who was famous for his ability in that art among those whom Italy had at the time, especially in the creation of figures. I have heard this man tell many times about the statues and sculptures that he[2] had seen at Rome, with such admiration and veneration that he seemed in recalling it to be transported beyond himself from the wonder of the thing. For he used to say that sometimes, passing with his friends by a place where some images of this sort could be seen, he had held back, looking in astonishment at their artistry, and, forgetting his company, had stood still so long that his companions had passed on five hundred steps and more. And when he would tell of the great excellence of these figures, and praise their authors beyond measure, he used to add in the end (in his own words): 'If only these images did not lack life, they would be better than living ones', as if to say that nature had been not only imitated by the genius of such artists but even surpassed.

Source

Gilbert, N., 1977, 'A letter of Giovanni Dondi dall'Orologio to Fra Guglielmo da Cremona', *Viator* 8: 322–5

Notes

1   The translation here is difficult. The text may mean 'and are highly prized by those who feel strongly about such things'.

2   'he' is an unnamed, but apparently eminent sculptor.

Reference

Alsop, 1982

69

Galeazzo Sforza describes the Medici Palace in 1459

On 17 April 1459, Galeazzo Maria Sforza, eldest son of Francesco, Duke of Milan, arrived in Florence for a short stay. The visit enabled him to meet Pope Pius II, passing through Florence on his way from Mantua to Rome, and to cement relations between Cosimo de Medici and the Sforza family.

For the time of his visit Galeazzo stayed in the Medici town palace, only recently completed. Letters written home to Milan by the Sforza group give a contemporary account of the palace and its contents. The first extract given here purported to be a letter from Galeazzo to his parents written on the day of his arrival, although it may actually be by his secretary. On the same day, one of the young Sforza's councillors, Niccolò de Carissimi da Parona, wrote a letter to Duke Francesco giving an account of his son's reception. Both these letters give a description of the Medici Palace.

Cosimo de Medici seems to have become a classical art collector at Florence in the 1420s, starting with carved gems, and perhaps coins and medals, and then adding classical sculpture. He may have been encouraged by the sculptor Donatello, who had his own collection of classical art, and to whom Cosimo gave sculptural commissions. Similarly the humanist Niccolo Niccoli and his circle were significant: Niccolo and Cosimo were close friends, and they visited Rome together in 1424. Cosimo may have inherited Niccolo's collection on his death in 1437. All of this material was presumably lodged in the new palace which Cosimo had built in Florence, and will have been visible to Galeazzo and his party.

GALEAZZO SFORZA

I took leave of their lordships and finally, accompanied by the great multitude of gentlemen and people, all of whom were on holiday by public proclamation as on Easter Day, I arrived here at the house of the magnificent Cosimo, where I discovered a house that is – as much in the handsomeness of the ceilings, height of the walls, smooth finish of the entrances and windows, number of chambers and salons, elegances of the studies, worth of the books, neatness and gracefulness of the gardens, as it is in the tapestry decorations, chests of inestimable workmanship and value, noble sculptures, designs of infinite kinds as well as of priceless silver – the most beautiful I may every have seen, or believe it possible to see. For, to tell of this house, for whomever might want worthily to discuss it and describe its parts, not my tongue, not the space of one day, and not of one month, but many – and the eloquence of many orators – would be necessary.

NICCOLO DE CARISSIMI

In the meantime the aforesaid count,[1] together with the company, went on a tour of this place, and especially of its noblest parts, such as some of the studios, chapels, salons, chambers, and garden, all of which are constructed and decorated with admirable mastery, decorated on every side with gold and fine marbles, with carvings and sculptures in relief, with pictures and inlays done in perspective by the most accomplished and perfect of masters even to the very benches and floors of the house; tapestries and household ornaments of gold and silk; silverware and bookcases that are endless and without number; then the vaults or rather ceilings of the chambers and salons, which are for the most part done in fine gold with diverse and various forms; then a garden done in the finest of polished marbles with diverse plants, which seem a thing not natural but painted. And among other things there is an adder[2] in the form of the device of Your Excellency,[3] and besides it there is the shield with the arms of the aforementioned Cosimo. This adder and arms are of new-planted grass in a piece of ground so that, the more the grass grows, the more that device will grow,[4] I am not saying these things distinctly, for it would not be possible, since they are things which can not only be expressed, but also imagined. And whoever sees them judges that they are celestial rather than earthly things, and everyone is agreed that this house is the most finished and ornate that the world has ever had or may have now, and that it is without comparison. In sum, it is believed by all that there is no other earthly paradise in the world than this. If Your Lordship were to see it, I take it for certain that it would cost you a good sum of money, because with the magnanimity and greatness of mind that you have, you too would want to do something worthy – and not only equal this but surpass it if that were possible. To me it seems like being in a new world, and I am of the opinion that in my days I shall never see anything worthier than this which I have seen and am first seeing. And not only I hold this opinion, but all the company here, who do nothing else but discuss it.

Source

Hatfield, R., 1970, 'Some Unknown Descriptions of the Medici Palace in 1459', *Art Bulletin* L11, 3 (Sept.): 228–9

Notes

1 'the aforesaid count' is Galeazzo Maria Sforza.
2 The adder, or viper, was on the arms of the Sforza family.
3 'your excellency' is Duke Francesco.
4 The notion of the devices of the two families in grass is probably intended to allude to the 'natural' growth of relations between Medici and Sforza.

Reference

Grombrich, 1966

70

Piero de Medici views his collections

Cosimo de Medici died in 1464, leaving his semi-crippled eldest son, Piero II Gottoso (the Gouty) as his heir: he was to rule Florence until his death from gout in 1469. Two inventories of Piero's possessions were taken, in 1456, before he inherited, and in 1465 afterwards. The 1465 inventory should therefore reflect those objects which he had inherited from his father. The inventory reveals that Cosimo's collections of antique coins, carved gems and vessels carved in hard stones had become very important by 1464. Between the two lists, Piero's gold medals (a term which includes classical coins) had risen from 53 to 100, his silver medals from 300 to 503, and the gemstones and vessels had also been similarly augmented.

Piero was in great pain and could not walk, although he was a man of stoical courage, as he proved at the time of his accession when a political faction in the city thought he was too ill to fight. We have an eyewitness account of how Piero related to his collection, and how enormous it had become in the time before his death. The account was written by Antonio Filarete, who heard it from an eyewitness, Nicodemus, who was the Milanese ambassador to Florence. Filarete inserted the reminiscence into his book on the ideal city, as a kind of lesson in good taste for rulers.

The description of Piero's activities is extremely interesting. He had lived all his life in the artistic magnificence of fifteenth-century Florence; the palace which he and his father inhabited was the first private building of its kind, and its room were filled with works like the paintings of the Labours of Hercules by Antonio Pollaiuolo, or the statues by Donatello of Judith and Holofernes, in the garden. Instead, what he wished to see passed before his eyes were the books, the classical works, the gems and the plate which had been gathered in the palace. It is clear that carved gems, precious metal coins and hardstone vessels held the highest place in the collector's hierarchy for Piero, as they had for those with access to the treasuries of the medieval centuries.

ANTONIO FILARETE, ON PIERO DE MEDICI

He takes pleasure and finds a pastime in the following. He has himself carried into [his] studio … When he arrives here, he looks at his books.

They seem like nothing but solid pieces of gold. They are most noble both within and without; in Latin and in the vulgar [tongue] to suit man's delight and pleasure. Sometimes he reads one or the other or has them read. He has so many different kinds that not one day but more than a month would be required to see and understand their dignity. Let us leave aside the reading and the authors of these books.[1] It is not necessary to list them, because he has them in every discipline, whether in Latin, Greek, or Italian, so long as they are worthy. He has honoured them, as you have understood, with fine script, miniatures, and ornaments of gold and silk, as a man who recognizes the dignity of their authors and through love of them has wished to honour their works in this manner. Then on another day he runs over all these volumes with his eye for his pleasure, to pass the time and to give recreation to his sight.

The following day, according to what I was told, he has effigies and portraits of all the emperors and noble men who have ever lived made in gold, silver, bronze, jewels, marble, or other materials. They are marvellous things to see. Their dignity is such that only looking at their portraits [wrought] in bronze – excluding those in gold, silver, and in other noble stones – fills his soul with delight and pleasure in their excellence. These give pleasure in two ways to anyone who understands and enjoys them as he does; first for the excellence of the image represented, secondly for the noble mastery of those ancient angelic spirits who with their sublime intellects [have] made such [ordinary] things as bronze, marble, and such materials acquire such great price. Valuable things such as gold and silver have become even greater through their mastery, for, as it is noted, there is nothing, from gems on, that is worth more than gold. They have made it worth more than gold by means of their skill.

He takes pleasure first from one and then from another. In one he praises the dignity of this image because it was done (by the) hand of man, and then in another that was more skillfully done, he states that it seems to have been done by nature rather than by man. When we see something made by the hand of Phidias or Praxiteles, we say that it does not seem by their hand. It appears to have come from heaven rather than to have been made by man. He takes the greatest pleasure and delight in these things. Another day he looks at his jewels and precious stones. He has a marvelous quantity of them of great value cut in different ways. He takes pleasure and delight in looking at them and in talking about the virtue and value of those he has. Another day [he looks] at vases of gold, silver, and other materials made nobly and at great expense and brought from different places. He delights greatly in these, praising their dignity and the mastery of their fabricators ...

In short, worthy and magnificent man that he is ... he delights in every worthy and strange thing and does not note the expense.

Source

Filarette, A., ed. Spencer, J. 1965, *Treatise on Architecture* vol. 1, New Haven, Yale University Press: 373–4

Note

1   The books were by Italian writers like Dante, and of theology; but chiefly they were by classical authors with special reference to Roman historians, poets, orators and thinkers.

Reference

Alsop, 1982

71

The inventory of the Medici Palace at the death of Lorenzo the Magnificent

In 1471 Lorenzo, grandson of Cosimo and son of Piero, went to Rome as chief of the Florentine embassy, and while there he acquired much of the magnificent collection of the late Pope Paul II, who as Cardinal Pietro Barbo had amassed a very large number of small antique bronzes, carved gems, tapestries and Byzantine miniature mosaics, together with some contemporary or recent paintings. Two of the most important of his pieces were the famous carved gem known as The Chalcedony which had belonged to Niccolo Niccoli, and the enormous Hellenistic double-sided cameo now known as the Tazza Farnese. This is a large piece of sardonyx carved with a Nile scene on one side and a mask of Medusa on the other. Both these pieces were acquired by Leonardo, together with his pick of the papal collection. It seems likely that Barbo had acquired this material, in part at least, as loot from Constantinople, and from dealers who were probably already shipping material into Italy from Greece and Asia Minor. Lorenzo himself had as his agents the staff of all the branches of the family bank.

An inventory of the contents of the palace was made following Lorenzo's death in 1492. The palace was followed systematically, room by room, with a list made of everything, and valuations of the individual pieces attached. It is not, however, complete: the sculpture is not listed, whether in the house or in the garden. While in Rome in 1471, Lorenzo is known to have acquired some expensive pieces of carved antique stonework, for example, and his agents in Rome and Naples also procured important pieces of statuary for him from excavations. What the whole inventory does show is the vast quantity of valuable goods of all kinds which, together with the artistic objects, had been accumulated in the palace.

TREASURES OF THE MEDICI PALACE

Nevertheless, with the help of the Medici inventory, so inestimably precious even in all its terseness, and of the scattered surviving fragments of the former furnishings, an attempt will be made below to arrive at a conception of what was assembled toward the end of the Quattrocento in the main rooms of the Medici palace, in rich and yet well-ordered, carefully planned abundance and opulence ...

Lorenzo Magnifico's private chamber, a rectangular room in the corner above the former loggia, has dimensions of about 9 by 10.5 meters and is 6.5 meters high, roofed with the surviving, powerfully articulated coffered ceiling of the first building period.

This room was also fairly extensively supplied with sturdy furniture, at once comfortable and luxurious. The inventory names first a *lettiera*[1] of considerable size (5½ braccia), and bedspread with decoration. The exterior was decorated with perspectival intarsia panelling and carved gilded heads and figures. There were also a *lettucio* [probably meaning a simple, light bedstead] and a cassone, decorated in a manner similar to the first piece of furniture mentioned, as well as a pair of chests gilded and painted with scenes from Petrarch's *Tronfi*. These *forzieri* and the aforementioned cassone served as containers for Lorenzo's wardrobe which the inventory enumerates piece by piece. The first thing on the wall above the pair of chests was a *spalliera* painted with falcons and golden coats of arms on a blue ground; farther up on the wall hung a velvet tapestry about seven meters wide. Beyond the chests was a long bench ... with arms of cypress wood with intarsia decoration. In the middle of the room stood a large table with a valuable cover spread over it; the only movable piece of sitting furniture cited in the inventory was the large armchair with colonnette balusters and intarsia decoration.

The decoration of the upper wall zones is mentioned next. We shall consider the pictures installed there in the order of their enumeration in the list of contents, since this presumably repeats the distribution of the original objects, proceeding along the walls and on the wall sections adjoining one another. The inventory writer begins with a marble Madonna relief in a carved gilt wood frame, hung probably near the entrance to the room from the hall.

Next he names two objects also framed as *colmi*, with allegorical [or perhaps cartographic] depictions of the Terra Santa and Spain: between these a round picture ... with the Triumph of Fame. There follows, probably in the corner near the door to the adjoining room, a small cupboard, ornately painted with images of a lady and two other figures [the former probably on the back wall inside, the latter on the doors]. A marble bust of Lorenzo's father Piero was set up above the cited door, and the bust of his mother, Lucrezia Tornabuoni, set up as a counterpart to it above the other door of the room. Another small decorative item follows: a rectangular alabaster relief in a little frame decorated with bone inlay.

Thereupon the inventory refers one after the other to a whole series of mosaics, mostly small: two heads of Christ of various sizes, three heads of individual saints [Peter, Paul, and Lorenzo's name patron St. Laurence] as well as two small secular pictures, also in mosaic, the head of a young girl and the *impresa* of Lorenzo's brother Giuliano in a round frame. Finally, three works of marble sculpture, specifically two nude figures, one standing, one seated, in high relief ... presumably antique sculpture: then a relief of the Ascension of Christ by Donatello. Last came a large horizontal rectangular *'panno di Fiandra'* [2.25 by 2.90 metres] with figures in front of the landscape and architectual scenery [*'arch e paesi e fighure'*]. In addition, the inventory cites the following objects ... a costly clockwork in gilded copper, four copper sconces decorated with leafwork, a gilded copper lily – a *palio* prize from the feast of John the Baptist – and as a rare curiosity, an ostrich egg and a mirror-glass sphere ... hung on a silken string ...

A principal portion of holdings in the Medici collections consisted of medals, among which the works of fifteenth-century *medailleurs* certainly by far predominated. The estate inventory of 1492 cites no less than 284 silver and 1844 bronze medals, in addition to 200 coins 'of various sorts'. The antique coins, however, were surely counted among these ...

A pronounced luxuriousness and lavish splendor of detail is manifest in the time of Lorenzo Magnifico in many other areas of artistic production and activity. This general trend of the period found particularly characteristic and direct embodiment in the precious small-scale world of such ornamental sculpture for the decoration of utilitarian objects, similar to elegant book illustration.

There is only one group of such highly refined tableware, demonstrably from Lorenzo's own possession and use, of which relatively many pieces have come down to us; in the Museo degli Argenti of the Pitti palace, in a display case in the next to the last room, are assembled no less than eighteen nobly formed bowls, tankards, and other table vessels of crystal and semiprecious stone. All are distinguished by the engraved initials 'LAUR.MED', as a mark of provenance. Most have feet and crown elements in studded or otherwise ornamented gold plate, sometimes enriched with enamel. The knobs sometimes appear as spheres marked with the emblematic diamond rings and provided with inset Medici arms in enamel.

To these we may now add thirty-two similar but often still more magificently equipped vessels from Lorenzo's household treasury, which came down to the later Pope Clement VII with the Medici legacy. They were later in 1532 adapted by him as reliquaries and consigned to the old Medici patronage church of San Lorenzo. They are still in its possession today, but are not accessible to visitors, and were on public display for the first time in the exhibition *Firenze Sacra* in 1933 ...

The following excerpt from the endless enumerations of the inventories may provide at least an overview of the range and the objects of Lorenzo's collecting interests. Thus here, along with certain precious stones of various sorts, are found above all the countless cameos, carnelians, and other antique carved stone work, most of them set off by some sort of gold mounting.[2] There are also many gems in precious rings and the like. Then come other gold ornaments, every possible decorative and utilitarian object in costly versions: belt buckles, Agnus-Dei salvers, hoards of rosaries, plus certain ink wells in elegant cast bronze, crystal drinking cups, silver salt cellars, decorated knives, show weapons, various small table clocks (*oriuoli*), etc. In any case, they are all exclusively objects which, through their material value or refined elegance of execution, could stimulate the collector's pride of possession and please the accustomed taste of the master of the house.

The same abundant treasure chests also hid many works of small-scale painting and sculpture and related genres of the more refined crafts. Thus there were a number of small images of religious subjects, sometimes in enamel or mosaic – and then probably of Byzantine origin, as is expressly noted in certain cases – sometimes in reliefs of ivory, alabaster, or gilded sheet silver, and among these certain reliquaries of the most ornate form with enamel decoration and sculptural ornament. There were a few small antique bronzes and, above all, the whole collection, containing about 2300 items, of portrait medals in bronze and silver, which was already discussed above. Finally, as particularly interesting pieces, there were many small paintings by known early Netherlandish masters; a Jerome in his cell by Jan van Eyck, a portrait of a woman by Petrus Christus, a small Deposition by Giotto, and a little Judith picture by Squarcione.

The sheer quantity of all these precious objects and rarities is enormous, and the same utilitarian and devotional objects sometimes occur in multiple versions. Thus it is clear that for their acquisition and retention it was hardly their actual function that was most decisive, but rather the insatiable passion for collecting. To possess such things in the greatest possible number and diversity and selection, to take them out occasionally for the pleasure of contemplating them or to be able to show them to specially favored guests of the house, surely in this lay the meaning and value of the collection for Lorenzo. It was not the only one of its kind in the period, but stood beyond all comparison in the range and quality of the individual pieces.

Source

Wackernagel, M., 1983 (trans. Luchs, A., 1981) *The World of the Florentine Renaissance Artist*, Princeton University Press: 163–6, 254–6

Notes

1 *Letriera* – bed.
2 The mountings belong to Lorenzo's time; the vessels themselves are of antique Roman or oriental provenance.

References

Alsop, 1982

Bibliography

Aberdeen Journal, Wednesday 29 March 1883

Alexander, J. and Pinski, P., 1987, *Age of Chivalry: Art in Plantagenet England 1200–1400*, London, Royal Academy of Arts and Weidenfeld & Nicholson

Alexander, M., 1966, *The Earliest English Poems*, London, Penguin Books

Alexander, M.C., 1976, 'Hortensius' speech in defence of Verres', *Phoenix* 30: 46–53

Alsop, J., 1982, *The Rare Art Traditions*, London, Thames & Hudson

André, J., 1949, *La vie et l' oeuvre d' Asinius Pollion*, Paris, Librairie C. Klincksieck

André, J.R. Bloch and Rouveret, A., 1981, *Pline l'Ancien Histoire Naturelle*, Book X[XXXVI] 26, introduction, translation and commentary by Paris, Budé, Belles Lettres

Annable, F. and Simpson, D., 1964, *Guide Catalogue of the Neolithic and Bronze Age Collections in Devizes Museum*, Devizes, Wiltshire Archaeological and Natural History Society

Arafat, K.W., 1992, 'Pausanias' attitude to antiquities' in *Bulletin of the British School at Athens* 87: 387–409

Arafat, K.W., 1995, 'Pausanias and the temple of Hera at Olympia in *Bulletin of the British School at Athens* 90: 461–73

Arendt, H., 1970, 'Introduction' in Benjamin, 1970: 1–55

Arrowsmith, W., 1966, 'Luxury and death in the Satyricon' in *Arion*, 5: 304–31 (also reprinted in *Essays in Classical Literature*, ed. by N. Rudd, Cambridge 1972)

Ashbee, P., 1960, *The Bronze Age Round Barrow in Britain*, London: Phoenix House

Austin, M.M. and Vidal-Naquet, P. 1977, *Economic and Social History of Ancient Greece: An Introduction*, Berkeley, University of California Press

Bateman, T., 1852, *Ten Years Diggings*, Sheffield

Beaujeu, J.M., 1982, 'A-t-il éxisté une direction des musées dans la Rome impériale?' in *Comptes Rendus de l'Academie des Inscriptions et Belles Lettres*, Nov.–Dec.: 671–88

Becatti, G., 1956, 'Letture Pliniane: Le opere d' arte nei monumenta Asini Pollionis e negli Horti Serviliani', in *Studi in Onore di Calderini e Paribeni*, Vol. 3, Milan, Ceschina: 199–210

Beckwith, J., 1964, *Early Medieval Art*, London, Thames & Hudson

Bieber, M., 1977, *Ancient Copies: Contribution to the History of Greek and Roman Art*, New York, New York University Press

Bekker, I. (ed.), 1838, *Georgius Cedrenus*, Vol. 1, University of Bonn Press

Benjamin, W., 1970, *Illuminations*, trans. H. John, London, Jonathan Cape

Bennett, T., 1995, *The Birth of the Museum. History, Theory, Politics*, London, Routledge

Benveniste, E., 1973, *Indo-European Language and Society*, trans by E. Palmer, London, Faber & Faber

Bland, R. and Johns, C., 1993, *The Holne Treasure*, British Museum, London

Boedecker, D., 1993, 'Hero cult and politics in Herodotus: The Bones of Orestes' in Dougherty, C. and Kurke, L. (eds), 1993: 164–77

Bol, P.C., 1972, *Die Skulpturen des Schiffsfund von Antikythera*, Berlin, Gebr. Mann

Borlase, Sir W., 1769, *Antiquities of Cornwall*, London

Bounia, A., 1998, 'The nature of collecting in the classical world: collections and collectors, c. 100 BCE – 100 CE', unpublished PhD thesis, University of Leicester, Department of Museum Studies

Bourdieu, P., 1984, *Distinction: A Social Critique of the Judgement of Taste*, London, Routledge & Kegan Paul

Bradley, R., 1990, *The Passage of Arms: an Archaeological Analysis of Prehistoric Hoards and Votive Deposits*, Cambridge University Press

Bromwich, R., 1978, *Trioedd Ynys Prydein: the Welsh Triads*, Cardiff, University of Wales Press

Brown, P., 1982, *Society and the Holy in Late Antiquity*, Berkeley, University of California Press

Bryson, N., 1994, 'Philostratus and the imaginary museum' in Goldhill, S. and Osborne, R. (eds): 255–283

Burkert, W., 1983, *Homo Necans: The Anthropology of Ancient Greek Sacrificial Ritual and Myth*, trans. P. Bing, Berkeley, University of California Press

Burkert, W., 1987, 'Offerings in perspective: surrender, distribution, exchange' in Linders and Nordquist (eds), 1987: 43–50

Colt Hoare, Sir R., 1812, *The Ancient History of Wiltshire*, Vol. 1, London

Carver, M., 1998, *Sutton Hoo, Burial Ground of Kings?*, London, British Museum

Chadwick, H. and N., 1932–1940 *The Growth of Literature* Vols 1–3, Cambridge University Press

Chevallier, R., 1991, *L'Artiste, le Collectionneur et le Faussaire: Pour une Sociologie de l'Art Romain*, Paris, Armand Colin

Chope Pearse, P., 1967, *Early Tours of Devon and Cornwall*, Newton Abbot, David & Charles

Coarelli, F., 1983, 'Il commercio delle opere d'arte in eta tardo-repubblicana' in *Dialogui di Archeologia* 1 (1): 45–53

Coffey, M., 1989, *Roman Satire*, Bristol, Bristol Classical Press

Conner, P., 1993, *Anglo-Saxon Exeter: A Tenth Century Cultural History*, Woodbridge, Boydell Press

Conte, G.B., 1994, *Latin Literature: A History*, trans. by J.B. Solodow, Baltimore, Johns Hopkins University Press

Cornfeld, G. (ed.), 1982, *Josephus – Jewish War*, Michigan, Zondervan Publishing House

Cottan, S., Dungworth D., Scott S. and Taylor, J. (eds), 1994, *Proceedings of the Fourth Annual Theoretical Roman Archaeology Conference*, Oxford, Oxbow Books

Couat, A., 1931, *Alexandrian Poetry under the first three Ptolemies, 324–222 BC*, with a supplementary chapter by E. Cahen; translated by James Loeb, London and New York, Heinemann and G.P. Putnam's Sons

Cunliffe, B., 1974, 'Chalton, Hants: the evolution of a landscape', *Antiquaries Journal* 53 (for 1973): 173–90

Cunliffe, B., 1972, 'The Late Iron Age metalwork from Bulbury, Dorset', *Antiquaries Journal* 52: 293–308

Cunliffe, B., 1978, *Iron Age Communities in Britain*, London, Routledge and Kegan Paul

Cunningham, I.C. (ed.), 1971, *Herodas, Mimiambi*, Oxford, Clarendon Press

Cunnington, E., 1884, 'On a hoard of Bronze Iron and Other Objects found in Belbury Camp, Dorset', *Archaeologia* 48: 115–17

D'Arms, J.H., 1981, *Commerce and Social Standing in Ancient Rome*, Cambridge, Mass., Harvard University Press

Dawe, R.D., 1993, *The Odyssey: translation and analysis*, Lewes, Book Guild Ltd

Déotte, J.-L., 1995, 'Rome, the archetypal museum, and the Louvre, the negation of division' in Pearce, S., 1995b: 215–32

Detienne, M. and Vernant J.-P. (eds), 1989, *The Cuisine of Sacrifice among the Greeks*, trans by P. Wissing, University of Chicago Press

Dimock, G.E., 1995, *Homer, Iliad*, 1st edition trans A.T. Murray, London, W. Heinemann

Dimock, G.E., 1995, *Homer, Odyssey*, 2nd edition, Loeb Classical Library, Cambridge, Mass., Harvard University Press

Dougherty, C. and Kurke, L. (eds), 1993, *Cultural Poetics in Archaic Greece: Cult, Performance, Politics*, Cambridge University Press

Drew, C.D., 1937, 'Two Bronze Age Barrows', *Proceedings of the Dorset Natural History and Archaeological Society* 58: 18–25

Ebert, F., 1950, 'Pinacotheca', *RE* 20, 2: 1389–94

Eddius, Stephanus, 'Life of Wilfred' in Webb, J. (ed.) 1970, *Lives of the Saints*, London, Penguin Books

Ehrhardt, C., 1966, 'The fate of the treasures of Delphi', *Phoenix*, 20: 228–30

Eicholz, D.E., 1971, *Pliny Natural History*, Vol. 1 (libri 36–37), Loeb Classical Library, London and Cambridge, Mass., Heinemann and Harvard University Press

Eisner, R., 1993, *Travelers to an Antique Land: The History and Literature of Travel to Greece*, Ann Arbor, University of Michigan Press

Elsner, J., 1994a, 'From the pyramids to Pausanias and Piglet: monuments, travel and writing' in Goldhill S. and Osborne, R. (eds): 224–54

Elsner, J., 1994b, 'A collector's model of desire: the house and museum of Sir John Soane' in Elsner, J. and Cardinal, R. (eds): 155–76

Elsner, J. and Cardinal R. (eds), 1994, *The Cultures of Collecting*, London, Reaktion Books

Elsner, J., 1997, 'The origin of the icon: pilgrimage, religion and visual culture in the Roman East as "resistance" to the centre' in Alcock S.E. (ed.), *The Early Roman Empire in the East*, Oxford, Oxbow Books: 178–99

Emanuele, D., 1989, 'Aes Corinthium: fact, fiction, and fake', *Phoenix*, 43(4): 347–58

Erasmus, D., 1849, *Pilgrimages to Saint Mary of Walsingham and Saint Thomas of Canterbury* (trans. Nichols, J.), Canterbury: 49, 55–6

Fairbanks, A., 1931, *Philostratus, Imagines – Callistratus, Descriptions*, Loeb Classical Library, London and New York, Heinemann and G.P. Putnam's Sons

Filarete, A., ed. Spencer J., 1965, *Treatise on Architecture* vol. 1, New Haven, Yale University Press

Findlen, P., 1994, *Possessing Nature: Museums, collecting, and scientific culture in early modern Italy*, Berkeley, University of California Press

Finley, M.I., 1979, *The World of Odysseus* (reprinted 3rd edn), Harmondsworth, Penguin

Firth, R., 1965, *Primitive Polynesian Economy*, London, Routledge & Kegan Paul.

FitzPatrick A., 1984, 'The Deposition of La Tene Metalwork' in Cunliffe, B. and Miles, D. (eds), *Aspects of the Iron Age in Central Southern England*, Oxford: 178–90

Forster Smith, C., 1951, *Thucydides, History of the Peloponnesian War*, Vol. 1, Loeb Classical Library, London and Cambridge, Mass., Heinemann and Harvard University Press

Fränkel, M., 1891, 'Gemälde-Sammlungen und Gemälde-Forschung in Pergamon', *JDAI*, 6, 48–60

Fraser, P.M., 1972, *Ptolemaic Alexandria*, Oxford, Clarendon Press

Friend, A., 1923 'Carolingian Art in the Abbey of St Denis', *Art Studies* 1: 67–75

Frisch, T., 1971, *Gothic Art 1140–c. 1450 Sources and Documents*, London

Fuchs, W., 1963, *Der Schiffsfund von Mahdia*, Tubingen, W. Wasmuth

Gantz, J. (ed.), 1976, *The Mabinogion*, London, Dent

Geary, P., 1979, *Furta Sacra: Thefts of Relics in the Central Middle Ages*, Princeton University Press

Gernet, L., 1981, 'The mythical idea of value' in *The Anthropology of Ancient Greece*, trans. by J. Hamilton and Blaise Nagy, Baltimore, Johns Hopkins University Press

Gilbert, N., 1977, 'A letter of Giovanni Dondi dall'Orologio to Fra Guglielmo da Cremona', *Viator* 8: 313–14

Godley, A.D., 1946, *Herodotus*, in 4 volumes, Vol. 1, Books 1 and 2, Loeb Classical Library, London and Cambridge, Mass., Heinemann and Harvard University Press

Gold, B. (ed.), 1982, *Literary and Artistic Patronage in Ancient Rome*, Austin, University of Texas Press

Goldhill, S. and Osborne, R. (eds), 1994, *Art and Text in Ancient Greece*, Cambridge, Cambridge University Press

Gray, D.H.F., 1954, 'Metal-working in Homer', *Journal of Hellenic Studies*, 74: 1–15

Greenwood, L.H.G., 1953, *Cicero: The Verrine Orations*, (in two volumes); *1: against Caecilius – against Verres*, Books 1 and 2, 1948; 2: Books 3, 4, and 5, Loeb Classical Library, London and Cambridge, Mass., Heinemann and Harvard University Press

Gregory, C.A., 1982, *Gifts and Commodities*, London, Academic Press

Grinsell, L.V., 1959, *Dorset Barrows*, Dorchester, Dorset Natural History and Archaeological Society

Grombrich, E., 1966, 'The Early Medici as Patrons of Art: A Survey of Primary Sources', *Norm and Form*, London: 35–7

Gros, P., 1976, *Aurea Templa: Recherches sur l'Architecture religieuse de Rome a l'époque d'August*, Rome, École Française de Rome

Gulick, Charles Burton, 1927, *Athenaeus, Deipnosophists*, in 6 volumes, Vol. 1, Loeb Classical Library, London and New York, Heinemann and G.P. Putnam and Sons

Hansen, E.V., 1971, *The Attalids of Pergamon*, Ithaca, N.Y. and London, Cornell University Press

Harris, D., 1995, *The Treasures of the Parthenon and Erechteion*, Oxford University Press

Hatfield, R., 1970, 'Some Unknown Descriptions of the Medici Palace in 1459', *Art Bulletin* LII, 3 (Sept.): 232–49

Healy, J.F., 1991, *Natural History – A Selection, Pliny the Elder*, trans. with an introduction, Harmondsworth, Penguin Books

Hellenkemper Sallies, G., (ed.), 1994, *Das Wrack. Der antike Schiffsfund von Madhia*, (Kataloge des Rheinischen Landsmuseums, 1.1–2, Bonn 1994), Rheinland, Verlag GmbH, Köln

Hicks, R.D., 1925, *Diogenes Laertius, Lives of Eminent Philosophers*, Loeb Classical Library, trans. in 2 vols., vol. 1, London and New York, W. Heinemann Ltd and G.P. Putnam's Sons

Hines, J., 1989, 'Ritual Hoarding in Migration-Period Scandinavia: A Review of Recent Interpretations', *Proceedings of the Prehistoric Society* 55: 193–205

Hitchins, Rev. M., 1806, 'Account of Antiquities discovered in Cornwall, the Rev. Malachy Hitchens, in a letter to the Rt. Hon Sir Joseph Banks, Bart KB PRS and PSA', *Archaeologia* 15: 118–21

Hobsbawn, E. and Ranger, T. (eds), 1983, *The Invention of Tradition*, Cambridge University Press

Holmes, U., 1953, *Daily Living in the Twelfth Century*, London, Duckworth

Hornblower, S., 1987, *Thucydides*, London, Duckworth

Horsfall, N., 1989, '"The uses of literacy" and the *Cena Trimalchionis*' in *Greece and Rome*, 36, 1: 74–89, 2: 194–209

Howard, S., 1986, 'Pergamene art collecting and its aftermath' in *Akten des XXV Internationalen Kongresses Für Kunstgeschichte, Wien 1983: IV/4. Der Zugang zum Kunstwerk: Schatzkammer, Salon, Ausstellung, 'Museum'*, Vienna, H. Buhlau: 25–36

Howell, P., 1980, *A Commentary on Book One of the Epigrams of Martial*, London, Athlone Press

Hubert, H. and Mauss, M., 1899, 'Essai sur la nature et la fonction du sacrifice', *Année Sociologique*, 2: 29–138

Hutton, R., 1993, *The Pagan Religions of the British Isles*, Oxford, Blackwell's

Hutton, R., 1997, *The Stations of the Sun*, Oxford University Press

Huxley, G., 1979, 'Bones for Orestes', *Greek, Roman and Byzantine Studies*, 20: 145–8

Isager, J., 1991, *Pliny on Art and Society: The Elder Pliny's Chapters on the History of Art*, London and New York, Routledge

James, R., 1938, 'Twelfth Century Interest in Classical Art' in Cate, J. and

Anderson, C. (eds), *Medieval and Historical Essays in Honour of James W. Thompson*, University of Chicago Press: 302–21

Jex-Blake, K. and Sellers, E., 1896, *The Elder Pliny's Chapters on the History of Art*, trans. by K. Jex-Blake with commentary and historical introduction by Sellers, E., London and New York, Macmillan

Johns, C. and Potter, T., 1983, *The Thetford Treasure: Roman Jewellery and Silver*, London, British Museum

Johns, C., 1994, 'Romano-British Precious Metal Hoards' in Cottan et al.: 107–17

Jones, G. and Jones, M., 1963, (ed. and trans.) *The Mabinogion*, London, Dent

Jones, H.L., 1954, *Strabo, Geography*, Vol. 4, Loeb Classical Library, London and Cambridge, Mass., Heinemann and Harvard University Press

Jones, W.H.S. and Ormerod, H.A., 1926, *Pausanias, Description of Greece*, Loeb Classical Library, London, Heinemann

Jones, W.H.S., 1963, *Pliny Natural History*, Vol. 7 (libri 28–32), London and Cambridge, Mass., Loeb Classical Library

Kent Hill, D., 1944, 'Hera, the sphinx', *Hesperia* 13: 353–60

Ker, Walter C.A., 1919, *Martial Epigrams* (in two volumes), Loeb Classical Library, London and Cambridge, Mass., Heinemann and Harvard University Press

Ker, W.P., 1957, *Epic and Romance: Essays on Medieval Literature*, New York, Dover

Knox, A.D. (ed.), 1922, *Herodas: The Mines and Fragments*, with notes by Walter Headlam, Cambridge University Press

Lafon, X., 1981, 'A propos de "villae" republicaines: Quelques notes sur les programmes decoratifs et les commanditaires', in *L'Art decoratif à Rome à la fin de la Republique et au debut du Principat*, Rome, École Française de Rome, Palais Farnèse: 151–72

Langdon, S., 1987, 'Gift exchange in Geometric sanctuaries' in Linders and Nordquist (eds): 107–13

Leach, E.W., 1982, 'Patrons, painters, and patterns: the anonymity of Romano-Campanian painting and the transition from the second to the third style' in Gold, B. (ed.): 135–73

Leach, E.W., 1988, *The Rhetoric of Space: Literary and Artistic Representations of Landscape in Republican and Augustan Rome*, Princeton University Press

Lehmann-Hartleben. K., 1941, 'The Images of Philostratus', *Art Bulletin*, XXIII: 33–47

Liebermann, F., 1889, *Die Heiligen Englands*, Hannover, 9–19

Linders, T. and Nordquist, G. (eds), 1987, *Gifts to the Gods, Proceedings of the Uppsala Symposium, 1985*, Uppsala, Boreas 15

Loomis, R.S. (ed.), 1959, *Arthurian Literature in the Middle Ages*, Oxford University Press

Lowenthal, D., 1985, *The Past is a Foreign Country*, Cambridge University Press

Lowth, R., 1759, *The Life of William of Wykham*, 2nd edition, London

Mango, C., 1963, 'Antique Statuary and the Byzantine Beholder', *Dumbarton Oaks Papers* 17: 55–75

Mango, C., Vickers, M. and Francis, E., 1992, 'The Palace of Lausus at Constantinople and its Collection of Ancient Statues', *Journal of History of Collections* 4, 1: 89–98

Marsden, B., 1974, *The Early Barrow Diggers*, Princes Risborough, Shire Publications

Marsden, B., 1984, *Pioneers of Prehistory*, Hesketh, Ormskirk and Northridge

Marvin, M., 1989, 'Copying the Roman sculpture: the replica series' in *Retaining the Original: Multiple Originals, Copies and Reproductions*, Washington DC, National Gallery of Art: 20, 29–45

Mauss, M., 1970, [1925], *The Gift: Forms and Functions of Exchange in Archaic Societies*, transl. by Ian Cunnison, London, Cohen & West

May, J.M., 1988, *Trials of Character: The Eloquence of Ciceronian Ethos*, Chapel Hill and London, North Carolina Press

Megaw, J.V.S. and Simpson, D., 1979, *Introduction to British Prehistory*, Leicester University Press

Miller, M., 1994, 'Treasure: interpreting Roman hoards' in Cottan et al.: 99–105

Moberley, G., 1898, *Life of William of Wykeham*, Winchester, Warner & Son

Momigliano, A., 1950, 'Ancient history and antiquarianism', *Journal of the Warburg and Courtauld Institutes*, 13: 285–315

Morford, M., 1986, 'Nero's patronage and participation in literature and the arts' *Aufstieg und Niedergang der Römischen Welt*, 2. 32.3: 2003–31

Morgan, C., 1990, *Athletes and Oracles: The Transformation in Olympia and Delphi in the eighth century BC*, Cambridge University Press

Morris, I., 1986, 'Gift and commodity in Archaic Greece', *Man* (N.S.) 21(1): 1–17

Morris, I., 1992, *Death-Ritual and Social Structure in Classical Antiquity*, Cambridge University Press

Morris, W. (trans.), 1963, *Volsunga Saga: the Story of the Volsungs and Niblungs*, New York, Collier Books

Murray, A.T., 1995, *Homer, Illiad*, Loeb Classical Library, London and Cambridge, Mass., Heinemann and Harvard University Press

Neudecker, R., 1988, *Die Skulpturen-ausstatung römischer Villen in Italien*, Mainz am Rhein, Verlag Philipp van Zabern

Newton, S., 1993, *The Origins of Beowulf and the Kingdom of East Anglia*, Ipswich, Boydell Press

Obelkevich, J. (ed.), 1979, *Religion and the People: 800–1700*, Chapel Hill, NC, Duke University Press

Oberhummer, E., 1933, 'Mouseion' in *RE*, 16, 1: 797–821

Oliver, G., 1861, *Lives of the Bishops of Exeter*, Exeter, William Roberts

Painter, K., 1977, *The Water Newton Early Christian Silver*, London, British Museum

Panofsky-Soergel, G. (ed.), 1979, *Abbot Suger on the Abbey Church of St Denis and its Art Treasures*, 2nd edition, Princeton University Press

Pape, M., 1975, *Griechische Kunstwerke aus Kriegsbeute und ihre öffentliche Aufstellung in Rom*, Hamburg, privately published

Pausanias – Description of Greece, 1898, trans. with a commentary by J.G. Frazer, in 6 volumes, Vol. 1, London, MacMillan

Pausanias, *Guide to Greece*, Vol. 1, *Central Greece*, 1971, translated with introduction by P. Levi, Harmondsworth, Penguin books

Pearce, S.M., 1995a, *On Collecting*, London, Routledge

Pearce, S.M. (ed.), 1995b, *Art in Museums*, New Research in Museum Studies 6, London, Athlone Press

Pearce, S.M., 1970–71, 'A Late Bronze Age Hoard from Glentanar', *Proceedings of the Society of Antiquaries of Scotland* 103: 57–64

Pearce, S.M., 1976–77, 'Amber beads from the late Bronze Age Hoard from Glentanar, Aberdeenshire', *Proceedings of Society of Antiquities of Scotland* 108: 124–9

Pearce, S.M., 1983, *The Bronze Age Metalwork of South Western Britain*, British Archaeological Series 120 (1 and 2), Oxford

Pellegrini, A., 1867, 'Orti di Asinio Pollione', *Bulletino dell' Instituto di Correspondenza Archaeologia per l' anno 1867*: 109–19

Perrin, Bernadotte 1914, *Plutarch's Lives*, Loeb Classical Library, London, W Heinemann Ltd.

Perrin, Bernadotte 1918, *Plutarch's Lives: Aemilius Paullus*, Vol. 6, Loeb Classical Library, London, W. Heinemann Ltd.

Perrin, Bernadotte, 1954, *Plutarch's Lives*, Vol. II, Loeb Classical Library, London, Heinemann

Peterson, T., 1920, *Cicero: A Biography*, Berkeley, University of California Press

Piggot, S., 1938, 'The Early Bronze Age in Wessex', *Proceedings of the Prehistoric Society* 4: 52–106

Piggot, S., 1968, *The Druids*, London, Penguin Books, Thames and Hudson

Polignac, F. de, 1995, *Cults, Territory, and the Origins of the Greek City-State*, trans. by Janet Lloyd, University of Chicago Press

Pollitt, J.J., 1974, *The Ancient View of Greek Art: Criticism, History, and Terminology*, New Haven and London, Yale University Press

Pollitt, J.J., 1978, 'The impact of Greek art on Rome', *Transactions of the American Philological Association* 108: 155–74

Pollitt, J.J., 1983 (2nd edition), *The Art of Rome, c.753 BC–337 AD Sources and Documents*, New Jersey

Pollitt, J.J., 1990, *The Art of Ancient Greece: Sources and Documents*, Cambridge University Press

Poole, A.L., 1958, *Domesday Book to Magna Carta 1087–1216*, Oxford, Clarendon Press

Poole, R., 1927, *Iannis Sareberiensis, Historia Pontificalis*, Oxford University Press

Poulton, R. and Scott, E., 1995, 'The Hoarding, Deposition and Use of Pewter in Roman Britain', in Scott E. (ed.), *Proceedings of Fifth Theoretical Roman Archaeology Conference*, Oxford, Oxbow Books: 116–32

Rackham, H., 1952, *Pliny the Elder, The Natural History*, Vol. 9 (libri 31–35), Loeb Classical Library, London, Heinemann

Rawson, E., 1985, *Intellectual Life in the Late Roman Republic*, London, Duckworth

Richardson, L., 1992, *A New Topographical Dictionary of Ancient Rome*, Baltimore and London, Johns Hopkins University Press

Ridyard, S., 1988, *The Royal Saints of Anglo-Saxon England*, Cambridge University Press

Rolfe, J.C., 1914, *Suetonius*, The Lives of the Caesars, in 2 volumes, Loeb Classical Library, vol. II, London and New York, Heinemann and Macmillan

Rolfe, J.C., *Suetonius, The Twelve Caesars*, in two volumes, 1: 1951, 2: 1979, Loeb Classical Library, London and Cambridge, Mass., Heinemann and Harvard University Press

Rollason, L.D., 'Lists of Saints' resting-places in Anglo-Saxon England', *Anglo-Saxon England* 7: 61–93

Rollason, D., 1989, *Saints and Relics in Anglo-Saxon England*, Oxford, Blackwell

Rose, K.F.C., 1971, *The Date and Author of the Satyricon*, Mnemosyne Supplement no. 16, Leiden

Rosenblatt, P.C., Walsh, R.P. and Jackson, A.J., 1976, *Grief and Mourning in Cross-cultural Perspective*, New York, HRAF Press

Rouveret, A., 1989, *Histoire et imaginaire de la peinture ancienne (Ve siècle av. J-C-Ier siècle ap. J.-C.)*, Rome, École Française de Rome

Roux, G., 1954, 'Le val des Muses et les Musées chez les auteurs anciens' *BCH*, 78: 22–48

Runciman, S., 1951, *A History of the Crusades*, Vol. 1, The First Crusade, Cambridge University Press

Rups, M., 1986, *Thesauros: A study of the Treasury Building as found in Greek sanctuaries*, PhD thesis, Johns Hopkins University, Ann Arbor, MI, University Microfilms International

Rushforth, G., 1919, 'Magister Gregorius *De Mirabilis Urbis Romae*: a new description of Rome in the twelfth century', *Journal of Roman Studies* IX: 14–58

Sage, Evan T., 1953, *Livy*, Vol. 9 (Books 31–34), Loeb Classical Library, London and Cambridge, Mass., Heinemann and Harvard University

Sauron, G., 1980, 'Templa serena: A propos de la "ville des Papyri" d'Herculaneum: contribution à l'étude des comportments aristocratiques romain à la fin de la Republique' *MEFR*, 92.1: 277–301

Schadla-Hall, T., 1989, *Tom Sheppard, Hull's Great Collector*, Beverley, Highgate Publications

Scheid-Tissinier, É., 1994, *Les usages du don chez Homere: Vocabulaire et pratiques*, Nancy, Presses Universitaires de Nancy

Schnapp, A., 1996, *The Discovery of the Past: The Origins of Archaeology*, London, British Museum Press

Schultz, E., 1990, 'Notes on the history of collecting and museums', *Journal of the History of Collections* 2(2): 205–18

Schweitzer, B., 1932, 'Xenocrates von Athen', Schriften der Königsberger Gelehrten Gesellschaft

Sélincourt, Aubrey, de, 1972, *Herodotus*, revised by A.R. Burn, Harmondsworth, Penguin Classics (originally published in 1954)

Serbat, G., 1986, 'Pline l'Ancien, État présent des études sur sa vie, son oeuvre et son influence', *Aufstieg und Niedergang der Römischen Welt*, 2.32.4: 2069–2200

Shackleton Bailey, D.R., 1965, *Cicero's Letters to Atticus*, Vol. 1, Cambridge

Shackleton Bailey, D.R. (ed.), 1978, *Cicero's Letters to his Friends*, Harmondsworth, Penguin Books

Shackleton Bailey, D.R., *Martial Epigrams*, Vols 1–3, Loeb Classical Library, London and Cambridge, Mass., Harvard University Press and Heinemann, 1993

Sharpe, R., 1899, *Calendar of Letter Books ... of the City of London*, London

Sheppard, T., 1907, 'Note on a British Chariot-Burial at Hunmanby in East Yorkshire', *Archaeological Journal* 19: 483–497

Shipley, F.W., 1924, *Velleius Paterculus – Compedium of Roman History*, Loeb Classical Library, London and New York, Heinemann and G.P. Putnam

Shotter, D., 1991, *Augustus Caesar*, Lancaster Pamphlets, London, Routledge

Slater, N.W., 1990, *Reading Petronius*, Baltimore and London, Johns Hopkins University Press

Smith, M.S. (ed.), 1975, *Petronius. Cena Trimalchionis*, Oxford, Clarendon Press

Sneyd, C., 1847, *A Relation ... of the island of England about the year 1500*, Camden Society, Vol. XXXVII: 83–4

Snodgrass, A., 1974, 'An ahistorical Homeric society?' *Journal of Hellenic Studies*, 94: 4–125

Snodgrass, A., 1980, *Archaic Greece: The Age of Experiment*, London: Dent & Sons

Stone, B., 1964, *Medieval English Verse*, London, Penguin Books

Strong, D.E., 1975, 'Roman museums' in Strong, D.E. (ed.), *Archaeological Theory and Practice*, New York, Seminar Press: 248–263

Strong, D.E., 1976, *Roman Art*, London, Pelican

Sullivan, J.P., 1985, *Literature and Politics in the Age of Nero*, Ithaca, New York, Cornell University Press

Sullivan, J.P., 1991, *Martial: the unexpected classic: A literary and historical study*, Cambridge University Press

Thackeray, H. St. J., 1956, *Josephus, The Jewish War*, Vol. 2: (Books 1–3), Loeb Classical Library, London and Cambridge, Mass., Heinemann and Harvard University Press

Tanner, J.J., 1995, 'The invention of art history: religion, society and artistic differentiation in ancient Greece', unpublished PhD thesis, University of Cambridge

Todd, M., 1992, *The Early Germans*, Oxford, Blackwell's

Tolkien, C., 1960, *The Saga of King Heidrek the Wise*, London, Nelson & Sons

Valenti, S., 1936, 'Cicerone collezionista', *Atene e Roma*, 3 (4): 236–270

van Wees H, 1992, *Status Warriors: War, Violence and Society in Homer and History*, Amsterdam, J.C. Gieben

Vermeule, C., 1967, 'Greek sculpture and Roman taste', *Bulletin of the Museum of Five Arts, Boston* 65 (342): 175–92

Vermeule, C., 1968, 'Graeco-Roman statues: Purpose and setting' (in two parts), *Burlington Magazine* 787–8 (CX), October–November: 545–58, 607–13

Vermeule, C., 1977, *Greek Sculpture and Roman Taste: The Purpose and Setting of Greco-Roman Art in Italy and the Greek Imperial East*, Ann Arbor, University of Michigan Press

Vernant, J.-P., 1983, *Myth and Thought among the Greeks*, London, Routledge & Kegan Paul

Vernant, J.-P., 1991, 'A general theory of sacrifice and slaying of the victim in the Greek Thusia' in Zeitlin, F. (ed.), 1991, *Mortals and Immortals: Collected Essays – J-P Vernant*, Princeton University Press

Vestergaard, E., 1987, 'The perpetual reconstruction of the past' in Hodder, I. (ed.) *Archaeology as Long Term History*, Cambridge University Press: 63–7

Veyne, P., 1961, 'Vie de Trimalchion', *Annales économies-sociétés-civilisations*, 16: 213–47

Ville, G., 1964, 'Les coupes de Trimalchion figurant des gladiateurs et une série de verres sigillés gaulois' in *Hommages à J. Bayet*, Brussels, Collection Latomus 70: 722–33

von Reden, S., 1994, *Exchange in Ancient Greece*, London, Duckworth

Wace, A.J., 1969, 'The Greeks and Romans as archaeologists' in Heizer, R.F. (ed.), *Man's Discovery of his Past*, Los Angeles, CA, Valo Alko Publications: 203–18

Wackernagel, M., 1938 (trans. Luchs A 1981) *The World of the Florentine Renaissance Artist*, Princeton University Press

Wait, G., 1985, *Ritual and Religion in Iron Age Britain*, British Archaeological Reports, British Series 149, Oxford

Wallace-Hadzill, A., 1994, *Houses and Society in Pompeii and Herculaneum*, Princeton, N.J., Princeton University Press

Walsh, P.G. (ed.), 1996, *Petronius: The Satyricon*, Oxford, Clarendon Press

Ward, B., 1982, *Miracles and the Medieval Mind*, Aldershot, Scolar Press

Warren, F., 1883 (ed.) *The Leofric Missal*, Oxford, Clarendon Press

Warmington, E.H., 1969, *Petronius: Satyricon*, Loeb Classical Library, London and Cambridge, Mass., Harvard University Press

Watson, G., 1988, *Phantasia in Classical Thought*, Galway University Press

Watson, G., 1994, 'The concept of "*phantasia*" from the late Hellenistic period to early Neoplatonism', *Augsteig und Niedergang der Römischen Welt*, II.36.7: 4765–4810

Watts, D., 1988, 'The Thetford Treasure: A Reappraisal', *Antiquaries Journal* 68: 55–68

Weinberg, G.D., Grace, V.R., Edwards, G.R., Robinson, H.S., Throckmorton, P. and Ralph, E.K., 1965, 'The Antikythera shipwreck reconsidered' in *TAPhS* (n.s), 55: 3–31

Weiner, A., 1992, *Inalienable Possessions: The paradox of keeping-while-giving*, Berkeley, University of California Press

Wernicke, K. 1894, 'Olympische Beiträge, II. Zur Geschichte des Heraion', *Jahrbuch der Deutchen Archäologischen Instituts* 9: 101–14

Williams, W. Glyn, *Cicero: The Letters to his Friends*, Vol. 1 1952, Vol. 2 1953, Vol. 3 1972, Vol. 4 1979, Loeb Classical Library, London and Cambridge, Mass., Heinemann and Harvard University Press

Woodruff, P., 1982, *Plato: Hippias Major*, Oxford, Blackwell

Wright, D., 1994, *Beowulf*, London, Penguin Books

Wulfram, H., 1988, *History of the Goths*, Berkeley, University of California Press

Index

Wilfrid of Northumbria 216
relic-collecting 190–92
William of Kilkenny 223
William of Wykeham, Bishop of Winchester, will of 220–22
Winchester
Bishop Henry of Blois bringing statues
from Rome to 211–13
relics at 194

Winchester College 220
women as collectors 158–60

Xenocrates 101
Xenophon 47, 102

Zeuxis 102
Zonaras 183
Zosimus 184